The Travel Addict's Puzzle

Around (most of) Half the World in 40 Days

Philip Gerald Brown

The right of Philip Gerald Brown to be identified as the Author of the Work has been asserted by him. All rights reserved.

Acknowledgements

I would like to thank my wife Liz because she told me I had to, and it is clear from some of the following pages that she has had a lot to put up with. I also thank my daughter Emily for the cover design and for helping me out on the occasions that my frustration with the computer thinking that it knew better than me bubbled over. Finally I would like to thank my son Henry for… um…. for promising that he might read the book.

Contents:

Part 1: China

1	Inside The Puzzle	1
2	Missing the Sights	14
3	To Travel Hopefully	26
4	The Intrepid Traveller	39

Part 2: Kazakhstan

5	Fitting Reality to Fantasy	52
6	Happy Hours	67
7	The Lazy Paradox	78
8	The Life of a Journey	93

Part 3: The Caucasus

9	Big Brother	110
10	Conquering the World	123
11	The Great Game	134
12	Fiction Trumps Truth	144

Part 4: Georgia

	13	Expecting the unexpected	158
	14	The Thrill of the Chase	171
	15	The Image Collector	185
	16	Seeing the Wood for the trees	202

Part 5: Turkey

	17	Arcadia	215
	18	Heart and Soul	227
	19	As You Like It	239
	20	Vivisection	251

Part 1: China

Chapter One: Inside the Puzzle

The time of day just seems wrong. I have never planned a trip so thoroughly but at 8 o'clock in the evening, after dinner and a couple of glasses of wine, it has an air of complete unreality. Long journeys should start in the morning and for a moment I regret booking an overnight train to Xian, but the alternative of over 12 hours in a hard seat is too long. A soft seat is little better and costs almost as much as a hard sleeper, so the night-train makes sense. I don my backpack and go down to the underground.

'Dear passengers, please hold the banister rail on the escalator', the disembodied voice on the Nanjing Metro is full of warmth and concern. *'No running or fighting on the stairs, walking in the opposite direction is forbidden'*- a steely edge has crept into her delivery and what is she talking about anyway? The Chinese don't run or fight. Rarely am I in a hurry but I have not been able to adjust to the pace of movement here. I thought that big cities were busy bustling places with everyone always anxious to be somewhere else. Nanjing has plenty of people on the move but the walking pace is so painfully slow that I am constantly trying to get past those in front; usually a group of young people strung across the pavement with their heads slumped over their mobile phones.

As for fighting; the history of the country is bloody enough, and not just from the emperors and warlords but from the ordinary people as well, that you could be forgiven for thinking that the populace is forever at each other's throats, but nothing could be further from the truth. Perhaps because of all their past hardships and travails, people put up with the discomforts and irritations of living in a packed city with a simple resignation and never seem to notice the annoying habits of their fellows. I ponder this as I, together with a crowded escalator of metro passengers, carefully edge round a young man who has decided that the top of a busy escalator is the ideal spot to stop and check his text messages.

The tube as ever is packed with young people and I observe a youth holding a large shocking-pink handbag. Most Chinese males are refreshingly free of machismo, the exceptions perhaps being businessmen who sit at round tables in restaurants with their legs wide apart amid the detritus of huge meals. They ply each other with cigarettes and become loud and red-faced by overindulgence in the evil rice spirit. The young man holds the bag proudly as it belongs to the pretty girl next to him and he views it as a sign of ownership. She looks equally content with the gallant upon whom she has bestowed her favour and who has now become her personal porter. Not all girls are able to use their beaus in this manner when seated on the underground, as in the summer months their skirts become so short that they need to keep their bags on their laps to maintain even a modicum of decorum.

Emerging into the twilight I observe a scooter rider insisting on the left side of the road, perhaps feeling that China should never have let America persuade it to change to 'the right' in exchange for a few Jeeps to help them fight the Japanese. No doubt America was hoping for some future export orders, but they did not count on the communist takeover and had to wait another 50 years before private car ownership was realised. Other road users simply do their best to drive around the scooter on the wrong side of the road; any hint of confrontation is avoided at all cost. There is really no right or wrong on the roads in China, there is only what you can get away with. I join a group of pedestrians trying to cross the road and wait for our numbers to swell to a point that we can edge out as a united group and force the motor traffic to stop. Although horns blare continuously and assertively there is little rancour. It is the law of the jungle, where you fight for position but accept success and defeat as part of the natural order of things.

Similarly when I arrive at the railway station the waiting room is packed with passengers sat on the floor surrounded by their belongings, but they will not even dream of asking someone who evidently got here earlier and claimed two extra seats for their own luggage to move a bag so that another person can use the seat. Always polite and helpful, the Chinese can also appear strangely indifferent to the comfort and feelings of their fellows.

The carriage is spotlessly clean and I make up my middle bunk with the duvet provided. I bought a small air cushion the other day and, half inflated and placed under the pillow it makes the bed more comfortable, but makes me feel old. It is sad if I have become so used to having two pillows at night that I need to resort to measures like this, which is something I would never have dreamed of doing when I was younger. I am not really sure if I have become soft and institutionalised or just better prepared and more appreciative of a little comfort. The train is certainly an institution and the guard exchanges a plastic card for my ticket, draws the curtains, and dead on 10 o'clock the lights go out. For the first time I am catching a Z-train, which has distinctive white coaches embellished with dark blue. Before bullet trains, which only operate on specially constructed lines, these would have been the fastest. This was not because they have a greater turn of speed but because they stop less frequently; Z 86 visits just one other station between Nanjing and Xian, a distance of over 1200 Km.

Xian is just my first stop and I don't intend to even spend a night there. I am travelling to Bulgaria for the summer and my route will take me through North West China, Kazakhstan, the Russian Caucasus, Georgia and Turkey. This is the first day that I could leave as yesterday was our 30th wedding anniversary and I have just 40 days before my wife, Liz, finishes work and flies to Sofia. Her job, which is to develop and maintain a high standard of teaching in the education centres operated by the company she works for, is what caused us to move from rural New Zealand. That journey had also been a bit of an adventure as I had persuaded Liz that we would travel overland through Malaysia, Thailand, Cambodia, Laos and Vietnam to get to China. The two of us travelling together had its rewards but also its challenges.

The trip did not get off to a good start. We left our home in the Wairarapa and caught the train to Wellington on the coldest New Zealand day in living memory. For many days the Tararua Mountains had been crowned with a mantle of white which seemed to beg you to make a climb up to the snow line, but on the day of our departure it was even snowing hard in the valley which is almost unheard of. We had plenty of time to fritter away in the capital before heading to the airport to catch our plane to Christchurch in the South Island, from where the following day we would fly to Kuala Lumpur. When flying is the only option (as it is to go anywhere from New Zealand), I at least like to stop for a night or two wherever we can on the journey, and so I had booked and paid for a night in a hotel in Christchurch where I was interested to see how the recovery from the February 2011 earthquake was progressing.

Our relaxed time rich attitude was abruptly shattered at the check-in desk at Wellington where we were told that the snow had closed Christchurch Airport and the next flight with space on it for us was the following Thursday. Ironically if we had allowed less time for our connection in Christchurch we would not have suffered any disruption as the airport was expected to re-open within hours, but we had become part of the backlog. This was disastrous as it meant that we would miss our flight to Kuala Lumpur, but we were not going to give up that easily. Our mood was now one of frantic activity. We caught the bus back into town after an intense session in the airport computer suite where we had booked places on the overnight ferry to Picton. We established that there was no public transport from there that would get us to Christchurch on time and so we tried to book a hire car online, but had failed to get confirmation from the rental company. Whether we were going to make it to the airport for our flight was far from certain, but a boat across the Cook Strait at least gave us a chance.

Gazing out of the bus window I was surprised to feel a certain thrill. All my travel plans hung in the balance, we had wasted money on a hotel room in Christchurch we couldn't use, the ferry and car would cost us extra, and I hate unnecessary expenditure, yet I felt elated. There was a kind of excitement at not just having a puzzle to solve but being inside the puzzle and living it. This would not have been the case if we were disrupted from just trying to follow a normal routine, but the allure of international travel seemed to lift us from the mundane to the romantic. In truth I felt myself to be Phileas Fogg racing across the wastes to beat the deadline. I have never been attracted to the adrenalin rush of things like bungee jumping or even rollercoaster rides, but I do get a thrill from travelling.

Liz, who is ever practical, spoke of claiming from her travel insurance, which she had insisted on buying despite my protestations that it is all a rip-off, while I was equally as staunch in my refusal to waste any more of our money by taking insurance for myself. I do get irritated by the attitude that it is somehow virtuous to pay inflated premiums to cover any eventuality, and that you are being wantonly reckless if you choose not to line the pockets of large companies which are little more than institutionalised highway robbers. Some people seem to think that buying insurance prevents you from the danger of having an accident rather than just a way that, if you are stubborn enough, you may be able to reclaim some money after the event. I was not too upset when she realised that she had dated it to start from the day we left the country, not the day we left home.

After a cold night on the ferry and a memorable drive sharing a car with a group of rugby fans, equally displaced and diverted as they returned from Australia, we arrived at Christchurch to find the airport open again and just in time for our flight. Getting there had been a challenge but it did remind me that when Liz and I work together we can be a good team.

Now that I am on my own I will miss her company and also feel denied that I will not have Liz to directly share my experiences with. But there is a frisson of excitement at travelling alone and, while two people can seem to be a closed group, as a single traveller I am by nature more exposed to my surroundings and the ebb and flow of the world around me. It is a cliché that travel is a journey of self-discovery, but I do want to use this trip as an opportunity to reflect on what is the underlying motivation behind both this current journey and my past travels. While my journey is taking me along the ancient Silk Road trade route, through the Central Asian Steppe, across the Caucasus Mountains and the breadth of what was Byzantium, I plan to think back to some of my other travels and mull over why I am driven to make these trips; what is it that makes a travel addict.

I have spent several nights on trains in China and have often found sleep easy as the carriage clicks and clacks and sways, but wake up if it stops for too long at a station, so I get a good night's sleep on the aptly titled and virtually non-stop 'Z' train. Now as we rattle through a small town I catch a glimpse of eight or ten workers in a uniform of bright pink shirts lined up in two ranks for their morning briefing. I have seen this all over China, especially outside spas and hairdressing salons, where the staff will be psyched up for the day ahead and sometimes put through a song and dance routine. Never have I seen anyone looking reluctant or disillusioned at this excruciating process as the Chinese simply do as they are told, seemingly without thought or question or self-conscious embarrassment.

This also reflects the positive attitude of nearly everyone. There is a paradox in that one of the oldest and most traditional of human cultures is now a thrusting modern economic giant that is literally bulldozing its way to a future as a world leader, and the citizens are being carried along on the tide of urban optimism. Despite the ever growing gap between rich and poor nearly everyone is significantly better off than they were. The country has moved from drab to colourful, from scarcity to abundance and from thrift to waste. The ease with which vast amounts of food and packaging is thrown away in a land where tens of millions have starved to death in living memory, I find astonishing.

I like to court sympathy by saying that I was born during rationing, which is true as food rationing continued in Britain until 1954. I wasn't aware of it at the time and was never forced to go hungry, but the virtues of thrift and avoiding waste were instilled into me. China has gone to the opposite extreme; food is available from every other doorway, most of it cheap and with little nutritional value, but food which would have saved lives and which is now treated with disdain. The Chinese appear to be immune to the stench of rotting meat and vegetation as half eaten filled buns, gelatinous sausage shapes and various body-parts-on-sticks are discarded in the street before being collected into overflowing bins piled with the city's leftovers.

The starvation suffered in the misguided and misnamed Great Leap Forward is in the nation's previous existence. The country has completely reinvented itself and put all the horrors of the past behind it. That sense of optimism can sometimes be felt in New Zealand which, as a young country with a small population and free of the class structure which stifles Britain and breeds so much cynicism, can take pride in its achievements with a youthful vigour. But you would have more chance of herding cats than of ordering a group of Kiwis to dress in a pink uniform and do a song and dance routine every morning before work!

In Xian I am going to be a proper tourist. Like a cruise ship passenger arriving at a new port and leaving their belongings in the cabin as they are shepherded onto a bus for a day-outing to see a famous sight, I deposit my backpack at left luggage and hop on a bus bound for the Terracotta Warriors.

The Terracotta Army was discovered to the east of Xian in 1974 by a group of farmers when they were digging a well. It is a mile east of the tomb of Qin Shi Huang, the First Emperor, who made Xian his capital and assumed the title of Emperor after unifying the warring factions in China. Qin Shi Huang is a huge figure in Chinese history and he was the start of more than two millennia of imperial rule. He undertook gigantic projects, including building the Great Wall and developing a national road system, all at the expense of innumerable lives. His reputation is that of a terrifying and totally ruthless narcissist who was himself terrified of death. His tomb and the estimated 8,000 strong clay army (of which about 2,000 have been uncovered so far), which were there to guard and protect it, was not built as a memorial but as a functioning resource for the after-life.

In addition to the warriors, an entire man-made necropolis for Qin Shi Huang has been found around the First Emperor's tomb mound. This complex was constructed as a microcosm of his imperial palace and consists of several offices, halls, stables and other buildings. There is no public admission to the area but I saw some of the artefacts on display in the museum on the Terracotta Army site. According to an historian writing a century after the First Emperor died, work on this mausoleum began in 246 BC soon after he ascended the throne at the age of 13. The full construction later involved 700,000 workers and the location was chosen for its geology; rich in gold and jade. He wrote that the First Emperor was buried with palaces, towers, valuable artefacts and other wonderful objects. According to this account, there were 100 rivers simulated with flowing mercury, and above them the ceiling was decorated with heavenly bodies, below which were the features of the land. The tomb itself appears to be a hermetically sealed space that is as big as a football pitch and located underneath the pyramidal tomb mound. The Chinese government, probably wisely, has not allowed it to be excavated for fear that techniques are not yet good enough to ensure the preservation of its contents.

Qin Shi Huang was clearly not convinced that he would be able to enjoy all this once he had shuffled off his mortal coil, as he put enormous effort into finding some kind of potion to give himself immortality. This involved utilising the talents of the best brains of the time and to prevent them from becoming distracted he burnt all their books and buried-alive many scholars who failed to meet expectations. Ironically it is thought that he finally met his end through mercury poisoning from ingesting a preparation which it was hoped would give him the immortality he craved.

The Terracotta Army is alright. Well it's extraordinary, magnificent, if I had no previous knowledge of it I would be blown away. But it is as I expected and no more. The entertainment value of stone figures is quite limited; they can't move or tell jokes and I don't get any sensation of awe as I might in a great cathedral. I would say that the world is richer for finding them, but as the only way to view them is to either gaze down into a pit or peer into a sealed glass case at some special exhibits, as an experience it is sterile. There's no special atmosphere to the place and a good photo would have done almost as well.

I suspect that I am not cut out to be a sightseer and now I am back in what seems to be my natural habitat of wandering the streets and soaking up the sounds and smells of the city. Xian can reasonably claim to be the start of the Silk Road and the Muslim Quarter overflows with stalls of dates and walnuts interspersed with griddles of flat bread and skewered meat, which is all very different from the markets and food stalls of Eastern China. I noticed from the train this morning that the agriculture has changed as rangy looking sheep scramble about the pasture, and the paddies of the Yangtze have given way to fields of wheat. The methods remain primitive but, as more and more of the population move to the ever expanding cities, it must fast be becoming a myth in the countryside that there is a limitless supply of Chinese labour, and the government is now making noises about the need to modernise the agricultural sector. I watch the crop being collected into sheaves; I think the only wheat sheaf I have seen before is on the inn sign of one of my favourite pubs.

I am interested in history, but for me the experience of travelling is about those who are alive today, and often that provides a trip to the past as well as to other cultures. Tucked away off a side street I come across an ancient wooden archway inscribed 'Mosque'. Smooth flagstones lead to what I can only think of as a lych-gate providing the entrance into a tranquil and perfectly symmetrical Chinese garden. Nobody bothers me but I am unsure how far I should enter, particularly as I am wearing shorts, and so retrace my steps. Five minutes later an elderly French couple stop me and communicate that they are looking for a mosque. I direct them as a local.

It is time to return to my cruise liner, or to be precise train 1043 (no letter prefix suggests that this is one of the slowest slow trains) which will take me overnight to Zhangye in Gansu Province. This train was significantly cheaper than any other doing the same trip and I wonder if it will be a good old green one with a yellow stripe along the side, and probably with no air-conditioning. Travelling in China demands a degree of planning, not least because train tickets get sold out so quickly. What makes life much easier is that there are several websites providing Chinese train timetables that are more reliable than my printed version, and some of them can also give current availability on any given train. What makes life less easy is that most of the tickets are sold before they come on sale. This is a quirk of the system that I have as yet been unable to fathom.

Before I realised the availability of railway ticket offices dotted about town I had to negotiate the bear pit of the station booking hall. As in other major cities, Nanjing railway station has more than 30 windows in the ticket hall, each of which has probably 50 people queuing at any given time, with a few rogues trying to push in at the front, so there are about 1,500 people in the building. Tickets can only be bought so many days in advance and at busy times can sell out in minutes. Over the national holiday in October you would probably have more chance of getting a ticket to Willie Wonka's chocolate factory than onto any train in China.

The little booking offices, which can be found around the city, provide an easier way to purchase a ticket for a small fee, and they usually have much shorter queues than the main station. There is one just around the corner from our apartment but I always seem to struggle with it. The woman who is often behind the counter is one of many Chinese people who seem to believe that foreigners belong to a different species and that any kind of communication with them, however clearly they articulate Mandarin, is impossible. I see her glazing over before I even open my mouth. At other times it is run by a middle aged man who anticipates language difficulties by keeping his mouth firmly shut and making a long and jumbled series of squiggles, dots and dashes on a scrappy piece of paper in the firm belief, also held by many of his countrymen, that while speech can be difficult to follow with foreigners, Chinese characters are universally understood.

There are things about the system, such as why I can get a ticket from one booking office but not another, that I don't understand but I am learning. I have recently realised that the number shown after some characters displayed above the window and which changes from time to time, is the number of days in advance that they are selling tickets. On this basis I calculated when I could get my ticket for train 1043 and caught the metro to a more enlightened ticket window.

I gave the destination, day of travel, train number and type of ticket I wanted when I got to the window and I was pleased that, not only was I not directed elsewhere but I was understood without having to show the piece of paper on which I had it all written as back-up. But the answer was 'meiyou', the ubiquitous Chinese phrase meaning 'there isn't', 'it's broken', 'I'm the wrong person to ask', I don't know what you're talking about', 'go away it's my tea break', 'I can't be bothered anyway'. While I was pondering which meaning was most applicable to this situation he said that I should return the following day. Having established when I could buy a ticket and with the website showing only 22 hard sleeper berths remaining, I was at the local booking office first thing in the morning. I was told to come back at 3 pm. Later I stood in the queue and studied my watch as the hands moved to exactly 3 o'clock. "Meiyou", come back tomorrow I was told. I caught the metro to another booking office and was told the same. I walked the 3 stops back home and, with no real hope of success, tried a third booking office on the way and got the ticket I wanted with no problem at all. China can be a challenging country to live in.

Today's china talks openly and unashamedly about a class system and evidence of a burgeoning middle class is everywhere, most obviously on the roads where jam-packed buses vie for space with Mercedes and Porsches. Curiously there are very few small cheap cars to separate the electric scooter riders from the BMW and Audi drivers. The new superfast trains offer first and second class accommodation, but the ordinary express trains still use the terms 'hard' and 'soft' seats or sleepers, with which we had become familiar when we first came to China on the Trans-Siberian Express. Now at Xian railway station I find that 1043 is an old green train with a yellow stripe of a type that used to be used throughout

East Europe and Russia as well as China. We first boarded a train like this in East Berlin in 1989 and travelled in similar carriages through Poland, across the breadth of the USSR and down into Manchuria.

I asked for a bottom bunk instead of the middle berth which I usually go for; as I am boarding the train at its point of departure my bed will not have been messed up by earlier passengers and it is late enough that I can claim it all for myself. It should also give me some entitlement to sitting by the window the following morning. I can cope without air conditioning but I can't get the windows open and it is hot and very humid. At my request the carriage attendant uses her key to open the window, and I try to distract myself with the Guardian prize crossword which I printed off before leaving Nanjing, while waiting for our departure to create some airflow. When it does, the old chap in the opposite bunk gets blown about so much that he apologetically has to close the window. It is fortunate that I am tired, and travelling west through the night the temperature gradually eases.

The man opposite proffers a hard-boiled egg but I spotted a dining car before I boarded. It was 3-4 carriages back and I make my way through the usual jumble of people and their belongings. Just before I reach it I am turned back with the dreaded 'meiyou', I really don't want instant noodles from the cart seller so I will do without breakfast and look forward to finding lunch in Zhangye. The city lies in the middle of the Hexi Corridor which is an ancient route through this mountainous area and probably one of the few stretches of the Silk Road where there was no viable alternative to take. Traders have been using this route, which is squeezed between the Tibetan Plateau and the Gobi Desert (a rock and a hard place if ever there was one), for over two millennia.

Chinese silk being transported west was certainly an important trade but it was by no means the only commodity that was carried. Precious stones, metals, spices, wool and even Arabian horses changed hands, and not just physical goods were exchanged; ideas and cultural customs also flowed along the route. China gained wealth and riches as an exporter of highly prized goods but some of her imports were of a more lasting quality, most notably Buddhism which was introduced to China from India about 2,000 years ago. The narrow passage that the ancient road utilised is over 1,000 km long, but the railway line seems somehow to have missed the corridor as we enter tunnel after tunnel, some of them exceptionally long. Tunnels are exciting mysterious places from the outside but unspeakably dull once you're inside one, and they make trying to read a book in a train carriage a particularly frustrating exercise.

So reflecting on the journey so far, it seems that the attraction of travel for me is to be able to wander around in real living places and that visiting museums, however splendid they are, does not really fulfil my needs; I found more of interest on the streets of Xian than I did looking at the Terracotta Army. There was also the bit about being inside a puzzle when our journey from New Zealand was disrupted. Being 'inside' feels important, that when travelling one becomes a part of the wider world rather than seeing it from the outside. I may need to think more about that.

Chapter Two: Missing the Sights

Zhangye looks more prosperous than I had imagined. With a population of about ¼ million, in China that gives it the feel of an English market town rather than a sprawling metropolis, and the wide tree lined streets are relatively quiet.

The city is in the middle of the Hexi Corridor, in an area that was a frontier for much of China's history as it formed a natural passage to the Central Asian portion of the empire, which was difficult to access by other routes. Zhangye is the birthplace of the fearsome thirteenth century Mongol leader Kublai Khan who was born in the Dafo temple, which is also the site of the longest reclining wooden Buddha in China, and which I have no plans to visit.

Kublai Khan was the grandson of Genghis Khan whose vast empire was divided between his four sons on his death. Kublai Khan's real power was limited to China and Mongolia together with the Korean Peninsula, though he still had influence over the rest of the Mongol Empire, which at that time stretched from the Pacific to the Black Sea and from Siberia to modern day Afghanistan, one fifth of the world's inhabited land area. In 1271 he assumed the role of Emperor of China and he is known as the founder of the Yuan Dynasty. Kublai Khan became the first non-Chinese Emperor to conquer all of China. He established his capital in what is now Beijing but returned to Mongolia in the summer to escape the heat, where he decreed the 'stately pleasure-dome' at Xanadu, celebrated in Coleridge's poem.

Marco Polo is said to have spent a year in Zhangye on his travels and presumably was aware that it was the birthplace of the Great Khan with whom his journeys were so closely connected. If the urge to travel can in any way be genetic, then he must have had a strong predisposition, as when he was born his father and uncle were travelling far from home and didn't return to Venice for another 16 years. In 1266 they met Kublai Khan in present day Beijing and were apparently the first Europeans that the Emperor had seen. Kublai Khan received the brothers with hospitality and asked them many questions regarding the European legal and political systems. He also enquired about the Pope and Church in Rome and he tasked them with delivering a letter to the Pope, requesting that an envoy bring him back the oil of the lamp of Jerusalem, which is anointing oil or myrrh. They had a problem because the papacy was vacant at the time and so returned to Venice where Marco Polo finally met his father and joined him and his uncle on their subsequent expeditions.

My travels are nothing compared to the adventures that they had. They set sail in 1271 and arrived at the port of Acre in modern day Israel, which was then still a Crusader stronghold. From there they rode on camels to the Persian port of Hormuz in the Gulf. No doubt having had enough of being on camelback they wanted to sail to China, but the ships available were not seaworthy, so they continued overland until they reached Kublai Khan's summer palace at Xanadu, three and a half years after leaving Venice, and presented him with the sacred oil from Jerusalem. Kublai Khan welcomed the family and took a shine to Marco who was about 21 years old at the time. He was given important government positions and became an envoy for the Emperor. It was much later, when he was a Genoese prisoner of war that Marco Polo related his travels to a fellow inmate who recorded his adventures and produced the book which it is said inspired Christopher Columbus.

I vow for the umpteenth time not to rely on Google maps as I am directed back nearly a mile to the bus station I must have passed half an hour ago. I think the problem is that new roads, railways and shopping malls spring up so quickly that even internet maps just can't keep pace with the development. As with all Chinese cities, it is difficult to imagine how it would have been hundreds of years ago. Any old remains are treated as a separate entity rather than as part of the continuing fabric of life in the town, and the street patterns as well as all the buildings are of recent origin. There is absolutely nothing that could possibly be a link to the city that Marco Polo lived in.

I have decided to visit an ancient site well out of town and I board a minibus bound for Mati Si. I'm going to give sightseeing another go at this temple which is built into the rock face. I am encouraged by the difficulty I have had in establishing if there is anywhere to stay. I had to recruit the help of a Chinese friend who, after a considerable time on internet and phone, came up with Mr Dong. He was unable to give a name for his hotel but said that any bus driver to Mati Si would know him. I like it already.

With breakdowns the journey takes over 2 hours and the pot-holed road skirts around the bottom of some dramatic jagged hills, with those in the distance ethereally capped with white, before suddenly and bizarrely coming to a new concrete surface with multi storey buildings freshly erected. The other remaining passengers are builders' labourers and the whole area seems to be still under construction. I notice that the driver is on his phone and after a few minutes have passed he directs me to a car and driver, who turns out to be Mr Dong. We drive through an enormous archway that is still being built and he indicates that I should go to a ticket office where I am obliged to make a purchase. This is an odd idea to me, that you have to pay to enter a village, but it is the norm in China for anywhere with anything that anybody may want to ever see, and those are the only places where accommodation may be available.

This accommodation is not one that I could take Liz to. The room has just enough space for a bed, which is rock hard even by Chinese standards. I am unsure what altitude we are at but it is decidedly chilly and the hotel has no heating. Downstairs off a courtyard he shows me the squat toilet with a bucket of water for flushing, but there is no bathroom. After the last two nights on trains I could do with a hot shower but the only washing facilities are an outside cold tap. The room does appear to be clean and the double bed has two duvets, one of which I can place underneath me to soften the solidity of the mattress somewhat. Mr Dong keeps coming up with something; first a key for the door, then a thermos flask of hot water- it is a basic human right in China that there is always access to water for tea, and finally he arrives with a pair of policemen.

It is a bit crowded with four of us in the room but they want to photograph my passport and get some more details such as what my profession is. They suggest teacher and I decide it is easiest to agree. They have a lot more questions but I can't understand most of what they say and they eventually give up and say goodbye. The hotel is one of a dozen identical buildings which make up the core of the village. One opposite with tables and chairs under an umbrella advertising Snow Beer is the police station. They are traditional style with columns and balconies and colourful decoration under the swept up tile roofs, but obviously of recent construction, which gives the feeling of being in a film set. A girl in traditional dress and a saffron robed monk hanging around the shop fronts do nothing to dispel this illusion.

It is a beautiful morning and I am ready to go. But go where; temple or mountain? I set off south up stream towards the pine forests thinking that as this is my whole day here, I can go for a long walk and not worry about time, but after a few yards I realise that as I have not had breakfast and have no food with me this is not a sensible option. There are no signs but walking north I soon find the Horseshoe Temple, which apparently got its name from a legend of a heavenly Pegasus leaving its mark as it flew past. It does look extraordinary with balconies of varying sizes carved out of the sandstone at different elevations and presumably connected by staircases inside the rock. But I am distracted by a sign that says sightseeing look out. The steps go up a long way but I am ready for some exercise and have plenty of time to return to the temple later.

After several hundred newish looking concrete steps I am looking down on the worked rock face. It was started in the fifth century and has really been a work in progress ever since, with the most dramatic stuff completed during the Ming Dynasty. It clearly looks to be not a single vision as bits have been excavated all along the sandstone cliff with some apparently prospering more than others. The path continues away from the temple and I end up on a horse track which leads steeply back down into the valley on the other side of the village, to which I return ready for breakfast.

No eggs today (meiyou), but a bowl of noodles glistening with chilli oil and finely chopped spring onions satisfies my appetite. After pottering around for a while I make my way back up to the temple but am hailed just as I get to the entrance. Two young lads I spoke to at dinner last night are on their way out and want me to go with them to another temple on the other side of the valley. I hesitate, but Wang Xiao Ming as he introduces himself (aka Andy) has good English and as I am unable to communicate more than basics in Chinese I like to take opportunities for more conversation when they arise, so off we go. It is very common for English speaking Chinese to give themselves an English name and is encouraged in some schools. I don't feel at all comfortable with the practice which seems to suggest a denial of one's own culture, but it can make introductions to people much easier.

One practicality I am trying to establish is what time I can catch a bus tomorrow. I get a different answer from everyone I ask and Wang Xi…., Andy says that it will be different tomorrow as it is a Sunday. The day of the week is usually irrelevant in China but I am a long way from home in Nanjing and maybe customs are different in this part of the country. This is borne out by a bus driver we ask who says that there will not be a bus back to the city tomorrow. Andy tells me that the alternative is to walk to a crossroads 4 km away. That does not sound too bad I say. 4 km or 10 km he replies. There is a bit of difference between those estimates I venture and he admits that he doesn't really have a clue how far it is. The temple we visit has a gorgeous display of colourful cavalry in remarkably good condition. Andy says that they were put there 3 years ago. The two lads scramble up into another cave at the back of the temple, which he tells me was dug at the same time as the statues were made. I had thought that even the Chinese couldn't fake ancient monuments carved out of a hillside, but it seems that I was wrong.

On returning to the village I still haven't seen inside the temple or explored the forests and mountains. Having twice been to the temple I decide to go the other way and am soon approached by a head-scarfed horsewoman. I had already turned down horse riding last night from a very insistent fellow but I make the mistake of asking how much and before I really think what I am doing I find myself on horseback. The horse moves off and I slide down the side of it still clinging to the iron ring pommel and with my feet in the stirrups. I shout out and am rescued but have lost some confidence in this venture and remember that earlier today I struggled on foot to get down a path filled with horseshoe prints, because it was so steep.

I had noticed the horses earlier in the day, about 30 of them with what I took to be a group of a similar number waiting to go trekking. I now realise that these were not customers but that each mount has its own handler, and that the experience I have agreed to, is to sit on a horse while it is being led around by the woman on foot. I would have preferred to have walked myself and consider offering to swap places with her. We make our way up the valley to a point where the river bed is a brilliant white with the sun glittering on it. She tells me to get off and continue on foot and, putting my glasses on, I realise that from this point up the whole river is frozen solid. No wonder I felt cold last night.

Back at the village the lady at the hotel tells me that a cultural show is soon to start at the Hall for Singing and Dancing. I find my way there and make the mistake of sitting at the front, where I immediately become the focus of attention, as the rest of the audience wait for the curtain to raise. Plenty of people are now in Mati Si but I am the only non-Chinese and fair game to be viewed as an entertaining curiosity when there is nothing better to see.

Being stared at and made to feel peculiar is an inescapable part of the life of a foreigner in China even in the large cities, let alone isolated corners of Gansu Province. Liz gets annoyed at people sneaking photos. Sometimes I am approached and asked if they can photograph me and, although I am not happy with being objectified in that way, I find it difficult to refuse. More often it will be done clandestinely, which I suspect I'm usually unaware of unless I'm with Liz, who is eagle-eyed in these matters. On one occasion we were in a railway station waiting room when she gave a cry of anguish and turned her head as if she had been bitten by something. I asked with concern what the matter was, only to be told that she had spotted a girl some distance away pointing her phone at us.

There is always a danger in taking an interest in people who are different in some way that the person gets lost and only the exterior features are seen. I suppose that is why feminists object to sensuous pictures of pretty girls, and I would imagine that the novelty of being a pop-star and being mobbed in the street would wear off quite quickly. Receiving that praise from those who don't know you as a person has to be a hollow reward. I have never been a celebrity (or a glamorous woman), but being something out of the ordinary in China can give an insight into what that experience may feel like.

One day I was wandering around the outskirts of Wuxi, an ancient city between Nanjing and Shanghai, and turned a corner just as three young factory girls came out of their place of work. They positively squealed with delight at seeing a foreigner and for a moment I felt that I could be a film star. The difference of course is that while they are put on a pedestal as super people, the attraction of a laowai (foreigner) is more akin to the wonder of something peculiar, like a performing monkey. But these girls had so little consciousness of anything other than wholesome wellbeing that I succumbed to their gleeful exclamations. I knew that really I was an oddity and not a celebrity as they fumbled in their handbags for their phones, but I gave a genuine smile and posed with them, giving the two-fingered sign required for photos in Asia, which used to mean 'peace' to hippies, but I'm unsure what it indicates now. Would I have acted differently if they hadn't been a group of pretty girls? Of course not!

At last the show starts and I am displaced as the main attraction. I don't understand a word of it, but the costumes are colourful, the dancing synchronised and the whole thing surprisingly professional. It's now too late or I'm too tired or both, to go to Mati Si temple but my priority tomorrow is to get back to Zhangye and catch the overnight train to the ancient oasis of Turpan.

I'm up early. According to the lady at the hotel, who has gained some credibility with me by correctly knowing the time of the cultural show, buses are at 7.30 and 8.00. My original plan to leave in the afternoon is too risky so I again hot foot it up to the temple. It is locked up. I console myself with the thought that really it is similar to a tunnel; intriguing from the outside but inside it can only be a dark dank flight of steps. Wandering back down I see a bus leaving on the road below. It's not yet 7.30.

The village is slowly coming to life and I again ask about bus times. 7.30 I am told. I show him my watch, it's now 7.40. He shouts across to a neighbour and explains the situation to me. I think what he is saying is that in 10 minutes someone with a motorbike will take me down the road to catch a bus from, presumably where I first got off and met Mr Dong. But then the hotel lady comes out and says that I should remain where I am. I sit on a step, pull out a book to read and await developments. At least I have plenty of time and if needs be I can walk 4 or 10 km to the crossroads. A frantic blaring of horns makes me jump up and hastily gather together my belongings as the same bus with the same driver that brought me here pulls up with an urgency that is not seen again for the rest of the journey.

So, I carefully planned this two day detour in order to visit an extraordinary and unique temple and to go walking in a beautiful mountainous area. I've successfully completed neither of these tasks but somehow my time still feels as if it has been well spent. Perhaps I just need to work harder at being a tourist, but tourist sights are not always what they are cracked up to be. I recall that visiting Agra and seeing the Taj Mahal was one of our least pleasant experiences of India as, what might otherwise have been a perfectly pleasant town had been turned into a den of thieves and con-artists and stripped of the charm and consideration usually found amongst the peoples of India.

It was only a few days after visiting the Taj Mahal that we reached the Golden Temple at Amritsar. Having worked for some years in the West

London suburb of Southall, with 80% of the population originating from the Punjab, I was keen to make this visit to the holiest place in the Sikh religion which I recall was also the scene of turbulent history during the time that I was in Southall. The Sikh activist Bhindranwale and his armed followers were holed up in the temple and Indira Gandhi mounted a major military operation to remove them, in which hundreds of civilians died. This assault on the temple was seen as an act of sacrilege and led directly to the assassination of the Prime Minister by her Sikh bodyguards not many months later. The Golden Temple is not such a well-known tourist attraction as the Taj Mahal, and troubles in the area have often caused the Punjab to be off limits to visitors, but we found a stunningly fabulous building. The golden facade shimmered as it sat serenely in its own tranquil lake but more importantly, in contrast to the stultified self-importance of the Taj, we experienced a living and breathing cultural centre which has stayed in my memory for many years.

Really it is not necessary to have any kind of attraction to enjoy the thrill of travel. The first time we went to China we spent day after day staring at identical snow covered birch trees from the window of the Trans-Siberian Express, and thought it hugely exciting. Of course there was also the sway and rattle of the train, the distinctive smells from the dining car, hot tea from the carriage samovar and thrilling gulps of freezing air when we stretched our legs at stations along the route.

There were also our fellow passengers. In the winter of 1989 we travelled all the way from Liverpool St. Station to Manchuria by train, except for the ferry from Harwich to The Hook. We were unaware what momentous times we were living in as we spent an evening in East Berlin just months before the wall came down. We experienced the austerity of communist Poland and saw Warsaw still being rebuilt from the destruction of the Second World War. The thought that Solidarity was little more than a year away from forming a government was not even a pipe dream. Finally, after a few months teaching in China, we were forced to leave in the wake of the uncertainty that followed the events in Tiananmen Square.

In the USSR all our travel and accommodation had to be arranged through the state run travel agency Intourist and the whole journey took on that seedy glamour that had been created by spy fiction writers. A clear demonstration that the dullest and seemingly most god forsaken places can still be romantic and exciting simply through an image created by works of fiction. When we missed our train because Intourist took us to the wrong railway station we insisted on being put on the next train despite the reluctance of the authorities to allow this. Consequently we escaped their practice of placing all foreigners together, so that they couldn't corrupt the locals, and were able to gain a proper experience of travelling with Russian citizens.

First there was the young naval officer, on his way to join his ship in Vladivostok, who viewed us with sullen distrust until we managed to produce a bottle of vodka. Unlike Russia today, where every other doorway sells alcohol, drink was hard to come by then without foreign currency or happening to be in the right queue at the right time. When he left the compartment our other travelling companion, a little busybody of a woman, rummaged through his things and produced a picture of a scantily clad woman which she showed us in disgust. We could only smile as we thought how overdressed the girl in the picture would be to feature on page three of The Sun newspaper.

After we changed trains at Irkutsk, in the middle of Siberia, we shared our accommodation with Maria. She was an older lady from Leningrad who boarded the train with a huge amount of luggage which she proceeded to unpack. All of it was edible. She stowed items of food in every corner and crevice of our compartment and still had more to stash away. It was only years later when I read about the Siege of Leningrad and realised the starvation and horror that she would have lived through when she was young, that I got a glimmer of insight into the emotional scars that she had carried into old age. When Chinese people began to board, the train became much livelier. With little or no concept of private space they would happily make themselves at home in any compartment and, with a Russian speaking Chinaman and an English speaking Chinese woman, after days of simply nodding and smiling, we could finally have conversations with Maria. It took time as our English was translated first into Chinese and then Russian and the process then reversed to get a reply, but one thing you have when travelling across the vastness of Russia by train, is time.

Back in Zhangye I am able to find a café with Wi-Fi and deal with urgent e-mails, such as how should Emily (our daughter at university in Auckland) best make gravy to go with a chicken she is roasting. I try to call Liz on Skype without success but catch a call from our neighbours in New Zealand. It strikes me as curious how such different existences can continue in the same dimension of time. I now need to return to the railway station to catch another overnight train, this time to the ancient Silk Road oasis of Turpan.

I am pleased with myself that I remembered to note the number of the bus I caught from Zhangye train station into town and I find a stop for a number 1. The buses here only have the number on the back of the vehicle, so you can see which one you want to catch after it has pulled away. Presumably as a solution to people missing their buses, they are colour coded and I see a green 4, a blue 3 and a pink 9 before I confidently hop onto a yellow bus. Even though it only has 20 odd seats the bus has a conductress who is clearly in charge and proud to wear the uniform of the bus company. New passengers are told where they must sit, but she is powerless to keep order when a fierce argument breaks out amongst passengers at the front of the vehicle. A large lady is still shouting even after she gets off at her stop.

I have ages to wait for the train as it is delayed but I am intrigued by a group of women who are giggling and laughing uncontrollably. They wipe tears from their eyes and try to cover their mouths but cannot contain themselves. This is not the China that I have come to know; two incidents in the space of an hour where people have completely lost control of their emotions. Like a noise that you are unaware of until it stops, I only now realise how tightly in control of their emotions and buttoned up the majority Han Chinese are.

I have again proved to be a poor tourist, not even getting inside the troglodyte temple, but it doesn't seem to matter too much, which reinforces the observation that tourist sites are not my main motivation for travel. Soaking up the atmosphere does seem to be important and that romantic notion of being somewhere exotic, whether it is a stop on the Silk Road or the old USSR with the ruthless brutality of the Cold War. The travel thing is not just about being in a living reality but also the romanticised fantasies that accompany those real places, and the way in which the two things can merge.

Chapter Three: To Travel Hopefully

Finally the train arrives at Zhangye station and I am on the move again. I love the feeling of steadily heading west, in no great hurry but making progress. The landscape is desert; dead flat with scrubby brown tussock. But looking south the plain ends abruptly in soaring snow topped mountains. Tomorrow I should be 500 metres below sea level, the lowest place on earth other than the Dead Sea, and I need to find a hotel with a shower.

This morning the tussock has gone. There is only an amorphous expanse of brown and grey. There is nothing of the beauty of the Arabian Desert with its apricot coloured dunes and clear blue sky. Here it is just desolate. Although it has not been noticeable, we have clearly descended a long way through the night to the extent that my bottle of water has imploded. Okay, not as much as when landing in a plane from 30,000 feet, but there is a good hiss of air as I unscrew the top and it crackles back into shape. I am now in Xinjiang Uyghur Autonomous Province. The land area is a bit bigger than France, Germany, Spain and Portugal combined, in fact you could probably throw in Belgium, the Netherlands and Luxembourg and I doubt that it would tip the scales. But only 4%-5% of it is habitable as the region is dominated by mountains and vast deserts.

Historically there have been no clearly defined borders to this land and although it was an integral part of China as long ago as the Han Dynasty, which was established soon after the death of the First Emperor, over the last two millennia it has at various times come under the control of Mongols, Tibetans and Russians. Uyghur nationalists believe that they are descended from a Turkic people who have occupied the land for thousands of years, but Chinese authorities claim that the Uyghurs were displaced from Mongolia in the ninth century and overran the Han people who had settled here long before them. On two occasions in the first half of the twentieth century the Uyghurs gained independence, but only as vassals of the USSR, aided and abetted by Mao Zedong who was intent on weakening the power of the Nationalist led Chinese Republic.

Uyghur protesters have used violent forms of terrorism to make their views known, including bus bombings and this has led to the authorities responding with harsh crackdowns on the population. Following a major attack in Urumqi market place in May 2014 which killed over 30 civilians the central government declared a 12 month war against terrorism in the region. Beijing has said that hundreds of Uyghurs have been trained by the Al-Qaeda terrorist network in Afghanistan, while Uyghur groups have criticised China for manufacturing a connection between the global war on terror and the Uyghur fight for independence. The Uyghurs, like their Central Asian cousins, are followers of Islam and there have been claims that China has repressed religious practice in the Province- Mosques certainly exist but the air is not filled with the calls to prayer heard in Muslim countries. Government policy has led to a huge influx of Han Chinese to the region in the last 20-30 years and, needless to say, the discovery of reserves of oil and gas has done nothing to ease the tensions.

I will be very surprised if I meet with any evidence of trouble other than perhaps a more attentive police presence than is usual in most of China, although there are several parts of the world where caution is needed despite the issues not being in the headlines. One such that I discovered when planning our trip from New Zealand to China is the Thai border with North East Malaysia. I had spent weeks poring over maps and train timetables. My most prized possession had become a map of Thailand and Vietnam, which actually included Malaysia, Cambodia and Laos and which took us all the way from Kuala Lumpur to China. It seemed remarkable to me that I had found this exotic gem with its promise of different landscapes, strange cultures and unforeseen happenings in somewhere as mundane as Palmerston North Paper Plus.

From studying this map and my other prized possession, the Thos. Cook Overseas Timetable, the jungle railway through Malaysia to the north east of the country looked the most interesting route to begin our journey, but I was somewhat taken aback to learn that crossing into Thailand at this point takes one to an area where several thousand people have been killed in recent years by a Muslim separatist movement. I found no indication of foreigners being targeted, but much of the activity is focused on the transport network with bombs on trains being an almost daily occurrence. Clearly none of this is considered newsworthy in developed countries with our free press being free to decide what it is that we want or need to know.

It was unlikely that we would encounter any problems on our travels, but equally we could just as easily take a different route, and wondering if a bomb is going to explode on the train you are boarding is not the kind of thrill we were looking for. In compensation for missing out on the train ride through the jungle I found a possible boat trip on the west side of the peninsular from Malaysia to Thailand, and so we arrived at Kuala Perlis. I say 'possible' because the information I scoured from the internet was contradictory. This area abounds with sea trips to outlying islands and at other times of the year the border can be crossed at Langkawi Island, but sadly there are no customs posts there in July. I had read a reference to a boat that goes round the coast to Satun in Thailand but an entry on a travel forum was adamant that there is no direct ferry to Thailand from Kuala Perlis. I nevertheless harboured a romantic notion of little boats bobbing about in a Mediterranean style fishing village and supplementing their income by taking passengers around the coast and maybe doing a little bit of smuggling on the side.

I had left Liz resting in the hotel room in Kuala Perlis while I went for a look around. Over the years this has become a familiar pattern. Arriving somewhere after a long and often uncomfortable journey we will find a place to stay and she'll lie on the bed and relax while I, however tired I am, feel compelled to immediately roam the surrounding streets. Whether we are in the middle of a teeming Indian city or a jungle village in Central America I am driven to try to give some context to our situation. Gazing out of a hotel window is never enough. I need to immerse myself into the rhythm of the place and gain some sense, not so much of belonging, but of how I fit in with my new environment. Footsore and struggling to remember the way back, I'll finally feel able to return and rest. Ideally I will get hold of a map.

The day before this had been in Kuala Lumpur after our flight from New Zealand, and I did manage to get lost. Knowing that we would not arrive until about midnight I'd booked a cheap windowless and rather dull hotel room in Chinatown, but outside the atmosphere was electric. The narrow streets and alleyways were full of colour and cheap glamour. They twisted and turned and after a while began to all look the same. I lost my sense of direction and struggled to remember anything that would act as a landmark. The hotel entrance was a simple doorway obscured by a clothing stall and it was with a great sense of relief that I eventually found it. Getting lost and then working out how to get back is a good way of getting a proper understanding of an area, but not when you are too tired and too late at night.

In the cold light of morning the geography appeared much simpler but Chinatown retained its allure. Steam rose from crooked passageways as giant woks bubbled with all manner of things and the streets between the terraced buildings overflowed with market stalls and cafes. Viewing this colourful scene I wondered how the world could swap this for MacDonald's and those other food chains. The sight of the 'golden arches' always fills me with sadness; I have no opinion of the food but these attempts to make everything and everywhere the same are a direct threat to the enjoyment of travelling. Why is the world so set on replacing individualism and difference with bland uniformity?

I have a nagging doubt about Kuala Lumpur's Chinatown. Too many of the eating places are geared for tourists and I suspect that it is being preserved, at least in part, as a tourist attraction rather than continuing as a living and breathing place of natural commerce. Nowhere in the city is there any great antiquity and before the nineteenth century Kuala Lumpur was simply the muddy confluence that gives it its name. Tin deposits attracted British colonial interest and Chinese miners, and now it has become a major city with expressways and skyscrapers but little depth of history. As usual, I was pleased to leave a big metropolis.

But in Kuala Perlis, which is a pleasant little seaside town in the extreme north-western corner of Malaysia, I had a purpose. From the day that Liz had accepted the job in China I had been planning this journey. Thoughts about how our life would be changed for the next so many years in an alien culture, where we would live, what I would be doing, all had to be put on hold because I was obsessed with the 3 or 4 weeks we had to spare to get there. Having found a cheap flight from New Zealand to Kuala Lumpur the rest would be overland, or at least over surface. Much as I love travelling by train, journeys by boat always seem to me to be the most adventurous, with bus travel being a poor third.

I anxiously looked for any clues as to the existence of an international ferry to continue our journey. The uncertainty is part of the thrill of travelling and adds to the sense of achievement when things do go right. I assured Liz that I had a plan 'B' but in truth it was pretty sketchy. There is a land border crossing through a national park but I was unclear how we would get there and, even if we could have got a bus to the Malay border, I think it would have involved quite a bit of walking to the park headquarters on the Thai side, which she would have complained about carrying packs.

So I was not just aimlessly exploring but I had a mission; to find a boat to take us to the next country on our list. My initial enquiries in Kuala Perlis only got me directed to the Langkawi ferry terminal, an impressive building that dominates life in the town as crowds gather and the road gets choked with traffic with the arrivals and departures of the ferries. I gazed out across the estuary and felt the task hopeless, but then I spotted a fishing boat, much further up river and presumably heading for its own harbour.

Twenty minutes later and I was in a different world. A real fish dock with men in rubber boots swilling buckets of water over concrete and tiles, plastic crates piled high amongst the remains of old rope and netting, the reek everywhere of fish mixed with diesel and ozone and the occasional small slimy fish underfoot, dead or dying with a desperate final flap. But best of all, proper wooden fishing boats with their blue paint peeling as the sun beat down on our position barely north of the equator. I expected to be challenged at any moment and told to move away but health and safety concerns have yet to reach this little corner, and when I heard a voice calling to me it was for me to untie a mooring rope for a boat about to depart. "boat-Satun" I asked with more hope than expectation. He didn't shake his head or raise his arms in miscomprehension but pointed to further down the quayside. "Satun boat, that way?" I looked for confirmation and got an affirmative.

Back in the hotel room I found it difficult not to appear smug but it was so satisfying to have found an oblique reference to something on a computer screen thousands of miles away, come to the place, turned names and lines on maps into real towns and features that can be seen, felt and understood and had my plans come to fruition. The boat I had been told would leave at 11.00 am. *"What about immigration?"* was all the praise I received, but of course she was right. Satun, I was pretty sure has Thai customs but we did need to properly exit Malaysia.

After breakfast the next day she sent me off to find a post office. I thought that this was ridiculous; we had only just left home and she wanted to send things out of her pack on to China. My main mission was to return to the fish dock. The previous day I had noticed a sign nearby that said 'Immigration'. I had tried to follow it but found nothing and assumed it was to do with the commercial fishing, but it was worth another look. I found it again but there was no obvious reason for the sign being there. I explored in every possible direction and eventually, tucked away down a dead end and backing onto the water's edge, I found an official looking doorway and inside a window, behind which sat a man in uniform who confirmed that he could exit-stamp our passports. Not only that but there were three more staff behind him, none of whom seemed to have anything, nor apart from us the prospect of anything to do; ever.

For once I would have been happy to sit and wait and watch the activity around the dock, but Liz still wanted to find her blessed post office, so we trudged along dusty roads carrying our packs and asking locals for directions. We were pointed to further and further out of town and I began to suspect that it did not exist. But I was wrong and she entered the building with the kind of triumph that I felt would have been worthy of finding an old wooden boat to ferry us across an international border. Liz was now in charge and she engaged the post office staff as if they were all bent on some great enterprise. There were discussions about weight, money, packaging and trips over the road to source a cardboard box and string. I was dispatched to the ATM. I had calculated on having just sufficient Malaysian Ringit left for the boat and this upset the perfection of my planning.

Then the woman behind the post office counter said that there was a miscalculation and more money was needed. It was pouring with rain and she had spent so much time on this project that we were in danger of missing the boat. I told Liz that she would have to wait until we got to Thailand, or better still abandon the whole stupid idea. Before we left New Zealand she had couriered a large box of belongings ahead and I failed to understand why she had packed stuff to carry that she clearly didn't need. She reluctantly agreed to abort the current mission, but was not happy about it and restated her determination to send these things on as soon as she had another opportunity. My observation that what she wanted to post to China probably came from there in the first place did not seem to help the situation.

Back at the dock the boat was leaving earlier than we had been told and we were quickly bundled into the hold under a big tarpaulin where wooden benches straddled the ten foot beam. I studied the other passengers, both of whom were rather frumpy looking women who sat bolt-upright on a bench amidships staring straight ahead at a thick black plastic cover. We perched on the gunwales and tasted the salt spray. The rain had stopped and I studied the shape of the mangrove fringed coastline and tried to plot our position on a diagrammatic map, which I had printed off the internet before we left home in anticipation of the journey. It doesn't get much better; crossing an international border in a small wooden boat unknown to any tourists and even the sun was coming out. This, I thought, is proper travel.

In Xinjiang my train arrives at the station for Turpan (or Tulufan as it is more widely known locally), but there is still about 50 km to go to get to the town proper. I am sure that there will be a bus going there if I can find it, but it is certainly not obvious. I ignore the usual gang milling around the station exit, although one follows me doggedly as I head for a row of buses, but they all look like tourist coaches and I have to double back and face my stalker. He is a large affable man who actually has reasonable English and his offer of a seat in his car with 3 other passengers looks like as good a deal as I am likely to get.

The catch I find is that unfortunately he doesn't have 3 others and the crowds from the train have now dispersed. He tells me that another train is due but ours was 2 hours late, and he is very vague about time. Luckily I am in no great hurry and get a large round of flat bread and a hard-boiled egg from an adjacent vendor for my breakfast, which I eat off the roof of his black Volkswagen Santana.

I am pleasantly surprised when the rattle of rails, loudspeaker announcements and a surge of activity all around, combine to herald the arrival of another train. The large affable man moves forward expectantly but gets a verbal barrage from another black Santana driver, but one whose car has official looking numbers stencilled on the side which ours clearly does not have. Looking mollified he retreats to his vehicle and says that we have to go. He does have one other passenger and I think that if we both have to pay double it's still not too dear, but he is made of sterner stuff and we set off to cruise the streets and demand of every pedestrian if they want a ride to Tulufan. It takes a while, and he is careful not to go too near to the station, whatever threat was made seems to have shaken him. Eventually we collect off the streets the passengers we need, people who were showing no sign that they wanted to go anywhere but who were somehow persuaded to casually clamber into the back of the car.

I've been in China long enough not to expect an oasis to consist of camels mooching around the date palms, but the car ride does show a contrasting landscape of stark desert dotted with mud brick buildings to luscious vineyards. The town itself of course is a standard grid pattern of wide avenues flattening out whatever was here before, although many of the modern buildings echo a different culture in their decoration of domes and turrets, intricately patterned tiles and ogee arches. The first hotel I try charges more than I want to pay but there doesn't seem to be an alternative. However, cheaper Chinese hotels often just have small entrances with no sign recognisable to me and looking above street level I can identify a likely building.

There is one unmarked door and peering inside I see the tell-tale sign of what I am looking for; a row of clocks ostensibly telling the time around the world. The price is right and the place would once have been a reasonable 3 star hotel but was clearly in need of complete refurbishment many years ago. In the corridor wallpaper is peeling off and the room I am shown has a worn stained carpet dotted with cigarette burns. An ancient television set sits on a cabinet with its door hanging off next to a matching chipped desk. There is also some graffiti on the wall, an act that the eastern Chinese would never dream of committing. But there is an en-suite bathroom, albeit with the bottom of the door rotted away, and it all looks reasonably clean. It will do for tonight. I think I hear a knock at the door but I am finally under a hot shower and whatever it is can wait.

The market is scattered around the back of a main street, rather than having a recognisable building of its own, but that doesn't detract from its atmosphere. Thinking that daily bowls of noodles are probably not the healthiest diet, I buy fruit and nuts for my lunch from a market trader dressed in a long cotton dress and headscarf, and I still have some flat bread left over from breakfast. One nice thing about Turpan is that I don't get stared at. I don't think that I have seen another foreigner here, but the locals are already a good mix of races and don't share the Han Chinese childlike fascination with anybody who is not exactly the same as them.

In the smaller towns people stare openly and are unfazed when I stare back at them. In the larger cities many people try to be more subtle, by keeping their heads straight when passing in the street but following with their eyes, which actually gives them a rather furtive appearance. Another group want to express their delight at finding something as extraordinary as a foreigner, with exclamations and enthusiastic greetings, as if you had suddenly appeared wearing a particularly clever form of fancy dress. This can be irritating when you are just trying to quietly go about your business, but the reaction that I really don't like is the parent pointing me out to their young child as if I was an exhibit in a zoo. If they are small enough they can hold them up to get a good view of you and they then expect you to smile sweetly at their offspring as if to say 'look at me aren't I a funny sort of creature'. I think that in Tulufan I am as obviously a foreigner as I am elsewhere in China, but nobody cares and so for once I can feel like a normal person.

After lunch, being a tourist I head for the museum. It is closed today. But the buses are running and to my mind travelling with the locals is more of a cultural experience than any museum. Here they have wooden slat seats which are probably preferable in the heat. As well as one of the lowest places on earth it is also about as far as you can get from any ocean, and this combination makes it one of the hottest as well. The maximum today in May is reported as being 35 C. Not hot enough to bother with air con but at least the windows are open. I catch a 101 which terminates after only a mile or so but it is a different world. I head up a beaten earth lane that a donkey cart is careering down and wander the back alleys. Pairs of heavy wooden gates are set into brick or mud brick walls that run continuously along the roadsides. Where these are open I look into courtyards with several low buildings and often beds laid out in the open; in one I see agricultural equipment, behind another I hear the baaing of sheep and at the end of the lane there is a vineyard. Now I can feel some connection with being in an oasis in the middle of a desert.

Barely an hour on the bus from the great depression of Turpan and only a third of the way to Urumqi, I catch a glimpse of brilliant white atop a distant range of mountains. The desert continues in dour bleakness until we reach some foothills which, if they were green would be attractive and inviting but in fact look forbidding and holding unknown danger. The landscape is becoming more interesting as we enter a dry valley which narrows to a gorge with steep faces of brown and grey rock on either side. And now some water as well, the same dull dun colour as the desert but a lively running stream which finally brings some natural movement to this unnatural place.

The Chinese Government has obviously been spending large sums of money here as we motor along a new dual-carriageway, with some local traffic still using the old road on the other side of the valley. Emerging from the rock face, presumably out of a tunnel are precast sections of concrete mounted on pillars which looks like a new rail line being built in the elevated fashion which is favoured for the superfast tracks. Coming into a much larger valley the snow tops are clear but ephemeral as they float in a jagged formation, their supporting grey mountains merging with the hazy gunmetal sky. And now at last I see camels; proper two-humped Bactrian camels with thick reddish brown fur that is moulting in great chunks. They are grazing in a massive wind farm, and the serried ranks of the turbines bring to my mind the lines of terracotta warriors guarding the First Emperor as he extends his rule into the afterlife.

Before we reach Urumqi the bus stops and everyone begins to get off. It is a police checkpoint. My passport is not where I usually keep it. I check and check again to no avail. With no passport I stay in my seat and notice a policeman boarding wearing a helmet and flak jacket and carrying a long wooden truncheon. I continue my fruitless search avoiding eye contact and am not challenged.

It is now 21 hours later and I hand over my passport for inspection. The police had ignored me when I failed to produce any identification yesterday, obviously more concerned about their own nationals than about foreigners, although ironically the police check on the bus back to

Turpan did ask for my passport. I gained some small satisfaction from simply saying 'meiyou' and staring at the officer as if to challenge him to do anything about it; his bluff called, he moved on. I had got off the bus in Urumqi and searched everywhere, completely unpacked my bag in the street, before buying a return ticket. Again on the way back, when I thought it could be in the pocket of the shirt I'd put in the plastic bag of clothes to be washed, I pulled everything out of my backpack. The remaining options in order of preference were a) at hotel reception, b) under the bed in the room I used, c) dropped somewhere in the street, d) stolen.

Back in Turpan I was relieved when the girl on the front desk of the hotel produced my passport as soon as I entered. They didn't return it to me when I checked in or out and I failed to realise the mistake. I remembered the knock on the door when I was under the shower. There was not enough time to get back to Urumqi for my overnight train to Yining so I had to book another night (at a slightly reduced rate) at the hotel. All very frustrating but I suppose part of the experience. As ever with these things it could have been worse. Not only do you need to show your passport to buy a train ticket but the passport number is printed on the ticket, so that a traveller's identity can always be checked. I had already got mine, so if it had not been for the police checkpoint I would have been in Yining before I realised it was missing, with less idea where I could have lost it and a three day return trip to Turpan. That would also have been problematic as without my passport I could neither book into a hotel nor buy a train ticket back, I would have been well and truly stuck.

This has knocked some of the stuffing out of the thrill of travelling for today and it hurt to have to retrace my steps, but turning plans and dreams into harsh realities is a definite motivation for me. I love the planning; studying maps, guides and train timetables and imagining how it is, and then turning all that into things that can be seen and touched and smelt, whether it is an old wooden boat or a decrepit hotel room- that is the buzz.

This is what I find so fascinating about travelling, the authentic experience of being part of something outside ones normal life, the draw of seeing other worlds as I trudge the streets of somewhere new, the sense of adventure of embarking on a journey, the romance of a picture book scene, the thrill of uncertainty as to what is around the next corner and the satisfaction of turning dry facts and lines on maps into something tangible. I need to be clear where I am, my position on the map and what the surroundings are like, and that is the beauty of travelling overland; it gives the ability to gain a proper feel of distances and how one part of the world relates to another.

Chapter Four: The Intrepid Traveller

I am annoyed with myself at losing my passport. I'm not always the most organised person, but I do like to think that I'm a seasoned traveller who should at least be able to remember to carry his passport with him. I spend a full hour queuing at Urumqi station for another ticket to Yining and get very irritated with the young tykes lolling around at the front trying to get those in the queue to buy tickets for them. I also have little tolerance for the absurd little woman behind me who complains that she gets whacked with my backpack when I look around the ticket office. I suggest that she not stand so close behind me, a solution that does not seem to have occurred to her. Looking at the other queues it does seem that there is only a few inches between people, perhaps they feel that by making the overall queue shorter they will get served quicker. In Nanjing it could be a defence against people pushing into the line, as the unwritten rules would prevent such interlopers being challenged, but Xinjiang is a very different part of the world and I am sure that anyone pushing in here would get short shrift.

I finally get my ticket and have several hours to kill before evening. I have been to Urumqi before. In 2002 we moved as a family from England to New Zealand and there was no way that I was going to travel all that distance by plane and see nothing of the journey. Consequently I travelled as much as possible overland, with our son Henry who was 11 at the time, while Liz and Emily went ahead. This proved to be a very expensive trip, as by the time we reached our new home Liz had opened a bank account and arranged a mortgage with which she had bought a house, a car and most of the local department store on interest free credit.

When we finally sold our house in England I thought that we could do something more interesting with the money than simply paying off the new mortgage, and so we purchased an apartment on the Black Sea coast of Bulgaria, near the ancient town of Sozopol where we had once had a very enjoyable holiday. This has turned out to be a disastrous investment and far too far for us to visit from New Zealand. Now that we are back in the northern hemisphere the plan is to at least make some use of it by going there for the summer holidays, which is why Bulgaria is my present destination.

On my first visit to Urumqi I was expecting to find a dusty frontier town and was shocked to arrive in a huge high rise city which was in the process of being rebuilt from the inside out. The only thing I think I recognise now is the statue in the station square. Then it had been crowded with people but now it is dominated by motor vehicles, as are the city streets which before could still accommodate donkey carts. I distinctly remember watching the progress of one as it plodded up the exit ramp of a newly-built multi-lane highway- the opposite way to the traffic flow. The pace of progress seems unstoppable.

I like cities to have a recognisable centre or at least some focal point to refer to. Urumqi is just a sprawl, but what could be thought of as the centre is reasonably pleasant. The road width is on a more human scale with just two lanes and they are lined with avenues of shade-giving trees which are protected by low metal railings. Unfortunately the pavements are far too wide which has made them usable as car parks. Even more unfortunately, because of the trees and metal railings vehicles only have access to these impromptu car parks from road junctions, and so walking along the pavement one is constantly harried by car horns. It is probably safer to walk in the road where the congestion is such that the traffic is barely moving. Waiting for a green light to cross the road I am badgered out of the way by a nasty little silver van intent on making complex manoeuvres on the pavement.

China really needs to do something about the motor vehicles which now rule the cities as dinosaurs once dominated the world. Private cars rarely venture out of town and the major highways are almost exclusively the domain of coaches, trucks and other commercial vehicles. But the upwardly mobile must have a car, and there is little point to that unless you drive it, despite the fact that city public transport is plentiful, cheap and a lot more convenient. The stress of driving in China can be measured by the desperate cacophony of car horns. Hangzhou, one of the wealthiest and most congested cities in the country, introduced a scheme of banning cars with odd or even registration numbers on alternate days. The rich responded by unscrewing the plates on their Mercedes and Maseratis and got away with it! The motor car is a monster that will increasingly destroy the quality of life in China unless drastic measures are taken; but what country of any political system takes drastic action against their wealthiest members? Okay I've had a bad couple of days; Liz would be calling me a grumpy old man.

And maybe she would be right. Independent travel provides the perspective to form ideas and opinions, but more than that, it forces one to make comparisons and formulate one's own views on issues. Otherwise it would be just an exercise in looking at the scenery and not giving any thought to what is happening all around. I think that this is particularly true for the older traveller, who is likely to have a firm value base from which to evaluate observations made and draw conclusions. Of course there is the danger of making sweeping generalisations and reinforcing stereotypical images, but the alternative is to pretend that there are no differences in peoples and cultures, and if that were so, there would be little point in ever leaving home. Understanding where one is in the world in terms of views and opinions as well as geography, is important to self-development and another reason to pack a rucksack and head off into unknown territory, even if it does make me a grumpy old man at times.

On the bus back to Urumqi station to catch the train to Yining the digital read out tells me that it is 7.40 pm and 37C. The time is misleading as we are still using Beijing time despite being thousands of kilometres further west. This also explains why my little compass disagrees with the sun, which is further east than one would expect for the time of day. I had planned to eat before boarding but I am not really hungry. I still have an apricot a few dates and some peanuts left over from Turpan market, as well as nearly half a bottle of red wine transferred to a plastic water bottle, and that should keep me going. As Turpan is renowned for its wine

I felt it a cultural duty to try a bottle but, unlike the rest of China, towns in Xinjiang province seem to have no western style supermarkets or, thankfully, any of the fast food chains which have muscled their way into the other cities.

I did find a little shop called a supermarket but it was run by Moslems and booze free. Not to be put off I tracked down, not really a shop but an old man sitting in front of some shelves upon which were dusty bottles of wine. They were either too expensive or pathetically weak. 5% is more what one would expect for beer. Having studied every bottle I felt obliged to buy something and compromised with a 7.5% red. It was disgusting. All it reminded me of was very sweet flat cherryade. I tried my best to get through it, I hate throwing things away and wasting alcohol is positively sinful, but in the end it had to go. I also jettisoned the remains of my flat bread which I had bought two days ago at the railway station while waiting for the large affable car driver to find more passengers. It had taken on a striking resemblance (and probably consistency) to the chamois leather that I remember my father used to use to wash his car. On retrieving my passport I celebrated by buying a much better bottle of Turpan wine, the last of which is now conveniently packed for lightness in a plastic drinks bottle.

On board another hard sleeper; it feels like home- and this one has the added benefit of lace curtains embroidered with camels. I could not get a zhong Pu, middle berth so I asked for a Shang Pu, bottom bunk and position myself by the window. A large man and his son plonk themselves down on my bed and start eating various unappetising items. It is nearly 9 pm so hopefully they won't expect to stay up too long. At least I've got possession of my pillow and duvet.

But now they expect me to move. I've got it wrong! Dad and son want their bed; Shang Pu is the top not the bottom. I retreat as gracefully as I can. The Chinese character for a middle berth is easy to recognise as it is the same as the first part of the name of the country; Zhonguo, the middle land. The symbol for the upper bunk is 'Shang' as in Shanghai, and really looks as if it should indicate the bottom not the top. As I think about it I realise that every Chinese name must have a clear meaning; in our alphabet there can be a jumble of letters which can be pronounced but not actually give any description. 'London' for example as a word may trace its roots to something intelligible but it means nothing to me other than a place name. In Chinese, as each character is a morpheme that makes some sense in its own right, and writing is only achieved by linking them together, it cannot be possible to form a word or a name that is meaningless.

At least sitting in the fold down seats in the corridor I get to talk to Nessie. She tells me that she works in intellectual property protection, and has the goodness to laugh when I suggest that it is the rest of the world that needs protecting from China. She is anxious about this trip because of terrorist activity and tells me that the meeting she is to attend in Yining had been postponed because of an earlier incident. I assure her that crossing the road in China is far more dangerous and ask her if she knows what the black and white markings on the roads are for. Her understanding of a zebra crossing, although she did not know its English name, is the same as mine. I then ask her why it is that people cannot cross the road on them and she explains that if motorists were to actually stop for pedestrians they would never get home. Pedestrians getting home are apparently less of a priority.

Nessie is a 26 year old girl feeling well out of her comfort zone in her own country which, to be fair is very large and diverse, and as a smart urban Han Chinese she does look as if she doesn't really belong out in what she views as the untamed frontier. Her English is good and she seems to regard me as something safe and secure in the alien and unpredictable world she has been thrust into. She tells me that her home is in Chongqing, a very large city which was in Sichuan province but is now a separate municipality, but she went to university in Guangdong and now lives and works in Guangzhou. I gather that her family are quite well off and she has had a good education, despite thinking that New Zealand is in Europe! She is one of perhaps the first generation of Chinese people to have opportunities and horizons which extend beyond simple survival.

This is causing her to be confused about what it is that she does want to do with her life, as inevitably freedom brings choice and responsibility.

The Shang Pu is hot and claustrophobic, but not too bad until the snoring starts. I don't always sleep too well on trains although I love the idea of rattling through the night, but I have never had a night like this. The combination of the lump opposite me and the slob in the bottom bunk is appalling and it is a relief when the lights come on at 6 o'clock. Nessie is horrified at her first experience of a sleeper train and, feeling defensive of one of my favoured means of transport, I try to assure her that it is not usually like this.

The language thing is still in my head as I also realise that, as Chinese cannot be read phonetically without understanding what each character means, the same piece of writing can be given a totally different pronunciation. Nessie tells me that she can understand a lot of written Japanese as the characters were originally from Chinese, but that the spoken language is completely foreign to her. It is the opposite of Hindi and Urdu, which are mutually intelligible as spoken languages but use entirely different forms of written script. It does explain why train ticket sellers and others are so keen to revert to writing when oral communication fails, as different Chinese dialects share the same characters and their meaning but may have little in common when spoken.

We resume our conversation from last night and I begin to understand that Nessie is feeling under some pressure to get married and that the expectation would then be for her to produce a child. She has a boyfriend who she seems to regard as being alright but she clearly doesn't have any strong emotional feelings towards him. She says that friends of her age in her home town are all married and producing children but that she isn't at all sure that that is what she wants at this time. I tell her that in European and other developed countries (like New Zealand) there has been a tendency, particularly for well educated people, to get married later than they would have done one or two generations ago, but I know that in

China a single girl is thought to be 'left on the shelf' when she reaches 30 years of age.

Nessie is relieved that there is someone to meet her at Yining station and she gets them to show me which bus I need to catch to get into town. There is an odd old part with a bazaar full of carpets, furs and tin ware and a line of horse carts which look designed for tourists, although there don't appear to be any or anything to attract visitors. The centre is the huge Peoples Square containing a massive TV screen which constantly belts out the same piece of music. By Chinese standards the roads and the streets are quiet, which doesn't make crossing the road any safer as it just enables the traffic to go faster. When the green light comes on for pedestrians, cars heading straight ahead are held up but those turning, career round the corner at a frantic pace, and when cars and pedestrians are allowed to occupy the same space in China, there can only be one winner.

One thing that is clear is that China has poured a vast amount of money into the region. The roads are superb and, as elsewhere in the country, building projects are in evidence at every turn. If Beijing's response to the threat of insurgency is to buy their way into the hearts and minds of the people then I think it is a tactic that is difficult to criticise. The region has been part of China at various stages in its history for a couple of thousand years, so it is not as if they have no proper claim to the territory and, although the majority of the people have more in common ethnically, culturally and religiously with the Central Asian republics, drawing national borders on that basis has been an appalling disaster everywhere from the Indian subcontinent to the island of Ireland.

The next morning I manage to board a minibus for Korgas, on the Kazakhstan border, where I am greeted by money changers. I don't trust these people at all but I do need to have some money for the other side and, as our income in China is more than our outgoings, it would be quite useful to exchange Yuan for Kazakh Tenge. Not knowing what the rate should be I only risk what is left in my pocket. They give me Tenge for 200 instead of the 300 Yuan I gave them, and I am amazed that I am able to wrest the whole bundle of notes from the man to demonstrate his error. I then notice a hotel and enquire from them what the exchange should be; better than I got but not hugely so. I negotiate with another operative and get closer to what the rate should be, but when I produce a plastic card he laughs and walks away. I call him back and point over the road to a bank. He comes with me to the ATM and walks with me most of the way to the border. I'm still not entirely sure what the exchange rate should be but if he had ripped me off too badly I think that he would have made himself scarce.

I love land border crossings; unlike so much in the modern world they are invariably individual and distinctive. Entering a new country is always a thrill; border guards strutting around displaying their weapons, the rarefied atmosphere of suspicion and distrust feeding the anxiety of fellow international travellers, and all this against the background of some isolated mountain crossing or last-ditch seedy town feeding off the tension generated by its proximity to the neighbouring country.

In this regard it was a complete disappointment when the boat we had caught from Malaysia docked at Satun in Thailand. The customs office was accessed through a window in a neat and tidy building set in well-manicured gardens on the seashore. There was no queue as we were the only travellers. One of the women on the boat turned out to be with the crew and the other had disappeared. The customs officials had friendly smiling faces and exchanged pleasantries as they stamped our passports, without even as much as a doubtful stare at the photo. This set the scene for Thailand as everywhere we went we found friendly smiling people, and I suspect that it would have seemed no different if we had entered the country just 50 miles away on the other side of the peninsula- where the bombs go off.

Thailand is the one country in South East Asia that has not experienced colonisation, even though it provided a geographical split of British territory between Burma and Malaya. One of the ways it maintained its sovereignty was by agreeing to cede chunks of land to possible aggressors in exchange for being left in peace. Consequently the border we crossed had shifted considerably over generations and, before an agreement with Britain in the early 20th century, it was a lot further south. Nevertheless the ethnic Malay population extends up the peninsula as the majority group, and this appears to be the cause of the unrest, although curiously nobody seems sure who is behind the violence or what they hope to achieve by it. Maybe it is because they have now become such a minority in Thailand, whereas the earlier border would have made the Muslim Malays a substantial part of Siam, as the country was then known, and given them a greater feeling of ownership of their country. Throughout the world borders that attempt to delineate religious boundaries and confuse nationality with religious beliefs seem to be a disaster. Our experience was of a country inhabited by friendly calm smiling people and it is difficult to comprehend how the degree of violence reported, or the unrest that simmers and erupts in Bangkok, can exist alongside the peaceful and apparently contented lifestyles we observed in Satun.

At this border with Kazakhstan the Chinese have predictably laid a four lane boulevard on their side, but for once there are no crowds and it is not even clear where the entrance is. Once inside I find an attempt to replicate an airport check-in with lines of light chrome poles supporting blue fabric barriers to channel the masses. There are just four people in the queue ahead of me.

I did have a bit of an issue getting a visa for Kazakhstan. First I had got a visa for Russia, which I obtained in an atmosphere of grudging distrust. It is usually necessary with these things to start at a further point of your journey and work backwards, so that you can demonstrate an ability to leave the country you are asking to enter. When I first turned up at the Kazakh Consulate in Shanghai I was told that they were closed for the National Day and that I would need to return the following week. It was clear from the information on the wall that the National Day had already happened but it seemed that they had decided to make it a National

Week instead. No doubt it is attitudes like these that makes the diplomatic corps around the world such a sought after profession.

I thought that I had allowed plenty of time, but my passport was then wanted by the Chinese authorities, because of some anally retentive piece of bureaucracy, and would not be returned soon enough to allow the Kazakh consulate the minimum of a week that they needed to glue a piece of paper into it. I had already bought my first two train tickets and was planning to leave the day after our 30th wedding anniversary. I was stuck. But then I remembered that I also have a British passport. As my newly acquired Russian visa was in my New Zealand passport I altered the application form to make it look as if I would be returning to China instead of travelling on to Russia. I dutifully attached the requested photocopy of my Chinese visa but I didn't point out that this was from a different document. In contrast to the Russians, the Kazakh authorities were polite and helpful and if they noticed the discrepancy, that my Chinese visa belonged to a different passport than the one that I had given them, they didn't question it. They would be well advised to take a leaf out of Kyrgyzstan's book and abolish visas altogether which would do wonders for their tourism industry.

So to leave China I produce my New Zealand passport containing my Chinese visa, but they don't want to let me out without a Kazakh visa so I then show them my UK passport. They are dumbstruck. More senior staff members are consulted with, more photo recognition examinations made, but they let me through. But through to where? I exit the building into a concrete yard with queues of big trucks carrying large bore pipes which I suspect are destined to siphon off some of Kazakhstan's reserves of oil.

I stand between two of the huge lorries and move forward with them as they inch their way past a sentry post. I cannot help recalling the time that Liz and I went through a drive-in bank in America- without a vehicle. After being stranded at bus stations miles away from the towns they were meant to serve we had realised the need to have a car in America, as the country is simply not geared to being negotiated by public transport. We then cottoned on to auto-drive-away companies, which are firms that arrange transportation of vehicles for long journeys to enable their owners to simply hop onto a plane. They recruit whoever they can find to do the driving, which provided us with free transport, other than petrol, right across the breadth of the United States. Understandably they ask for a significant deposit which, having made delivery in New York, they refunded us by cheque. We didn't have enough money left to even get to the airport for our flight back to England without getting it cashed but the only bank that was open was a drive-through.

I admit to being quite amused by the incongruity of us standing in line with packs on our backs in a queue of big American cars, but the humour was clearly not shared, as when it came to our turn a loudspeaker announced that we could not use the bank without a vehicle. As we took up so little space the next in line was alongside us and the driver kindly motioned that I give him the cheque. But the disembodied female was not to be thwarted so easily and announced that it was necessary to be in the car. I looked for and got permission to take the passenger seat and exchanged views with the driver on meaningless bureaucracy. It was one of those situations that proved serendipitous as he was going close to JFK Airport and gave us a lift. I would have liked to have seen the teller's expression as we shoved our backpacks into the boot and happily drove off.

In the line of trucks with giant pipes I am not surprised when I get challenged by armed soldiers who actually try to be helpful and eventually get me onto a bus. It is a sleeper bus but with just 20 berths; 5 rows of bunks on both sides and a large carpeted area in between. I only once travelled overnight on a bus which was when Henry and I were travelling to New Zealand. We went from Kunming in South West China to near the Laos border. That one slept twice as many with a third row of bunks down the middle and 5 across at the back. That is it would have done if sleep had been possible. Unfortunately the road was yet to be built and every time I dozed off we would descend into a pit and gradually grind our way back up again.

The co-driver demands what I feel is an unreasonable amount for what must be a very short journey through the border. I know that I have no choice and after making my protestations known I stump up the money and smile ruefully, which seems to make some sort of connection with my host. My fellow passengers are, I guess, all from Kazakhstan and their clothing, the carpet and the piles of duvets all reflect the richness of colour and pattern of Central Asia.

It would have been a long and tedious walk to the other border through what feels like a vacuum, insulating China from the rest of the world. But China is no longer insular; it is an integral part of the world economic order. Trade and commerce have leapt ahead in a country where the vast majority of citizens do not feel the same pressures that Nessie, the privileged young girl I met on the train is coping with, and whose grasp of the world doesn't even reach her country's own borders.

I don't know that the last day or two has given me any more insight into the travel bug; I suppose that coping with the challenges, like visas and money changers, and overcoming those hurdles gives some sense of achievement. I'm far from convinced that it would be less attractive if it was easier, but then I would not want to go on a tour with everything organised for me as that would definitely take away some of the pleasure and satisfaction of getting to the right place unaided. The thrill and challenge of the unexpected is certainly a draw, and managing to come through in one piece does give a good feeling. More than that; it fulfils a more primitive need to demonstrate an independence rather than interdependence- that survival is possible without all the supports of home and a modern lifestyle. It is a reaffirmation of the ability to live by one's own wits and not be totally reliant on the cocoon that our societies have constructed around us all.

Of course casting oneself adrift in an alien world is inevitably going to stimulate an emotional response, and maybe this is something that I want. I consider myself to be an emotionally stable person who doesn't have extremes of elation or depression, and it could be that travel addicts like me need to create situations or circumstances where they experience more polarised states of affect. I recall seeing racing drivers being interviewed just after they've been hurtling around at breakneck speed, and they invariably speak very matter-of-factly as if they needed something hair raising to revitalise them. I particularly have in mind the Scottish rally driver Colin McCrae, who would slide around gravel roads bursting with frenetic energy, become airborne over uneven humps and sometimes finish upside down against a tree, and then wind down his window and talk as if he'd been taking elderly relatives out for a drive in the Surrey countryside. I wonder if they are people who are drawn to their sport because they need to kick-start their emotional systems with adrenalin fuelled mayhem, without which their worlds would be flat and boring. But travelling is different and satisfies the needs of a different character. It is not for those who are looking for instant gratification; it is playing a long game and at a pace where it can be rolled around the tongue and savoured.

Part 2: Kazakhstan

Chapter Five: Fitting Reality to Fantasy

Emerging from Kazakh customs I am undecided what to do; I could start walking and see if I can find a bus stop but I have no idea how far away that could be and I am not entirely sure how far my current deal may take me, or if it is still current. I think that they only agreed to take me to the other border, but I feel that I have paid too much for just a journey through no-man's-land, and that the sleeper bus may take me further. I join some other bus passengers and find a seat in the shade to read a book while awaiting developments. These come in the form of the co-driver who offers me a ride to Almaty for twice the price of the short trip we'd already made. I'm not exactly sure how far it is, but it must be a few hundred kilometres and so this seems a reasonable deal and the easiest thing to do. I hand over my Kazakh Tenge and try to spot fellow passengers so that I can be sure of getting on the right bus when it arrives.

There is no Great Wall on this border but it feels as if we have come outside the fortress of China and into the wild open spaces. Travelling across the desert in China there was little or no habitation but I was aware of busy rail lines, freshly built highways and evidence everywhere of human endeavour, even if only manifested by a smart new 200 km long wire fence lining the rail track and serving no apparent purpose. The wide tarmac rolled up to the broad Chinese customs building and ended there. Life is very different on this side of the border.

I have been invited to take a top bunk at the back but I feel more like a rodeo rider than a bus passenger. The road is not tar sealed and I need to wedge myself in and hang onto a metal safety bar to avoid being tumble dried as we hit bumps and pot holes without warning. Through the window I see a landscape of flat scrub which does not appear to support any form of agriculture, but as we proceed there is some livestock, a mixture of sheep and goats grazing, but no enclosures. The occasional village has squat detached wooden houses with corrugated iron roofs and some have wooden shutters which gives them a cottagey appearance. There are few other vehicles on the open road but I spot a couple of boxy Ladas in a village and when we stop at a service station there is a profusion of Audi 100's of a certain age. This is very strange in what has clearly never been a wealthy area and I wonder if there is an interesting story to it.

As we get nearer to Almaty the road improves but not enough to be able to read or write and even taking a swig of water has to be carefully timed. I was anxious to get my money's worth on this journey after paying over the odds just to get between the Chinese and Kazakh border posts, but I would have happily settled for less than the 7 hours it has taken as we are dropped at the edge of the city. There is no alternative to taking a taxi and all that is available is an unmarked car with no meter. I throw my bag in the back and ask the price. I've no real idea how far it is or what it should cost but I indicate that it is too much and move to get out. He knocks a third off and I resume my seat. I'm probably still being ripped off but that's almost inevitable when first arriving in a new country- and I am tired.

Almaty is by far the largest city in Kazakhstan with a population of about 1 ½ million, nearly 10% of the country's total population of 16 million. It used to be the capital until 1997 when that was moved to Astana, which actually means 'capital' in Kazakh, and which I visited en-route to New Zealand in 2002. At that time it looked like a newly built and futuristic showpiece, but it has only become the political centre as Almaty remains the country's commercial heart, with the stock exchange and largest banks located here. The Stock exchange is the biggest in Central Asia and is responsible for a large proportion of the Country's economy. Almaty literally means 'city of apple trees' and the surrounding area is said to be the genetic home for many varieties of apples and the true beginnings of the domestic apple. The tourist blurb extrapolates from this that the city can lay claim to being the actual site of The Garden of Eden! If New York finds out that this is the city of the big apple they will probably sue.

Almaty has a reputation for high hotel prices so I am satisfied with the standard of my cheap room which reminds me of student accommodation, with a single bed and fitted furniture. There is an en-suite toilet and I ask if it should have a shower but I am told that it is down the corridor. I can live with that. After being woken by biting mosquitoes I set out to explore the town. Like Urumqi it lacks a focal centre, but it is different. Not just different from Chinese cities but individual. Everywhere is greenery; all the thoroughfares are avenues, and I keep coming upon parks and fountains liberally endowed with places to sit and watch the world go by. During the 13 hours that I spent on buses, trains and taxis yesterday I always seemed to be in sight of some snow-capped mountains, but never as close to them as now. The prospect to the south of town is filled with a magnificent range of glistening white peaks which are always in view, and so I can give my compass the day off. Unfortunately that doesn't prevent me from getting lost- several times.

I recently replaced my compass with a very handy small round one that I can look at discreetly. My previous one suffered on our flight to Kuala Lumpur as I discovered when we got to Thailand. After we got off the boat in Satun on our journey to China we caught a bus, which was painted shocking pink with baby blue upholstery, and travelled further north to the town of Trang. We were dropped off at the bus station and I tried to get some idea of where the town centre was, but at midday close to the equator the sun was of little help. I slid my old compass out of my pocket surreptitiously as I feel a bit of an idiot using a compass to find my way around a town. It somehow seems inappropriate, in the same way as middle-class urban mums ferrying their children to kindergarten in a Land Rover. It should be used to navigate over hill and dale, which is what I imagine it was designed for, but I actually find it very helpful in towns. It is really useful to literally get ones bearings in urban areas, particularly when emerging from the underground. At least it would have been if it had worked. Air travel didn't seem to have agreed with it, and there was a large bubble which pushed the needle around the dial. Vigorous shaking produced several smaller bubbles and with a bit of practice I could get it to point North- in any direction. *"This way"* I told Liz with more confidence than I felt.

I became aware of a car crawling alongside. *"Hello"* said a voice. I ignored it. Throughout the world it seems millions of people can say 'hello', but not another single English word, and believe that this is sufficient for a conversation. Sometimes there is a genuine desire to want to communicate but more often it feels like being made fun of for being different. It sadly seems to be part of human nature that 'difference' is to be either feared or ridiculed instead of valued and celebrated. Without it travel for its own sake would be pointless and the greater the difference the more enticing the prospect. This must count as another reason for travelling, and a laudable one- to experience the cultures of other people in the world and gain an understanding of what their lives are like; identifying the points of difference and the needs and aspirations that appear to be universally common throughout human societies.

Too often 'hello' is said in the hope of getting a reaction from an oddity, as a child may by poking an insect with a stick, but this one was persistent. I assumed a taxi, but when I eventually turned to look I was surprised to see a police car. As we were in Thailand the policeman was smiling but indicated that we should get in the car where he introduced himself as an officer of the Tourist Police. He handed us various leaflets and a business card to prove it, and insisted that he give us a lift into town. After a short distance Liz commented that it would have been too far to walk and our policeman agreed avidly. A bit further on and she was making noises of incredulity at our foolhardiness of even considering doing the journey on foot. She and the officer were now getting on like a house on fire as they warmed to their only topic of conversation and took pitying glances at the one who had embarked upon such a suicidal mission. In truth it would have been a long hot walk.

We came to Trang because it is on the railway line, and we were dropped off in a large bustling square by the train station. The longest journey I have ever made was when we moved from England to New Zealand and our son Henry travelled with me overland, mainly by train, through Russia, Kazakhstan, China and South East Asia. I told Liz that we had a routine when we arrived somewhere to first buy a ticket for the next part of the journey and then find a place to stay and finally get some food. I proposed getting a train ticket for tomorrow but she was hungry and had already spotted a cafe she liked the look of. From there she surveyed the square and identified a suitable hotel. None of this mattered, as when I finally got to the railway station the smiling lady behind the window gave me some fruit as a gift but told me that we couldn't buy tickets for our train until the next day.

Walking around Trang I realised that the great draw of the place was that it is completely nondescript. As such it is far more representative of Thailand than a tourist attraction and free of complications such as sights that one is expected to look at. Seeing famous world landmarks is not a motivation for me to travel and I must be one of the few people to have visited Cambodia and not seen Angkor Wat. I did feel almost guilty about that and it was an omission that I rectified later on in the trip.

From our room we looked out over to a hill, topped with a giant Buddhist statue which I decided I would like to take a closer look at. Not into climbing hills, Liz was still in search of a post office, after her failure in Kuala Perlis to forward her belongings, so I set off on my own. First I came across a monastery with singing coming from the temple. I would have liked to have loitered there for a while by the open doorway and soaked up the atmosphere, but feeling self-conscious and out of place I continued my quest. The statue was immediately above but I could see no way up. After another hours walk I realised that I had come to the other side of the hill and by crossing some waste ground I found a path up to the extraordinary massive multi-tiered wedding cake of a monument. It seemed to be in disrepair and becoming overgrown but when I reached the foot of the huge statue there were fresh flowers and burning incense.

I wished that I knew what I was looking at and its significance for the local people. I felt sure that if I was more knowledgeable about things like that, I could get much more enjoyment from my travels but available time is always taken up with the practicalities. Even when we have arrived somewhere I still seem driven to study the map and consult train timetables. I know that I need to spend more time learning about where I am instead of just getting there.

Liz was happy that she had finally sent her parcel. It cost double what it would have done from Kuala Perlis but she has a wonderful ability to not worry about money. This is a potential source of friction between us travelling together; I was taught as a child to 'take care of the pennies and the pounds will take care of themselves' and I tend to be perhaps overly economical with money and hate to see things wasted. Liz's pragmatic attitude is to live for the present, and if you run out just borrow some more. The difficulty is that what I see as her extravagance makes me want to cut back on our spending which causes her to react in the opposite manner and thus a vicious cycle is set up. It's a bit like when you can't hear a person very clearly so you speak louder to encourage them to do the same, instead of which they feel that you are talking louder than needed and lower their volume in the hope that you will follow suit. Although we hadn't said so explicitly I think we were both trying to make some allowance for each other on this journey, and I settled for a pained expression for which I received a thump on the arm.

We hadn't always been so polarised in our attitudes and I recalled that nearly a quarter of a century ago, when we first came to China, we were much more of the same mind. I reflected on this when we had the opportunity to return to the town in China where we had lived all those years ago. Liz's work was taking her to the north east of China and with a bit of jiggery pokery we had contrived to stop off in Shenyang while in transit from Beijing.

I felt both excited and apprehensive; it was here that we had lived and worked in 1989 and the place holds a kind of mythical status in our personal history. It was our big adventure, at least our first one, and I desperately wanted to find things that I recognised and that could link the past to the present. I wasn't sure why this was so important, I have clear memories of the city, and we have a photograph album of our time there. There was no need to revisit sites to reminisce but I did feel, more than a desire, an actual need to make a connection with the past. Maybe it was my former self rather than the place that I wanted to find a link to. When last in Shenyang I had most of my working life still ahead of me and gloried in having no idea which direction it would take. Returning I was not many years from retirement age and with two grown up children. I wouldn't want to change anything if I could, but maybe I just wanted to gain a glimpse of that old self again.

We got off the train and out into a cold wet snow. There was a long queue for taxis and, more worryingly, very few cabs arriving. It had been cold when we alighted from the trans-Siberian express in 1989 after train journeys through West and East Germany, Poland and the USSR. Then our train had been several hours late and there was no one to meet us in the thrilling darkness. We had some adventures before finally finding a hotel for the night, but this time we were booked into the Liaoning Hotel which I remembered as being on a roundabout containing possibly the largest statue of Mao in all of China. It's not all that far from the station and I pulled my compass from my pocket and suggested that we walk north. Liz pointed out that as we were at the north railway station we would be going away from town and I realised that, contrary to what I had thought, I had not recognised the area in front of the station; it wasn't even the same railway station.

But it was the same Liaoning hotel and the same Mao statue. I knew that most of the city would be changed beyond recognition and that it is many times bigger than it was, but the hotel, which was built in 1928, was splendid. There are very few old buildings in use in China. There are plenty of historic sites but they are dry and devoid of life. I was thrilled that the

Liaoning Hotel and the other buildings which face the roundabout, the centrepiece of which is the monumental Mao with his arm outstretched in that familiar gesture, had somehow survived as an oasis in a desert of the looming skyscrapers of the modern city.

In 1989 they turned us away from here, probably not for lack of room but because they weren't allowed, or didn't know if they were allowed to accept foreigners. This time they were much more welcoming and the place was magnificent. We delighted in the highly polished dark wood, graceful pillars and high ornate ceilings. For some reason the hotel is only given three stars but to my mind it is palatial, and it appeared to be looked after with great care and pride. I suppose that it's over the top but due to its age it gets away with it, whereas the extreme opulence of China's newer posh hotels, with enormous lobby's full of leather and gold paint and even containing miniature mountain ranges and waterfalls, just seem absurd.

The China Medical University where we had lived and worked was still shown on the Google map. The nearby streets which had contained a jumble of shacks and eating houses had been replaced by high rise shopping malls, but the facade of the old hospital was still recognisable and behind it we found the university campus. It was never pretty but strolling around we found an advanced state of decay. Cracks in the walls of the buildings matched those in the tarmac paths and, even in the centre of the city, it felt that nature would recover the area as mould and vegetation found a hold. The place was not yet deserted but there were signs to a new campus and a billboard with pictures of redevelopment plans. The piece missing was that we didn't recognise the building where we had lived.

Liz was in the hotel but I came out for an evening walk and found myself back at the old university. A bare concrete construction in the centre was the sports grandstand that I remembered being built in 1989, surrounded in bamboo scaffolding. I used that as a point of reference and bingo. Our guest house must have been a building that appeared to be larger than either Liz or I remembered it as being. I sauntered in and avoided eye contact with the woman in a glass reception area. This was it. A simple corridor, our room was to the right and to the left and at the end I found the small kitchen where Mrs Wei made jiaozi, dumplings filled with pork and garlic chives, which we loved. We thought it was smaller because there is no connection with the rest of the building, which is accessed by an outside staircase. Before we left town I showed Liz this strange remnant of our memories which had been suspended in time all the years that we had done so many different things.

If we had come a year later I am sure we would not have found any trace. But does it matter? Before we came back to China I had no great desire to revisit the place. Why was I so driven to find it? What it did was to make tangible the link between the China we used to know and our new experiences. It is blindingly obvious that the country has undergone enormous change, I had understood that, but it hadn't made any impression on me at an emotional level. In Shenyang we found another modern Chinese city but with enough of the old still recognisable that we could relate one to the other. It is easy to understand these things with one's head but, as doubting Thomas's we needed to see and feel where we had been, so that we could properly get a true understanding that modern urban China has actually grown from the seed that still exists in our imperfect memories.

Next stop was Changchun, further to the frozen north-east, or east-north (Dongbei), as anything that can be done or expressed in reverse, invariably is in China. It was throat-grippingly cold. Immediately stepping off the train Changchun felt different. There was a robust coarseness about the people, perhaps reflecting the harsh climate. It is not exactly a frontier town but there was some of that sense of pushiness and volatility, almost a slightly manic edge to the whole atmosphere. The orderly calm of the Han, underpinned with a dread of confrontation, was not in evidence as a taxi driver tried to negotiate an outrageous sum from us and refused to consider using the meter. A gangly man with a pronounced limp, probably from a road accident, halved the others demand and led us to his contraption.

We squeezed into the three-wheeler and lurched off across the pavement and into the teeth of the oncoming traffic. After several hundred metres a red light, obeyed by other road users, afforded the opportunity to cross to the correct side of the road. But not for long, he was clearly only intent on using the hypotenuse to follow the shortest route and we were back head on with the opposing flow of traffic, and then side on as we went through another red light. Did I say only 'slightly manic?' we arrived at the hotel via the cycle path having crossed a busy city with several sets of traffic lights and not having once come to a complete standstill.

From our room on the seventeenth floor I gazed out at square blocks of grey and brown buildings punctuated by tall smoking brick chimneys where the essential heating is produced and piped into factories and apartments. It looked strangely familiar and I realised that it could have been a scene from a painting by Lowrie, but when I looked down there were electric scooters instead of stick figures.

Changchun is China's Detroit and from the train I had watched a succession of car transporters ferrying new vehicles south down the highway. For once I found a good city map which covered a sensible area of the centre, was clear and double sided with roads marked in Chinese and pinyin on either side. My only criticism was that it didn't show a scale but I quickly got the hang of distances. In a booklet I had found a reference to an Automobile Cultural Park which sounded as if it could be very interesting, but I couldn't find out much on the internet other than an item saying that it should be open by 2007. If it had been finished back then, I would have expected there to have been more information. I was about to give up when I spotted it clearly marked on the map, which also indicated bus routes.

Of course it is when maps are not clear or are inaccurate that you have to keep pulling them out of your pocket and staring at the confusion. I walked directly, if ponderously over the iced pavements, to the terminus of the number 10 bus and only then opened the map to follow our route. Inside the bus was warm and clammy and I removed my duck down jacket. Chinese people are far more concerned at protecting themselves from the cold by wearing multiple layers on the lower halves of their bodies, and I observed a fellow passenger with his legs outstretched revealing his clothing choices. He was wearing a thin pair of shoes with cheap nylon socks but heavy cotton trousers which were not quite long enough to cover a thick pair of tights, which in turn had pyjama bottoms poking out of their ends.

This habit strikes me as being odd as I have always thought that it is the core that needs to be kept warm, which is why we wear jumpers and maybe a vest. It is just another example of the way that anything that can be different in China is; but I also have a theory. Instead of wearing nappies, Chinese children are clothed in trousers with a slit in the back which conveniently opens out when they squat down, which they are liable to do anywhere. In fact this has now changed and modern toddlers wear a disposable nappy protruding through the hole in the special design of trousers, but that would not have been the experience of most of today's adults. My theory is that after a childhood of walking around with a cold bottom all winter, when they get to the age that they can choose their own clothing many Chinese resolve to keep warm that part of their anatomy at all costs.

The map showed that the Automobile Cultural Park covered a large area and I got off at a stop along its eastern flank, but I couldn't find a way in. Trudging along the icy streets I eventually got to the west of the park and gained entry into an area of parkland with a large lake but no evidence of anything else. There was a big barn like building back on the other side which I felt could house some kind of exhibition, but when I finally gained entry I was in a poultry and vegetable market. I continued to walk around hopefully but the only explanation was that this had been something that was planned but never materialised. Shame; I would like to have found out what an Automobile Cultural park is.

In Almaty my problem with navigating is to do with distance rather than the absence of what I am looking for. While the town is on a simple grid pattern and I have a photocopied map that is reasonably accurate, there are no street signs. To get around it is necessary to calculate the number of blocks to the required destination and count them off as you walk. But there are always little roads that may or may not be shown on the map, and even if there aren't I end up daydreaming and losing count of where I am. It is then necessary to find a bus route and look for a suitable stop. I discovered that many bus shelters contain excellent large scale maps of the centre with a 'You Are Here' blob showing the current position, so that you can calculate how many blocks it is to where you want to go and start the process all over again. Shops are few and far between but there is no shortage of civic buildings, some of which are quite grand. The architecture in general is of the stolid suet pudding nature associated with the Soviet Union. Most of it is unremarkable, but old enough to feel that it has stories to tell, while not so ancient as to be self-conscious and want to display itself as being of special interest.

The itinerary I hatched before leaving Nanjing was to next get into a mountain area by catching an overnight train tonight to Tjulkubus where the nearby village of Zhabagly can provide homestays with hiking and horse trekking. I am less enthused about this plan now, mainly because I need a day to get my energy back and I have already lost a day chasing after my passport. Another reason that I am tempted to stay in Almaty for a second night, is that I have read that tickets for the Abay State Opera and Ballet Theatre can be very cheap. I am intent on exploring this option before I make a decision although I am also aware that the availability of train tickets could be the ultimate factor.

The theatre is housed in a magnificent lemon and white meringue of a classical building but the posters I can see do not look encouraging. About to turn away I spot an isolated noticeboard with what could be today's date on it and the word 'Tpabhata'. From my little knowledge of the Cyrillic alphabet I think this could be La Traviata, which at least I've heard of although I know nothing about it. The box office is not yet open so I find breakfast in a café with Wi-Fi and use the marvel of modern technology to learn more. The plot seems a bit thin but at least it should be possible to follow it and I expect that I will recognise some of the music.

Back at the box office the cheapest tickets sell for about the cost of a pint of beer. I choose the front of the circle, which looks to me to be the ideal spot, although seats in the stalls are more expensive. I am a bit surprised that on the day of the performance I could have had just about any seat in the theatre, but I am also quite excited about the prospect of a night at the opera, or early evening anyway; it starts at 5 pm. I have never been to the opera before and I feel that having turned 60, this is the right time to experience it. I would usually be more attracted by a mountain visit, but I will find plenty more opportunities for that on my journey whereas this is possibly something that I could do nowhere else at a price which I can easily afford.

I book another night at the hotel and seek a train ticket to Turkestan for tomorrow. I am told that this is not available until the following day, but two nights in Almaty is enough. I expect that the overnight train I originally planned to catch to the mountain area is also fully booked so that some change of plan was inevitable. After consulting maps and guides I am back at the train booking office and get a platzcart ticket (equivalent to a Chinese hard sleeper) to Taraz, just over halfway to Turkestan. The only real drawback is that the train arrives there at 4 am.

I arrive in good time for the performance and, while the orchestra is tuning up, I am free to explore the building, which is exactly how I expect an opera house to be. There is an abundance of marble and gold gilt, glittering chandeliers are suspended from the ceilings and ornamental mouldings decorate every nook and cranny. It is completely over the top- perfect. The audience drifts in a few at a time but I estimate that there are about 700 seats, and at 5 pm I can only count 70 people. My research mentioned just six main characters but when the curtain goes up the performers nearly outnumber those in the auditorium. I do recognise the music- for the first ten minutes, but not really for the next couple of hours. I suppose that this is the result of listening to Classic FM, with its culled pop-song-length excerpts of the most accessible bits of classical music, but I'm happy with the popular classics and could never cope with the serious stuff played on highbrow BBC Radio 3.

The set is spectacular, the costumes lavish and the playing and the singing is perfectly good to my ears. It must be massively subsidised. I could have gone for a cheaper ticket as everyone except me has now moved to the most expensive seats, regardless of what they have paid for. But I still think I have the best position and am slightly cheered at the interval to see that the theatre is now about a quarter full. There is a bar where I remain the odd one out as the other customers order coffee from a Nescafe machine and I point to a bottle of red wine on the shelf. She finds an open bottle in the fridge, but I suppose that if they only sell one glass an evening it is the best place to store it. I smuggle it back into the auditorium and cup my hands around the Paris Goblet to warm it. So, I'm pleased that I came and I have enjoyed it in parts, although I day dreamed through quite a bit. I think that perhaps I'm still not quite old enough to appreciate opera.

It is ironic that having identified that the authentic experience of exotic cultures is one of the draws of travel, I should end up watching European culture in Kazakhstan. But then from a post-modernist perspective there is no such thing as an agreed authentic experience, as what is felt by one person may be experienced completely differently by another. The freedom of travel provides the opportunity to seek out whatever reality is required to satisfy the needs of an idyllic fantasy. Many people would never dream of going to the opera and would be bored to tears if they did, as indeed I would probably have been a few years ago, but it provided for me an experience which I was able to match up to the enjoyable fulfilment of some romantic image. Travel can be restrictive to the narrow confines of a railway track but it also opens up all kinds of stimuli which are not available to those who stay at home.

Chapter Six: Happy Hours

I am very used to Chinese trains but I am unsure what facilities will be available on Kazakh rail and so I spend the morning looking for a supermarket. These modern cathedrals for the worship of consumerism are now easily found in Eastern China but do not seem to have penetrated Central Asian culture, and dried up when I reached Xinjiang Province.

In Nanjing our nearest one is a Wal-mart, an American chain store which I believe to be the largest in the world, but the branch in Nanjing largely stocks only Chinese goods. The next main contender is Carrefour from France and in other cities I have found Tesco's, but home-grown Chinese ventures are now proliferating. This seems to be the way that China absorbs things from other countries; to first bring in foreign companies to introduce the new ways and then allow Chinese businesses to copy them. All these supermarkets follow the same lay-out and they have their own foibles which would probably not be acceptable to a population with less of an ovine tendency.

The trolley-friendly escalators carry you to the floor selling everything that you have no interest in buying and give no indication how you can get from there to the food items. From experience of wandering aimlessly around shelves of pots and pans and rails of cheap cotton clothing, and feeling not just an idiot but a trapped idiot, as the only visible means of escape would involve running the wrong way down the moving metal ramp I came up on, I now know to head to the corner diagonally opposite. Here, hidden behind stacks of packets of tissue paper, boxes of soap powder and plastic bottles of shampoo, is the access to the next floor.

The supermarket concept has been welcomed in China for a variety of reasons, but particularly for the ease of access it provides to air conditioning. It can provide welcome relief from the fierce heat of summer in Nanjing, said to be one of China's four furnaces, but also a place of refuge in the cruel cutting cold of winter in the city. Much more cost effective than heating your own home, (which in any case the Chinese don't do, they just put on padded pyjamas), and more comfortable than visiting your friends' unheated homes, is to meet in the supermarket. One group of old men, who could be a local chapter of Last of the Summer Wine, regularly spend their winter days in Walmart. They can be found in a section selling outdoor and camping furniture, sat in a circle on the folding chairs. I don't know what the reaction to this would be in a store in America, but here the golden rule of no confrontation means that they are allowed to use the shop as a community centre. Anyway they don't present a problem to anyone- unless of course someone wants to buy a folding chair.

Other Chinese who need to escape from the extremes of the Nanjing climate are the card players. These are actually a significant proportion of the population, although outnumbered by card game spectators. On street corners, down narrow alleys and in every park middle-aged men and women play cards, always surrounded by a larger group of people who just quietly observe the unfolding dramas. In very hot or exceptionally chilly weather, the less hardy seek refuge in odd corners of the shopping malls where they upturn supermarket trolleys to provide a playing surface. If you have sufficient cheek you can do almost anything in China. The one thing I can't get away with is parking my bike outside Wal-Mart. Nobody turns a hair at cars driving along the pavement, but there is someone employed for the sole purpose of preventing bicycles being left outside the shop. On the occasions that I have tried he has become very agitated and waved his arms about, although he seemed reluctant to come too close to me.

The avoidance of confrontation is not the same as shying away from any contact or having any concept of respect for the privacy of others, and people often look into my basket, interested to see what things a foreigner might buy. Standing at the check-out on one occasion the young lad behind me was particularly nosy and peered at all my shopping. I scowled and, to make him aware of what he was doing, deliberately and purposefully leant over his trolley to inspect his purchases. My ruse completely backfired as he saw this as a welcome escalation of our burgeoning cultural exchange and, with a sheepish grin he picked up a bottle of wine I had chosen in order to study it more closely. All I could do then was to laugh and he joined in, although I don't know what he thought the joke was.

The food is invariably divided into sections. The meat is predominately pork; any beef is several times the price and fresh lamb non-existent. Chicken is also available, boneless skinless breast meat is cheaper than scrawny bits of wings and drumsticks as in this part of China they seem to prefer skin and bones to lean meat, which makes ordering in a restaurant a challenge. At least you can buy poultry that you know is fresh, as in one corner ducks and chickens are kept in cages and seem unperturbed when one of their number is taken out, beheaded, put in a bag and handed to a customer. The fish are nearly as fresh but not quite, as several of the large carp in the tank float upside down and the rest slowly suffocate in slimy water. Bullfrogs fare better and make quite a din. Occasionally one will escape and hop around the aisles. The turtles are less fortunate as they are wrapped in netting to restrict their movement. But every supermarket in this part of China is distinguished more than anything else by the pervasive smell of durian. This stuff is not to everyone's taste and according to Wikipedia the giant knobbly fruit has been described as like eating sweet raspberry blancmange- in the lavatory.

Almaty might not contain these splendours but surely the biggest city in Kazakhstan has more than a New Zealand corner dairy, which is about all I've found so far. It takes a lot of traipsing around the city and I am almost ready to give up before I find what I want. Again I am impressed that it is an individual shop and different to any supermarket I have been in before. I am greeted by a shelf full of a great variety of bottled beers and choose a cloudy unfiltered brew. There is also a section for pulling draft beer into large plastic bottles. I select bread, cheese, tomatoes and olives before I come across another shelf full of the same varieties of beer. I am tempted to buy an avocado as they are almost unobtainable in China, but it costs nearly as much as half a litre of vodka (which has also found its way into my basket), and I pick up strawberries instead. They are cheap and cause me to wonder if Wimbledon is due to start soon. I know that I tend to get too carried away with economising and that Liz would tell me to just get what I want and not bother about the cost, but I am conscious that she is currently the main money earner and I would like to live within my means. I pass another shelf full of the same beers on my way to the checkout. These people know their priorities.

The contrast between here and China really hits home when I get to the railway station. The system, even in relatively small towns in China, is to queue to put all baggage through an x-ray machine and be frisked with an electronic baton before locating the correct waiting room. When the digital display for the required train number goes green a crush of passengers go through the ticket check and usually over a covered bridge to the appropriate platform and have their tickets checked again before boarding. Here I saunter through the ecclesiastical marble station onto the platform and follow others who cross the tracks to a waiting train, which I am sure started life dark green with a yellow stripe along the side but the green has now been repainted with the bright blue of the national flag. Later arrivals are delayed as a very long goods train slowly makes its way along the line I have just crossed but we are well underway before anyone asks to see my ticket.

Platzcart is the equivalent of hard sleeper but the layout is different. Instead of the three-tier bunks, this carriage has twin bunks but with a further pair lengthways alongside the other window, where in China there would be drop-down seats. I assume that the carriage has more width and I know that the old Soviet Union uses a different gauge of track to anyone else; twice I have travelled by train into or out of the old USSR and waited several hours at the border crossings for the carriages to be lifted off the wheels and suspended, while bogies of a different beam are brought in to replace the previous ones. I believe that adopting a different gauge was a deliberate defensive strategy against invasion by rail. This sounds odd to people such as myself from island nations, but I suppose that if military control of the line was achieved it would be a very fast way to advance.

The seats have only a thin plastic covering but there are bundles of mattresses on the higher bunks, although it all looks a little shabby compared to the slick Chinese carriageways.

As the ninth largest country in the world but with a population of just 16 million, the Kazakh government encourages population growth. Many of those in this carriage have listened to the call and there are babies everywhere. I vacate the main lower bunks to the young family who will use them and take a seat in what will convert to the lower of the side bunks. I am fortunate to get talking with Nailya, a middle aged woman who is one of the very few Kazakhs I have come across who can speak English. Russian of course is the main second language. We have a pleasant and relaxed conversation, making comments or asking questions as they arise with no pressure to talk and long periods just looking out of the window.

The landscape is flat but greener than I had expected and supporting some stock, tended by herdsmen on horseback. Nailya is critical of the government as she believes that the riches from the great mineral wealth of the country are not filtering down to the ordinary people and that corruption is rife. I am relieved when bags of fresh linen are distributed, which even include a hand towel, and the forbidding looking bedding can be turned into something acceptable to sleep in. Having made my bed in the upper bunk I clamber into it and stretch out. My feet and half my legs overhang the end of the bed. Maybe this carriage is not wider after all.

Some people would think that I'm getting too old for backpacking but I really wouldn't want to travel any other way. We have friends who book to travel to exotic destinations on group tours because they don't feel confident to just go on their own. The irony of course is that 30 or 40 years ago, when they would actually have been far less able to manage the challenges of foreign travel, they wouldn't have batted an eye lid at heading off to an unknown destination with just a change of clothes a sleeping bag and enough cash to get back home.

It may be that I still haven't really grown up properly. I sometimes find it difficult to remember that I'm no longer young and have always been slow in moving on to the next stage of life, although I seem to have reversed this trend in now becoming semi-retired (with some confusion around the 'semi' bit). I recall being sat in the church daydreaming at a nephews wedding. I always daydream in churches, I think it is deep-set Pavlovian reaction to having had to sit through Latin masses as a child and not understand a single word of it. On this occasion I suddenly realised with a shock that the old people around me, dressed in their responsible Sunday best, were actually my own generation; siblings, in-laws and cousins. As you get older time passes more quickly and I think that my sense of identity is struggling to keep up with the pace of physical change.

Travelling through Thailand on our way to China we left Trang on the train heading north and crossed to the other side of the peninsula. I was due to celebrate my 61st birthday the day after and for the occasion, and the only time on that trip, I had booked a place for us to stay in advance. It was on an island off the east coast, called Koh Tao. There is an overnight ferry to Koh Tao which I resolved that we should catch, not just because being a slow boat it was cheap but as it also seemed to me to be more adventurous. Liz was concerned that we would have nowhere to sleep but as I hadn't told her that there was a fast daylight alternative she didn't argue.

Boat journeys, particularly at night, are often the most memorable and I reminded her of many years ago when we sailed into the reflection of a broad pink sunset from La Paz to Mazatlan eating cheese, olives and tortillas on the deck, all washed down with tequila and guava juice. We had been on our way to South America and had started the journey with a cheap flight from London to New York. After crossing the United States from coast to coast we had gone down the 1,000 mile long peninsula of Baja California before taking the boat to the Mexican mainland. Unfortunately we ran out of time in Nicaragua and have still never been to South America. I hope that we will get there someday, but for me experiencing the travelling has always been more important than reaching a destination.

This attitude to travel has resulted in some difference of opinion over the years as Liz always wants to go from A to B by the fastest possible route, while I plan to enjoy the journey. If I got my way when travelling in England, she would often drive while I would be juggling Ordnance Survey maps with my old AA book and the Good Beer Guide. I would find narrow lanes to connect pretty villages, believing that one should never use an 'A' road when an unclassified byway was available, and find a country pub for a lunch stop. Regardless of the distance to be travelled I always felt that the journey should take all day. For many years I ignored the abbreviations in the old black AA book of 'e.e.', 'dec.' and 'perp.' that came under village descriptions but then I acquired an interest in old architecture. This added another dimension to travels around the country with a volume of Pevsner's Buildings of Britain in the glove box and old church's added to old pubs as favoured places to explore. Sadly gothic architecture joined trips-across-the-channel as a casualty of our change of hemisphere, as it is an interest that I couldn't maintain once we moved to New Zealand.

I was pleased that I had allowed plenty of time to get to the Koh Tao ferry because we got stuck at Surat Thani railway station, which is several miles west of where the boat departs. At first I tried to ignore an officious little man, who demanded to know where we were going, as I assumed that catching a bus or failing that a taxi would be a simple process. I was wrong and even he struggled to find us any transport. This appeared to be his role in life and presumably lack of public transport is a local problem. My frustration was that we were powerless to do anything other than wait as I was sure that leaving the station would completely scupper our chances. Eventually he found what appeared to be a private car to take us and we negotiated a fair price. I was happy to be moving again, movement is soothing and I let the sights and sounds of the townscape wash over me until the smiling young driver dropped us at our destination.

We arrived at the quay near Surat Thani and located the ferry which was much smaller than I had imagined it to be. The tickets cost double what I expected but they assured us that we would get a berth. On board we found a closed deck with limited headroom and 20 single foam mattresses on each side. They were so tightly packed that there was no visible floor space. Allegedly there was a toilet at the back of the vessel but getting there would involve climbing over every sleeping body in between. Gradually the deck filled with young travellers, all apparently unconcerned at the accommodation, and for the first time I began to feel old. So much for: 'independent travel being so easy' and 'I can't understand why all our friends don't do the same'; never had a sardine simile seemed so apt. We survived of course but when morning came we were shocked to see the apparent inability of the crew to handle the boat as they attempted to come to shore, eventually sending the youngest among their number into the calm sea to swim to the jetty with the mooring rope.

Koh Tao was lovely. After we had found some breakfast Liz waited at the jetty for our lift to the accommodation while I had a look around. The little port slowly came to life with a mixture of traditional fishing boats and tourist craft. A huge and exceptionally ugly catamaran arrived laden with passengers in its sterile air conditioned confines. Further along the port area I watched cargo being driven onto a rusting hulk with wide jaws swallowing an assortment of trucks and rickety carts through its bow. A few yards inland I discovered a group of little lanes with an assortment of shops, cafes and bars. A second-hand bookshop advertised discount ferry tickets and I arranged the next part of our travels, which was the ferry to Chumphon.

When I was initially studying the map I was attracted to Koh Tao because we could arrive from the south and continue our journey with another ferry heading north. I knew that this was ridiculous because when we boarded the train at Chumphon, 3 days after we alighted at Surat Thani we would be just 2 hours further up the line. Nevertheless it seemed important to me that we were continuing our travels rather than taking a detour. I cannot adequately explain why this is and from an objective standpoint it seems to smack of an obsessive/compulsive nature. I wonder if I really want to continue to reflect upon my motivation for travelling!

Liz was happy, and why wouldn't she have been? We were in the idyllic paradise of the travel brochure. A cosy little sand fringed bay with a couple of brightly painted long-tailed boats bobbing up and down, one with a Thai flag fluttering in a gentle breeze. She seemed unconcerned that our little thatched cabin was pretty basic (it may have been my birthday but I was not going to waste too much on somewhere to sleep). It also seemed to come with a cat. A sleek black animal that was so demonstrative and so certain that we belonged together that, although I generally prefer dogs to cats, I couldn't but smile at the joyous noises it made whenever we returned to our temporary little home. In an ideal world it would have got into the roof which, every now and then, exploded into a frenzy of activity. I suggested that it was birds up there, Liz knew that it was rodents but hey! It was happy-hour at the bar.

Usually beer or wine drinkers, we decided to try the half price cocktails. Not what I expected they were creamy white and came in yellow china cups. They both tasted delicious but I thought mine to be slightly better although I couldn't remember what it was called. We were sitting on a wooden deck on tapestry style cushions overlooking the sea as the sun sank down at speed, as it always does in the tropics. The waiter brought two more drinks, a red one and a green one, and explained that we had been given the wrong order but could now keep them all. The new arrivals weren't as good as the cocktails that came by mistake, which we then realised were the same. And neither were the next ones we got in before happy-hour finished.

When I booked this place Liz saw some pictures and said that it looked far too nice to only stay one night, so for the first time since we left home we had a day with no travelling. After a few minutes sitting on the beach I decided to go for a walk keeping to the coast as much as I could. I had a great day trying to follow the dotted lines on the map I acquired which indicated footpaths. The terrain was hilly and the buildings, while geared to tourism, were all low-rise. Away from the island's small town the tracks were deserted and development did not appear to have gained too strong a hold. When I finally returned Liz was relaxed and looking forward to happy-hour, at the end of which, through an enjoyable process of elimination, we established that the cocktails brought to us the day before in error were Mango Colada, and that they were still our favourites.

I'm in a very different place now as it's still dark in Kazakhstan and also raining. It's not yet 4 am as the train nears Taraz but everyone in our section of the carriage is up. They are interested in my movements (as well as how old I am) and I explain that I could not get a ticket through to Turkestan and so have come part way. I wasn't expecting to see much rain in the Kazakh steppe and I am told that it is unusual but welcome; everywhere it seems is affected by climate change. When we get off Nailya accompanies me to the ticket office and translates my needs. There is a train at 5 am but she says that the only place available is the top bunk of three and will not be at all comfortable. This confuses me as I thought that the top platform was for baggage, and also on overnight trains in most countries the bottom berth can be used for seating during the day. There is another train at 8 am, which is not too long to wait, and I accept their advice and buy a ticket on the 041 for Turkestan. This turns out to be exactly the right decision, as Nailya then invites me to her house for breakfast.

As she tells me that she is a doctor, I am expecting something a little grander than the sheet metal door set in the crumbling soviet apartment block we arrive at. After fumbling in her bag for a while, she makes a phone call and keys are dropped from an upstairs window. We climb several flights of bare concrete steps and enter a cramped apartment, with wallpaper peeling off in one room, and she introduces me to her parents who are in their seventies. Neither of them can speak English but they have a lively curiosity and seem to be a happy and contented couple.

Breakfast exceeds all my expectations as a very tasty vegetable soup with meat balls is followed by plates of cherries, dried fruit, and nuts including almonds and cashews, and homemade cheese. There is plenty of bread and tea poured into bowls with milk. We squat on the carpet at a low table to eat and I make the mistake of asking if the round cap with a peak in the centre that Nailya's father is wearing has any religious significance, as in China they seem to be a badge indicating a Moslem. I am told not and he leaves the table to return immediately with a hat as a gift for me, which I would be to reluctant to wear even if it were not several sizes too small.

I am wondering if doctors don't get the same recognition, or at least remuneration, in Kazakhstan as in other countries when Nailya shows me some photographs of her last holiday. She travelled through Spain, Italy and France before going on to attend the graduation of her nephew who was at university in Scotland. Clearly it is a matter of priorities and perhaps one of culture also, as I imagine that ideas of home ownership and taking pride in a well maintained living environment are of less importance here than in the culture that I was brought up in. Finally Nailya and her father take me back to the railway station and she writes down her telephone number for me in case I run into difficulties as I journey through Kazakhstan; what a lovely family.

Chapter Seven: The Lazy Paradox

Travelling further west, the next step through the steppe, the landscape becomes harsher. It is flat as far as the eye can see and the mountains seem now only a distant memory. The ground is pale brown and bare save for stunted shrubs which look as if they would prefer to be elsewhere. Inside the carriage things are brighter, as most women wear colourful cotton dresses with large patterns on them that look as if they would not have been completely out of place in 1950's Britain, but would certainly indicate something foreign today. I notice an older woman in a cherry red waistcoat of felt material embroidered with silver thread which I take to be some form of local dress. There is a paradox here; if you visit a tourist attraction you are very likely to find people wearing a national costume as part of the display, but if it is worn naturally as part of everyday dress, then it merges with the background and becomes unremarkable. So there is a danger that it is only when interesting cultural differences are falsely created that they are clearly seen and appreciated; when they are not contrived and highlighted they simply get lost in the crowd. Maybe this is why I prefer wandering the streets to visiting the sights.

We arrive at the train station in Turkestan but before I head into town I want to get my next ticket- to Aral. The booking clerk writes down numbers and I point to 15.00, I assume a train leaving at 3 pm tomorrow. When I get my ticket it is for an early morning train which will not even go overnight, but arrive quite late in the evening. Not what I really wanted but now that it is all printed out I don't think it can be changed. Next time I will check the train number I want and ask for that. It means that I only have this evening to see the sights, which is not too big a problem, but it is becoming clear to me that in Kazakhstan you buy a bed on the train, whether you are travelling overnight or not, which is a waste on this train going from 8 am to 9 pm.

I am pleased that I read that Turkestan has the finest architectural masterpiece in the country as I would not have known otherwise. The Sufi

Yasaui lived about a thousand years ago but his mausoleum was built a few centuries later by order of Timur. The big dome is nice and the tiles are pretty but as a whole it doesn't work for me; the walls seem too high and the proportions are just not right to my mind. I do like that the atmosphere of the whole sandy, Spartan area which is evocative of dusty Silk Road adventures and I dutifully take a few snaps with my phone, its camera being the only real use that I have for it at present. I use WIFI (here pronounced wiffy) wherever I can find it to keep in touch with Liz using my small computer.

I feel a bit of a philistine; not only have I failed to appreciate the jewel in the crown of Kazakh architecture but I am spending more time studying Turkestan railway station than I did the Sufi Yasaui mausoleum. Of course I am obliged to spend time here waiting for my train and it does look like a palace, sedately commanding its own quiet square. Inside there are heavy solid wooden doors and panelling above which the wallpaper bears large intricate patterns. No it doesn't- on closer inspection it's not wallpaper at all, it has all been painstakingly painted by hand. The whole building is lovingly presented to the glory of my god, the god of travel.

I am still puzzling what it is that makes me have to keep travelling, but after just two nights in the paradisiacal setting of Koh Tao I was eager to continue the journey. I don't really know how people are content to stay in one place for a whole week-long holiday. It isn't that I expected the next place to be any better. On the contrary I knew that it wouldn't be as pleasant, but I also knew that it would be different and provide new stimulation. This is a great motivation for me; the laziness of travel. All you have to do is move and you are constantly bombarded with fresh views of the world. Once you have a ticket to ride it is no longer necessary to invent an activity or provide entertainment, just sit back and let it all come to you. It seems a paradox but, far from being the manifestation of an adventurous spirit, the attraction of travel comes down to idleness and a reluctance to take any real initiative.

We left our Island paradise for the Thai mainland on a small ferry boat I would describe as a launch. It was about 20 metres long and seemed to be a mix of wood and fibreglass all painted white and not quite as ugly as the more modern catamarans. We sat with our fellow passengers with our legs dangling over the side and our backs against a superstructure housing a large cabin. With visions of money and passports disappearing under the waves I strapped my bag to my leg and held onto the guard rail. Always preferring to sit outside on boat journeys I had ignored the cabin but saw that it was furnished with up-market armchairs and was totally empty. Presumably a first class area that nobody wanted to pay extra to use and which had become a complete waste of space. The boat docked at a long wooden pier in the middle of nowhere and we followed the crowd to arrive at a bus stop with a shop selling food and drink. Two buses were stationed within sight but obstinately refused to move to collect their passengers and we waited in the midday heat. When, presumably it was felt that the shop could do no more business, drivers appeared and we boarded for downtown Chumphon.

The plan was to catch an overnight train to Bangkok. The most cursory glance at the map shows that to go anywhere other than Myanmar requires passing through the Thai capital. I would have liked to have travelled through what was Burma. My father was in the army there during the Second World War and, although he never spoke much about the country, it was one of the first foreign places that I tried to imagine as a child. Sadly it was not possible to traverse the country other than by flying in and out; any land entry could only be a detour, returning through the same border, which is anathema to my view of a journey as a one-way trip. I do seem to have a certain preciousness about the shape of my route and, although I am happy to meander, taking side trips spoils the concept of travelling from one point to another, albeit circuitously. I have since travelled through Myanmar, which has relaxed many of its restrictions, and I entered the country at its southernmost point where it shares the narrow Isthmus of Kra with Thailand. First I had to get to the Thai border town of Rangon.

I had finally found my way to Pheng Nga bus station on the back of a motorcycle, the bus having dumped me unceremoniously on the main highway 5 Km away. A girl sitting behind a simple table on the pavement told me with a confident official air that the bus to Rangon would leave at 10 am the next day, and that she could sell me a ticket but not until the morning.

I was back in good time but the girl had been replaced by an older man who spoke no English. He indicated an adjacent blood red vehicle and pointed to 9.40 on his watch. At 9.40 I got back off the bus and enquired what time it would reach Rangon, as I thought this would be an indication of whether it was going to get further than a tour of local villages, which is what it appeared to be most suited for. In reply he wrote down 60 Baht which I took to be the fare and which failed to ease my concern as the girl the evening before had quoted 170 for the ticket.

I gingerly touched some of the bodywork which gave under slight pressure and seemed to have been repaired with some kind of woven fabric and then painted over. The green plastic seats could accommodate five abreast and I noted my gradual decline in comfort levels as I had moved northward, from a luxury detached armchair I climbed into at Singapore, through buses with reclining seats set in pairs in Malaysia and then an only slightly dilapidated double-decker in the deep south of Thailand.

Before 10 O'clock we were under way and the driver was unabashed when I stated Rangon and offered my 60 Baht. I had located myself behind the back door, which was permanently secured open with a knotted bungee strap, in a seat which afforded extra legroom. We turned right out of the bus station and with the sun now on our right I felt a small glow that we were heading north, which my map showed as a minor road, rather than back to the main Phuket highway. A few more locals clambered aboard as we nuzzled through the town traffic and soon we were bowling along a narrow tarmac strip with corrugated iron roofed bungalows displaying colourful washing lines, breaking up the density of banana and palm trees.

And for the first time since I had left Singapore I was properly travelling; country smells blew through the open doors and windows, the road wound a route through a density of green foliage and I was in and a part of it all. Why, I wondered, had I even bothered to travel in those luxury coaches, as cut off from my surroundings as if I was 30,000 feet up in a jet plane and with a bland view of mile after mile of motorway. I couldn't even breathe the same air as the outside world as I relaxed in a super luxurious false air-conditioned, (actually uncomfortably refrigerated) environment. I smiled in satisfaction as the primitive suspension bounced, seemingly with joy, over the twisting road.

The blood red machine only made it a quarter of the way to Rangon before it joined the main road and all the passengers alighted. Half an hour later I was on board another only-slightly-dilapidated double-decker which annoyingly had the ventilation ducts screwed in the open position and blasting a constant draught for all they were worth. This modification was quickly forgiven once we were under way and, occupying the rear seat, I soon felt a much stronger counter-blast of hot air funnelled up from the engine. The vehicle had no opening windows and must have originally been air-conditioned but this had been superseded with loops of flex festooned from the roof and connected to whirring electric fans. This bus was clearly a little more than only-slightly-dilapidated but it strove to maintain appearances by the addition of rounds of silky decoration hung from a kind of pelmet running around the top of the windows, which reminded me of the frilly knickers that lady tennis players used to wear before that touch of femininity became incompatible with the groaning and screaming each time racket connects with ball. This decoration succeeded in adding an element of claustrophobia to the over-heated interior and blocking much of the view.

Ranong proved to be a dull dusty town strung along a noisy road and with a rubbish-choked shallow brown river, but its importance was as a stepping stone to the main focus of my travels. As a child I viewed a day trip to Boulogne as something impossibly exotic which filled the mind with all kinds of images of foreign adventure. Over the decades I have continued to be thrilled by travelling to different parts of the world but there is a constant need to up the ante, to recapture the buzz of that first foray into foreign parts. I have now been reduced to a state of mind where I am almost blasé about catching a few buses to travel up through South East Asia. But from Ranong I had another destination in view, a land shrouded in mystery and a way of life likely to have been little changed since before I was born.

The next morning I caught a sawngthaew to the pier. These vehicles, which provide narrow wooden benches for passengers to perch on, are ubiquitous throughout the region but Ranong has its own style. The fleet is based on old Datsuns with all the bodywork behind the windscreen removed to the level of the floor pan and replaced with a wooden superstructure which includes the mandatory double row of benches running along the sides of the vehicle. I suppose you could say that they are coach built but, without the kind of chassis used on pre-war vehicles, the operation must have included a huge amount of strengthening and I noticed a thick metal bar above the windscreen. No doors are provided and the driver has the same cushioned wooden slat seat as the passengers which must give him a numb bum after a day at the wheel.

I found the area around the pier to be much more atmospheric, with a stinking fish market, food stalls where local workers sat idly drinking tea and a hive of activity on the water with boats of all sizes jostling for position. I passed through Thai immigration, joined half a dozen other passengers on a long-tailed wooden boat and donned the life jacket I was given. The helmsman wielded a shaft 15-20 feet long with the outboard motor at one end and the propeller at the other. This he could swing through 300 degrees to place anywhere in the water and provide thrust in any direction around the stern of the boat. Twenty minutes later we had crossed the estuary of the River Pagyan and I gained my first glimpse of Myanmar, or more evocatively, Burma.

I suppose that the main difference between the two sides of the river was in my head, as the draw of travel is often linked to associations with a romantic name as much as to the reality that is found, and the latter can be disappointing if it fails to equate with the minds preconceived perceptions. Kawthaung didn't disappoint. I stepped off the boat into a jumble of quayside activity and surveyed the scene to decide where I should first explore, but before I got more than a few yards the boatman said that I should follow him and he took me to another layer of bureaucracy where I was allocated a spy.

He wasn't introduced as such but he clearly had a responsibility for ensuring that I remained within the bounds of a foreign tourist. He did admit to being in the army although, as a slightly overweight young man dressed casually and with an unsatisfactory growth of facial hair, he had little in the way of a military demeanour and he told me that he was completing his 3 years National Service. Early on in our conversation he explained that some people give him a tip and I suggested that these may be Americans as there is not a culture of tipping in either New Zealand or, more importantly, Myanmar.

Once he had ensured that I was booked into an overpriced hotel designated to take foreigners and that I had a boat ticket to leave early the next morning paid for at a foreigners' rate and in US dollars, his work was done and he asked me openly for money. I responded to his frankness by explaining that I had no intention of offering any kind of financial support to his government, even if they didn't pay their soldiers well, and our brief and bizarre relationship came to an unsatisfactory close as my spy appeared to retreat into a kind of sulk.

The question of what drives me to travel seems to be more complex than I had at first imagined. The adventure and romance is fairly obvious. Experiencing and appreciating other cultures all seems very worthy but the concept of travel being a lazy option rather less so, although nonetheless interesting, and to be brutally honest far from inconsistent with my character. Laziness, or sloth which seems very similar, is one of the seven deadly sins and something which our society is most intolerant of. Some people are more intelligent than others, some better looking and some lazier. But while people can gain sympathy for not having been blessed at birth with fine features or a large brain, if you are said to be 'born lazy' it just makes the sufferer even more culpable. The only other sector of society to be discriminated against so unfairly is the overweight. Thankfully I'm not fat and lazy as that is a condition which is truly unforgivable. I can live with that, but I am less happy about the rigid attitudes I seem to have, such as being unwilling to make side trips. I don't really think that I have too many obsessive/compulsive traits and I wonder if it's somehow akin to the compulsion to collect things. Collectors develop similar notions of wanting perfection and balance in their chosen field, although any such pastime has now become associated with a socially inept personality, so maybe I'm digging a bigger hole for myself here.

When I was a child we all collected something; if it wasn't stamps or train numbers it would be sets of picture cards out of packets of tea or bits of plastic given away with breakfast cereals. Living in West London I actually collected aircraft numbers from Heathrow. In our pre-teenage years my mate and I would catch the bus to the Queens Building where the modern age was manifested in plate glass and bright red plastic chairs. Steeped in the intoxication of burning aviation fuel and the manic shriek of the first jetliners, we would cross off the numbers we read on the tail fins of the Comets, Caravelles and Boeing 707's we spotted, using a book specifically published by Ian Allen for that purpose. No one made derogatory comments about our outer clothing and we were part of the modern sixties, unlike my elder brother who had hung around Feltham marshalling yard spotting the numbers on diesel shunting engines.

I'm not clear how that links with my travels where I have nothing to show at the end of a journey. Liz will take a few photos but we rarely look at them again, and I'm not one of those people who have a list of all the countries in the world to cross off. But making collections of things does somehow seem to be the same mentality and it is an idea I will try to develop as the journey continues.

When I am at home or at work and thinking about travelling, everything about it seems appealing. Even being delayed in an airport lounge is tinged with a glamour that makes it all acceptable. The reality is different. We were back on the Thai mainland at Chumphon railway station waiting for the train to Bangkok which should have been there 40 minutes beforehand and, instead of the relaxed resignation and deigned allowance that I exhibit in my daydreams, I wanted it there right away! Walking up and down the platform failed to make it materialise but just as darkness was setting in, there was a whoosh of activity and train 178 made its grand entrance. I love sleeping on trains; the swaying motion, the rhythmic rattle and, best of all, the knowledge that you are travelling. Our 'hard-sleeper' carriage was a bit clinical, and it had air conditioning so the windows wouldn't open, but we were on a train in a glamorous land and moving on to the next place. Life felt good.

I had been to Bangkok before and had no great desire to do so again. For me it is one place that cannot be redeemed by an exotic image. It is overcrowded choked with traffic and worst of all has no proper centre. Siam Square is an area on a map rather than a visual point of reference and apart from the Chao Phraya River (which the city seems to have targeted and missed) there is nothing but mile after mile of urban development in every direction. The wonderful images of exotic floating markets which are seen in travel brochures do I believe exist, but so many miles out of the city that getting there and back would take days.

I have found that the smaller the settlement the truer the experience of being in a foreign place and that big cities around the world become more and more like each other. Liz agreed that we should negotiate the obstacle of Bangkok as quickly as we could. And we did. We stepped onto the platform at Hualamphong and made our way to the station concourse where the departures board showed one of the two daily trains to Aranyaprathet leaving at 6.55 am. We had 3 minutes. Quickly finding the platform I spotted a smiling young woman in uniform and indicated that we wanted to catch the train but had no tickets. She exchanged a few words with the guard, we boarded and the train lumbered out with a slow but persistent swaying motion. We'd beaten Bangkok.

Railway lines cut through the hearts and souls of cities. Nothing is softened or censored. There are no facades visible from the carriage window and there is no prettification or attempt to woo the onlooker with shop fronts, avenues or civic buildings. From the train you see the unabridged naked truth of the city, and Bangkok is uglier than most. We gently trawled through mile after mile of slums where the city's dirty washing is hung out for all to see. Precarious structures of wood and plastic are wedged in to fill gaps and forgotten corners, and those at the bottom of the heap sift through the heaps of rubbish discarded by those from higher up.

We were on a local train with only 3rd class carriages and the world came to us with the ebb and flow of passengers and food vendors chanting their array of produce. As city gave way to soft pastoral countryside there was evidence of a pride taken in the small communities. I don't know if they have a Best Kept Station Competition, but the frequent stops seemed to vie to be the best presented with bright paintwork, floral displays and immaculately uniformed personnel armed with whistles and flags. Gradually we adjusted to the pace and rhythm of the train. As long as this can be achieved the slowness is of no consequence as one is attuned to being part of the whole and taking in the surroundings as they present themselves. Journeys where you feel the need to move at a more energetic level than the transport you are in is prepared to travel at, is as frustrating as listening to music played at the wrong speed, while on the other hand, being whisked away at a furious pace when you are wanting a gentle relaxed trip is at best the waste of a journey. As a horse and its rider need to be of one mind, so must travellers be in harmony with their transport. We arrived at the terminus 6 hours, but only 250 km later and quickly had to change pace.

Tuk-tuk drivers crowded the platform and one, a burly woman in her forties, claimed us as her prize. I knew that Poipet is the kind of border crossing where people make a living by preying on the ignorance and gullibility of strangers and that we had to be on our guard. Arguments about a fare at the end of a journey when you know you are being ripped off are unpleasant and can be quite upsetting, so we made sure that the price was agreed before we boarded her motorised chariot. Although she wanted nearly as much as the train from Bangkok cost, it was still only a few dollars and it was the major scams that I was wary of. At full throttle we inched past a more heavily laden machine and, entering into the spirit of our change from flat to frenetic, I gestured to the other passengers that we were willing our mount on to get ahead of them. With the border in sight we veered off the road and were deposited at the immigration office.

No queues, energetic officials, a simple form to sign to get the relevant visa; this seemed too good to be true. And of course it was. As passengers arrived by the tuk-tuk load they were processed as quickly as possible without even entering the building but with the emphasis on paying a large amount of money. Our driver didn't need to overcharge us for the journey because no doubt she got a commission on delivering victims to be fleeced. We declined and headed for the border hoping that we would find a proper visa office further on. Then we were joined by a middle aged man wanting to know where we were going in Cambodia. He said that he would drive us to Battambang in a Toyota Camry for $60 US and promised that we would have the vehicle to ourselves. I suggested that $40 would be a fair price but I wasn't too interested as I was more concerned about getting across the border into Poipet. He pointed us in the direction of the real visa office and said that he would see us later.

I was unclear if the first place we were taken to had false customs officials or real ones doing some freelance work in their own time. I suspected the latter as even in the proper building we were invited to pay well over the official amount. I received a scowl when I pointed to a large sign that stated that the price should be $20, but they took our money and passports. I realised that they didn't want to make too much fuss and draw the attention of other travellers to the discrepancy in the advertised rate and what they were trying to charge, but we had an anxious wait as others were returned their documentation but our passports failed to reappear. Eventually they were returned with the appropriate visa and we made our way into no-man's-land.

The buffer zone between opposing borders is often a tense stretch of ground, whether it is in an isolated mountain area or Check-Point Charlie, where the spy would always get shot on their lonely walk towards the arms of their saviours. This one was just bizarre. There was a wholly different world operating in the short stretch of road between the border posts. It bustled with activity and energy as locals vied to take advantage of bewildered travellers but it was dominated by the garish neon lights of casinos.

Gambling is illegal in Thailand so there is an attraction for Thais to cross the border in order to have a flutter, and presumably Cambodia welcomes their money. I am not sure who has control over the areas between border posts, which can be a short walk or, as in entering Kazakhstan from China, a decent bus ride. It may be that the Cambodians have deliberately moved their customs post back to create the space to build these casinos and enable Thais to spend their money without the bother and international bureaucracy of entering another country. However it has come about, this mini Las Vegas in the limbo created between the two countries is very curious.

The man with the Toyota Camry found us again but I really didn't trust anyone in that place and I was reminded that it was the promise of a similar ride to Cambodia that ended up in an impossibly hot and claustrophobic minibus. On that occasion I had been travelling with our daughter, Emily. With little or no public transport available where we were in Laos we had, against my better judgement, joined a tourist trip to Cambodia. Setting off sat in the passenger seat of a big Toyota was fine but as the journey progressed, in a manner which brought to my mind wartime British Pilots being helped by the French resistance, we were passed to other vehicles with larger groups of people and finally crammed into the dreaded minibus.

When Liz and I finally cleared immigration at Poipet we doubled back into no-man's-land and found a cafe where we could get a well-earned lunch and soak up the unique atmosphere of that extraordinary frontier. I wasn't too disappointed that the Toyota man didn't reappear and we eventually found a proper sized bus bound for Battambang.

Kazakhstan is far too large a country to be able to cross by bus and thankfully the USSR has left a legacy of over 15,000 km of rail line. Despite the ancient rolling stock the Kazakhs do seem to take a pride in their railway, and at Turkestan station I watch the fruit vendors carefully sweeping their section of the platform as they set up their stalls for the day. I board my train for Aral but who's this sleeping in my bed? I check with the conductor that I have the correct berth in the hope that he will do something about it, but he doesn't look as if he is going to evict anyone on my behalf. I have to shake the interloper violently to get a response and tell him to sling his hook.

The youngster bears no malice and once awake he smiles and is able to speak a little English. He (and the train) are from Bishkek in Kyrgyzstan and are on a 3 day journey to Moscow where he hopes to get a job earning more money than he can at home. He tells me that the cost of his ticket is equivalent to a month's wages where he comes from so this a major adventure for him.

My other travelling companions are also from Bishkek and, at 9 am I turn down their offer of beer. At 10 o'clock they will not take no for an answer as they produce a 200ml flask of vodka. I am disappointed a little later when they ask for money as I had felt that they simply wanted to share, although I do seem to recall reading about a culture in Russia where 3 or more strangers will split the cost of a bottle of vodka. But then I have the solution; I find a plastic water bottle into which, to save carrying a heavy glass bottle, I had decanted the half litre of vodka that had found its way into my shopping basket in Almaty. I carefully refill their small bottle and honour is satisfied. They are very impressed and get the one who can speak English to ask if it is American alcohol. I had told him that my home is in New Zealand but failed to convince them that this is not a part of America.

It is nearly 9 pm as we finally reach the dusty little town of Aral. A whole day on the train brings the reality of the size of Kazakhstan home. After we left Turkestan it was 7 hours before I saw a proper road and vehicles, and that I'm pretty sure was the Cosmodrome; the Baikonur Cosmodrome was the world's first as well as being the largest operational rocket launch site. It is located in the desolation of the steppe, about 200 kilometres east of the Aral Sea and is now leased by the Kazakh government back to the Russians, currently until 2050. It was originally built by the Soviet Union in the late 1950s as the base of operations for its space programme and it was from here that Yuri Gagarin made the first manned spaceflight in human history. I remember listening to that piece of history being made on the radio at primary school, and it somehow seems odd that in such a very different age this is still the launch site for all Russian spacecraft.

Apart from the space station we had occasionally passed through villages and they appeared to have been built to a pattern; the low brown dwellings dominated by a substantial water tower and with a larger building, perhaps a school, which in most cases was deserted and crumbling. I saw no roads and the railway was the only visible connection with the rest of the world. There was little or no evidence of any agriculture, but once or twice I caught a glimpse of the River Syr Darya, which had once fed the Aral Sea until over ambitious irrigation projects starved it of its sustenance and caused the sea water to retreat.

After wandering the streets of what is really just a village, I find Aral's only hotel. The surly blonde Russian woman at reception charges more than I had yet paid in Kazakhstan and says that there is no shower. It would be more accurate to say that there is no water as the tap produces a dribble which just enables me to clean my teeth. The top floor of the hotel is completely shut off and probably falling down. The whole building has the feel of having been built by a very amateur DIY fiend; all the concrete steps up the stairs are of different depths and the corridor floor is lowest in the middle where it has had the most feet upon it. Even inside the room the corners are finished with mounds of cement and lying on the bed I can see that the doorway is crooked. I nevertheless sleep well and, finding people sat around a table eating in the morning, I wonder if breakfast is included. The blonde woman gives a curt 'no'.

I find where the sea was. Some boats have been placed here but it is contrived, the real ship graveyard of abandoned vessels that were left high and dry is many miles away. In the main road several women are bent double using short brushes to clean the street. They are working hard but as the whole small town is covered in a thick layer of fine silt it seems a fruitless task. I suppose that in a fishing port where the sea disappeared 40 years ago, any opportunity to create work needs to be taken. Most places are shut but I find an open doorway and enter a bar full of men drinking beer and vodka. It is 8 am. By going into the kitchen and pointing I manage to order bread, eggs and coffee and the world begins to look a bit better.

There is an organisation that arranges trips to the sea and I find an English speaking man in its office. The cost for a jeep and driver is excessive because there is only one of me. He says that there was another tourist last week but that is of little help now. I try to think where I have seen other foreigners since I was in Xian on the first day of my journey, but all that I can remember is a couple sat at a table where I had breakfast in Almaty. My route through the rest of Kazakhstan does not feature in any guide or article on the internet that I can find, so I do not anticipate meeting foreign tourists any time soon. I like the idea that I am off any tourist trail but then think that it smacks of some kind of inverted snobbery; that I want to see myself as a fearless adventurer. In truth I'm just catching trains and buses from one place to another, and if no one else wants to be where I am or go where I am going, it is hardly anything to be proud about.

Chapter Eight: The Life of a Journey

I am walking back to Aral railway station as I need to plan the next step of my journey, which will take me to the north of the Caspian Sea towards Russia. There is a scrum formed at the ticket window, which was closed when I arrived last night so that I was unable to get my next ticket as soon as I would have liked. The only train to Makat leaves at 1 o'clock in the morning which is not ideal, and nor is it available. I ask if I can take that train as far as Kandygach, which I have seen on a map as being where the line running south west towards Astrakhan leaves the main route for Moscow. This is affirmative but I am not going to rush this time and leave the ticket office to see if there is an earlier alternative. Yes, train 027 leaves just after 5 pm, a much better time and I return to get a platzcart ticket. She writes down 05.06 which I take as being the arrival time, a bit earlier than I would have liked but still. Hang on. 05.06 is today's date, when I check the ticket I see that I arrive at 2.03 am. Oh dear.

This time my part of the train has a group of Uzbeks from Tashkent who are also going to Moscow. No wonder that it has grown into the largest city in Europe, if it is drawing in hopefuls looking for its golden paved streets with every train carriage arriving from the far corners of the old Soviet Union. They are pleasant enough and when a group of their mates turn up from another compartment with a pack of cards, I indicate that I want to go to bed soon and they dutifully troop off somewhere else. I manage to get a bit of sleep before being ejected into the dark of the night where it takes me a few minutes to even locate the station building.

I have come to the sad conclusion that the rail timetable internet site I was hoping to rely on is wholly inaccurate. It has the right train numbers but the times are all over the place and so I have to rely on what information I can glean from station staff and information boards, both of which only communicate in Kazakh. The good news is that, with the help of Timor, a young medical student on his way back to university in Astana, I have now got tickets right through to Astrakhan in Russia. The less good news is that I have to wait until this afternoon to catch my first train and alight from it in Atyrau at 1 am tomorrow. I tell Timor that my daughter is doing a medical science degree in Auckland, but he also has little idea where New Zealand is. I don't know what geography is taught in this country; maybe an understanding of the layout of the world is less important when you live in the middle of a vast continent and have no seafaring history, but to me it is a basic human need to know where you are in relation to everything else. I am advised to stay in the station as this is not a safe place to wander around. I think that the booking clerk is being melodramatic but I can't see much in the dark anyway.

Kazakhstan doesn't strike me as being a dangerous country, although I suspect that Nailya was correct when she said that the mineral wealth has not greatly improved the living standards of the bulk of the population who remain in relative poverty, and the country may well have significant more petty crime than China. Some of my travelling companions leaving their homes in other Central Asian republics to seek their fortunes in Moscow have certainly appeared a bit rough around the edges, but I haven't felt too uncomfortable or at all threatened by their presence.

The harsh truth, for those who share my background, is that while we think of foreignness as being linked to danger and the unknown, it is our own Anglo-Saxon culture that exhibits more day to day violence than is experienced in any Asian country. It is the United Kingdom that produces the worst soccer hooligans, the United States that has such a ridiculously lenient attitude to gun toting that its citizens seem to be forever shooting each other, and even in clean green New Zealand we have disturbing levels of domestic violence and child abuse. Nor is terrorism confined to foreign fundamentalist fanatics; I remember the bombing campaigns of the IRA, which ironically had to stop after the September 11th 2001 terrorist attacks on New York. President George W's War on Terror, and countries harbouring those who supported terrorists, highlighted the hypocrisy of his anti-terrorist rhetoric while American organisations funded Irish Nationalists to enable them to buy explosives. The United

States Government finally had to act to curtail their activities and the cash starved IRA came to the negotiation table.

In China I feel completely safe walking down the darkest most poverty-stricken alleyways of the biggest cities at any time of day or night. The most dangerous aspect of life is undoubtedly crossing the road. On the streets the normal rules of law and order break down and it is a tooth and claw fight for survival. A green light for pedestrians is an invitation to get bowled over by cars and buses turning into the road you are trying to cross, and all two-wheeled traffic assumes that none of the rules apply to them anyway. It is a common sight to see, often young people, struggling with limps or deformities, presumably caused by road accidents. These are the walking wounded, victims of the war of the roads, who probably lacked sufficient funds to get their broken bones set properly.

The most dangerous thing to attempt in China is to use a zebra crossing. Not often, but every now and then a vehicle will stop, and it is invariably a bus containing a suffocating crush of travellers. What can you do while the long-suffering bus passengers sweat it out? Walk out and peer around the blunt front end by the driver as big black BMW's accelerate past a stationary bus, in the total absence of any convention of giving an inch to anyone else on the road, whether they are on foot, riding a bike or driving an ambulance. For anyone who has the nerve to do it, it is safer to emulate the old ladies with shopping bags who refuse to accept that motor traffic has come to China. They step off the kerb looking straight ahead and maintain a constant if slow pace until they reach the other side, regardless of what is happening around them. On most occasions they survive and are the true rulers of the road, as dirty great trucks and sleek Mercedes-Benz alike, steer a course to avoid them.

Whatever the perceived dangers of Kandygach are, they don't include being run over, and when daylight comes I go to explore the settlement, which is an invention of the railway, and a little town has developed around the lines. There is a pleasantly rural feel to the place, as cows are herded along the street and agricultural land vies for space with rows of houses, which are the usual plastered brick with iron roofs, but many have gable ends constructed of wood which is laid in attractive intricate patterns. But there is not much to entertain a traveller on a 12 hour stopover and I will be very pleased to be on the move again.

We had no such delays on our journey through South East Asia and as ever, I was thrilled to be in another country to see what experiences it might bring, when we exited Thailand. The first thing we noticed was the distinctive Cambodian architecture. The narrow fronted 3 or 4 story buildings looked like slices of wedding cake. They were iced pastel pink, blue or yellow with decorative hard white icing for the ornate balconies and window surrounds. The sides were windowless slabs left in sandy coloured cement as if just sliced off the whole cake and irrelevant to the decoration.

We had been moving constantly by boat, train, tuk-tuk and bus for 30 hours and had got further than I thought that we would have in the time. As the bus rolled into Battambang Liz spotted an imposing looking hotel she liked the appearance of. As usual I thought it looked too expensive but I had resolved to let her choose where we would stay. This was a good strategy for several reasons: as she had no interest in planning our route or timetable it gave her some say and control over our trip and, although I would have stayed in more basic hotels, the middle range options were still good value. Most importantly, it meant that she couldn't blame me if an establishment failed to live up to her expectations.

The hotel she chose was great. It was clean and comfortable with friendly staff and only US$18 including breakfast. The Cambodian currency is the Riel but American dollars are accepted for anything other than the smallest items and you could probably travel through the whole country without using local money. As Liz doesn't bother to look at the map she didn't know that we could have gone straight to Siem Reap from Poipet and that we were travelling along two sides of a triangle. The only reason we were in Battambang was because we could catch a boat from there to Siem Reap rather than using the bus, and I did not want to miss the chance of getting on the water. The hotel even arranged the tickets and transport for the morning departure.

The morning departure for my boat on my trip through Myanmar meant that I was up at 3 o'clock the next morning in Kawthaung. I wasn't surprised that the streets and alleys were deserted as I moved from one pool of light offered by a street lamp to the next. Stripped of the confusion of goods for sale but leaving the ghostly shapes of stall stands and carts, all made of dark weathered wood, the town seemed more than ever to be caught in a time warp. But as I neared the pier the spirits took the form of a crowd, muted by the darkness or perhaps dazed at the unaccustomed hour of their wakefulness, and moving mechanically to the food stalls that had sprung up in the road to serve rice with unknown dishes of dark lumps in sauce. I found a pink plastic seat at a temporary table and asked for coffee, which came made from a sweet milky powder. I drifted into idle daydreaming and it was with a shock that I looked up and realised that the crowd had melted away. I hurriedly strode to the pier end and the back end of a throng of passengers boarding the sleek white ferry.

The Myeik archipelago is said to be beautiful, but at four in the morning no-one seemed very interested. Once it was light I divided my time between the plastic upholstered reclining seat and the rear deck, shared by smokers and those enjoying the flow of air as we carved a rut through the calm blue Andaman Sea. Twice the boat slowed to a halt in order to rendezvous with fishing boats which took off a few passengers. No habitation was in sight and I remembered reading of 'water gypsy's' who live nomadic lives fishing between the 800 odd islands.

From the pier at Dawei an old bus took me into the town centre and I finally established that the traffic rule is to drive on the right. This had been unclear in the jumble of trucks and motorbikes in Kawthaung and also confusing as every vehicle that I saw was right-hand-drive. I found Dawei to be another basic but pleasant town and with a large temple area which is a riot of bright colours set against the glittering gold mass of the stupa. Buildings of varying shapes and sizes and housing different gods and bodhisattvas are scattered throughout the complex providing a spectacle, but somehow seeming in competition with each other and lacking any sense of a unified whole.

Once I had more than explored the centre of town I decided to make my way to the largest reclining Buddha in the country, a few miles distant. Armed with the destination written in the impossible Burmese squiggles I set off in the right general direction, hoping to flag down a sawngthaew. I eventually got one to stop but when I displayed my squiggles he indicated that he was taking a different road and I kept walking until I came to the junction. A tractor stopped and I pulled myself onto a wooden trailer, but after only a few yards the farmer waved down a truck and I clambered into the cab next to a red-robed monk. They dropped me at the destination and refused any payment. The statue was truly massive and wearing that beatific Buddhist expression which seemed to justify its superhuman scale, as the feminine moon-like features gazed indulgently down at us mere mortals. The only other visitor was a man with a motorbike who asked the usual questions of what country I was from before his English dried up and I was reminded, not for the first time, at how refreshingly unsophisticated the country is at exploiting its sights of interest.

On the return journey I was waved at and called to excitedly by a group of 4 boys on 2 bikes. I thought that I may have been the only foreigner in this relative backwater of the country, and Kawthaung is only really patronised by day-trippers looking to extend their Thai visas, but in fact I saw a few foreign faces in Dawei, although I suspect that it is a fairly recent phenomenon and young and old alike are keen to give a friendly greeting or just a pleasant smile. This is in contrast to some countries where a greeting from an adult is often the precursor to some sales pitch and from children can smack of impudence. I was deeply disappointed that as soon as the cyclists had passed I heard them laughing with that harsh edge of mockery used by the ignorant when they come across something of difference. But when I turned round I saw that in their enthusiasm, and to the huge amusement of the other pair, one set of bikers had wobbled to disaster and one of them was in the process of climbing out of a ditch. My joining in the laughter was sufficient for the victims to appreciate the humour in their situation and they all erupted with glee to heartily enjoy all the slings and arrows of outrageous fortune as only a bunch of young boys can.

I bought a ticket to Ye, which has the recommendation of not featuring in any guide to the country that I have seen, and boarded the fancy air-conditioned bus. I didn't like it. Particularly when the seat in front was reclined and I was squeezed into a space which barely allowed me to move a limb. The distance wasn't too great but unfortunately the road had not been built, or to be accurate was being completely rebuilt and widened and with several new bridges under construction. On many occasions we came to a complete standstill while the vehicle appeared to pluck up the courage to navigate a vertiginous new earthwork or temporary bridge around newly placed concrete pylons.

When I was told to alight I was surprised that I was the only passenger getting off and not, as I had assumed, at the town bus station. We didn't appear to be anywhere in particular and I took the only option available which was to climb onto the back of a waiting motorbike. Perhaps the surest indication that Myanmar tourism is still in its infancy is the lack of necessity to bargain for simple things or even to ask the price, which on my travels throughout the country was always very fair. Any unnecessary advantage taken of tourists is at the hands of the state, not individuals. I was told that the journey to Ye would take four hours but in fact it was six, the last two in darkness, so I was pleased to get to a guesthouse and head out to find dinner. It was actually a shock; usually I arrive somewhere, poke about, walk around, get my bearings and, probably after a bit of walking around in circles find somewhere to stay. Here I had stepped off a bus and 5 minutes later I was booked into a simple guesthouse and walking along the side of a wide river heading for dinner in what seemed a very pretty spot, but the suddenness of it all was quite disorienting.

I liked Ye. The town is very spread out but that gives it the feel of a collection of villages with palm thatched wooded houses built on stilts along roads of red packed earth. But how was I meant to leave? I wasn't too clear how I'd even arrived and I could see nowhere that resembled a bus stop, let alone a ticket office. I did see one long-distance coach trundling down a main road but the next could have been hours away and likely not stop for me if I did try to flag it down anyway. Really I'd had enough of bus travel. There is a railway station in Ye but my initial enquiries lead to no more than a general wave of the hand such as may be given by someone who wants to be helpful but really has very little idea of the answer to the question. I determinedly headed west until I came to the railway line and followed it until I found the station. The platform looked busy, I presumed in anticipation of the arrival of a train, but when I got closer I saw that they were all vendors of various food items rather than passengers, which at least proved that trains do arrive sometime. In fact the train was due at 14.38 I was informed, which meant that it would be nine o'clock and dark again when I got to Mawlamyine, but it had to do.

I was back at the station in good time and looked around the local streets for some lunch. There were several possible options but only one looked well patronised, although no one was actually eating and I got a negative response when I asked for food. I realised that I was in the equivalent of a pub and that it was Saturday lunchtime and so ordered a beer. A little later I was presented with a small bowl of broth which I tried with some trepidation but found to be very tasty potatoes and beans in chicken stock. When I finished the bowl it was refilled and I got another beer to wash it down. The clientele were all young males but then a woman with a huge comb holding her hair up appeared and directed a tirade at one of our number at a table where they were all well into the local whisky. This brought back happy memories of Sunday lunchtimes in an English pub in that glorious two hours of pre-prandial drinking, before the custom was lost forever by a change to the licensing laws which allowed the pubs to be open all day. Less was so much more.

A big screen was showing Peter Jackson's Hobbit, but the live drama was much more gripping as a particularly tall moustachioed man wearing a black singlet, and perhaps a little drunk, began to make good-natured fun of a friend across the room. I had no idea what he was saying but the tone was becoming increasingly challenging and he eventually left to return a few minutes later with a small black cockerel. Now feeling part of the community I paid my bill and followed most of the other patrons out to a piece of dusty ground to see what would unfold. Another bird had been produced which, judging from the gaps in its plumage, had had more pugilistic experience, and they eyed each other with pure malevolence. They came together with a furious flurry but broke of the engagement after a couple of seconds. This pattern was repeated over and over again and, despite their posturing I was beginning to think that their hearts weren't really in this fight.

But what was I doing there anyway? In my culture cockfighting is banned because of its cruelty; I don't support unnecessary cruelty to animals, but here I was giving mental judgements that the birds were not displaying enough vicious killer instinct! The conundrum was neatly caught by camera. For once I got a good picture from my phone and it showed feathers flying as they went hammer and tongs at each other illustrating the extreme barbarity of the contest. We like to take pictures of things that are unusual or extreme; there is little point in snapping stuff that can be seen in our everyday lives. There is an inherent boastfulness in this that is the basis of all boring holiday snaps and is why I tend to shy away from photography. But the essence of my action picture was such that, even just showing it to my wife, I would need to try to explain that it wasn't actually as bloody as it looked and thus totally undermine the whole reason for taking it. So why was I there at all? I left the scene and found the train waiting at the station.

It is a well-used metaphor to say that life is a journey, but maybe a journey is also a kind of life. An entity in itself with a beginning, a middle and an end, and developing its own characteristics as it proceeds. A person on a journey is influenced and changed by the surroundings and what happens to them as they travel. At the end they are a slightly different person and their experiences have been absorbed into their being. So part of the thrill of travelling is not knowing exactly how you will come out at the other end!

I was thinking about this when Liz and I were in Cambodia. To my shame I realised that I had been to Battambang before. It was when travelling with our daughter Emily, but I had forgotten its name. I would have liked to have gone down a side street to see where we had stayed on that occasion, but I sensed that Liz was somewhat ambivalent about being taken round sites of my previous travels. In fairness it is probably like being made to traipse about in the dust and heat to view someone's boring holiday snaps.

I noticed a familiar triangular area and I recalled from my previous visit that it had been used as a bus terminus, but was now grassed over. It looked much better than it did before but I felt uneasy about it, as if they had tampered with my memory of the place. This is illogical as nothing stays the same. But is it these memories of scenes, locked away as a never changing still frame, which I collect? I can accept that they are only a snapshot in time but it is still brutal to be confronted with the reality that the mental picture is no longer a true and accurate one. I could have taken a photograph which would have preserved the image, although it would not have occurred to me to photograph a grotty bus stop. I do not choose the mental pictures that get trapped in my head, and if I used a camera I would then have an external object. The memories and experiences I have had are a part of me and I have grown with them. I cannot put myself in a photo album. Travelling through different landscapes is like applying successive coats of clear varnish, some of which sticks and becomes part of the whole while the rest is washed away.

Points along the route, even just an odd shaped corner of an insignificant town, form a part of an experience which helps to define the person you are. This I think is what I felt about the attraction of travel being akin to building a collection. The practice of collecting things in childhood is to do with establishing a personal identity. Following the life-cycle of a journey also develops and enhances an individual's sense of self and amasses a collection of images which are absorbed into ones being and become the building blocks of one's personal history and character.

If a journey is a life mine has gone off the rails as I have more than exhausted all that Kandygach has to offer. But finally my train arrives and I am relieved to finally be on the move again and heading south west to Atyrau which is virtually on the Caspian Sea. I am now used to the routine on a Kazakh train; first I evict whoever is in my place, and then wait to be issued with my clean sheets and towel. The etiquette is to remove ones linen and leave it in a pile before reaching your destination. Most of the trains I have been on have been decades old and still showing signs of the original solid fuel fired samovar, although they have been modernised to gas or electric and the conductress no longer has to keep a fire constantly burning to make the tea. I have a lower bunk again in platzcart which has used linen on it and before long a very overweight mother of several appears. The compartment is knee deep in small children. I show her my ticket and she pleadingly asks if I will take the upper bunk. After a moments reflection I accept both graciously and gratefully.

Lying in my position elevated from the worst of the mayhem of young children I find that my toes are curling uncontrollably in a kind of cramp. I blame the Kazakhs love of having gold teeth. I assume that ethical dentists don't replace healthy teeth so they first have to destroy the ones they are born with. I watch a man make his tea and count seven sugar cubes he adds to the small cup, from a box he has on the table. The large woman in the compartment is less exact and has a packet of granulated which she pours into her cup; it must nearly be a saturated solution. Annoyingly this predilection for sweetness seems to have ousted salt from every dining table in favour of a bowl of sugar and I have been unable to replace what I have lost in the sweat and the heat of my travels. The conductress wakes everyone just before 11.30 for our 1 o'clock arrival at Atyrau which seems overenthusiastic to me, but we all dutifully strip our beds and dump the linen in a big pile while she goes round tidying up the carriage.

At Atyrau I am fortunate to get the last bed available in the station retiring rooms, a kind of simple hotel for travellers situated above the ticket office and waiting room. I remember that we used similar railway retiring rooms a lot, many years ago when we were travelling around India. It is a bed in a very hot dormitory but I manage to get my head down for a few hours. I am unimpressed in the morning to be told that there is no shower and I have to settle for a stand up wash at a sink with a cold tap.

I have all day to explore Atyrau before my next train, which will take me across the Russian border to Astrakhan, but I am unsure where to get off the bus as nothing looks like a town centre. Having crossed the Ural River it must be about here, and now I am in European Kazakhstan. They have erected wrought iron sculptures either side of the river stating the appropriate continent to prove it. That's nonsense surely. I don't believe that this river is a border between continents and we are still a long way east of Turkey, which no one claims is European, other than the relatively small area west of the Bosphorus as it divides Istanbul. Logic then dictates that lands to the east of the Black Sea, which includes the Caucasus region, belong to Asia. I remember seeing from the Trans-Siberian Express, way to the north of here, a little marker stone to show where (for the first time in my life) we left Europe, but I'm pretty sure that it was in the Ural Mountains, not the only moderately wide sluggish moving Ural River.

As in the rest of Kazakhstan that I have seen, there are very few shops in Atyrau. The town is full of banks and ATM machines but it is not clear what the money can be spent on. I don't need to buy anything but I would like to feel the buzz of being in the heart of the town- and that is the problem; these towns have no heart. I find a huge newly built square but as it is only occupied by gardeners it seems to be an add-on rather than a focal point. I would like some breakfast but the only cafes or restaurants I can find don't open until midday according to signs on their doors. There is one that also advertises WI-FI so I think I will stave off hunger until lunch time and then try to contact home.

I'm not sure what to do about money. I suspect that no one will want Kazakh Tenge once I have left the country, but I may not have enough for lunch and I don't really want the embarrassment of having to rush to the ATM to pay the bill whilst making incomprehensible gestures, or frantically patting all my pockets searching for cash, which is a routine known in New Zealand as the Australian Hakka. I do manage to find some kind of supermarket and satisfy myself that I can spend any excess Tenge there, and so make a visit to one of the many holes-in-the-wall, and now it is time for lunch.

I can't decipher anything on the menu but hear mentioned 'business lunch' and say that I will have one of those, whatever it is. It is alright but nothing memorable and the waitress keeps trying to get the table lamp to work despite my waving her away. I am unable to raise Liz on Skype but have a conversation with my brother-in-law in England. I can imagine exactly where he is sitting, in a completely different world to the one that I currently inhabit. This must surely be another reason to travel; the ability not to immerse oneself into an alien world but to skim it- to live it but at the same time to belong elsewhere and to experience the bizarre thrill of the physical world and the emotional being in complete juxtaposition. Before I leave I unplug my re-charged little computer and turn the table lamp back on for them.

In the distance the sun is glinting off golden domes which I first mistake for a mosque, but these have the pinched tops of cake decorations my mother used to use or, for those who never sampled my mother's baking, of confections such as St. Basils in Moscow or the Brighton Pavilion. The subtle difference in the shape of the dome reflects the divergence of belief; while Moslems revere Jesus as a great prophet, they don't buy into the Holy Trinity bit, and maintain that there is only one God, which rules out divinity for Jesus Christ (and Mohamed). Of course not everyone has had the advantage of early schooling from Irish nuns, who were able to simply solve the conundrum of there being three-in-one by reference to a picture of a shamrock. With God-the-father in Heaven and Jesus in Palestine I was left with the assumption that it was the Holy Ghost who hailed from the Emerald Isle. As the Christian church survived its first 300 odd years without the idea of Jesus being divine, there is perhaps less difference between these two enormously powerful religions than the media would have us believe.

There used to be a very rude and very right wing morning news presenter on New Zealand television. I used to watch it sometimes because the alternative channel was even worse, and it amused me that he looked like Bugs Bunny. One morning (before he was sacked for making racist remarks), he adopted an indignant self-righteous tone to read correspondence from one of his more ignorant viewers, who demanded to know why 'we' should give any respect to the beliefs of Muslim's when 'they' clearly afford none to Christianity.

I once visited an Islamic information centre in Dubai, where I was told that not only is Jesus (peace be upon him) revered as a great prophet, but that the Islamic creed extends to a belief in even the more improbable claims of Christianity, such as the virgin birth and his ascension into heaven. This last I think is a challenge for Christians in the modern world, as he is clearly said to have literally risen up into the clouds, presumably on a nice calm day. Apart from the meteorology, our current knowledge of the solar system would then have him eternally stuck in orbit. The idea of Jesus whizzing around in constant danger of colliding with a piece of space junk seems undignified at best. The Muslims I spoke to at least gave some kind of answer, rather than the stock 'mystery of faith' response to anything clearly illogical. They reassured me that there are seven concentric sets of heavens and Jesus is safely well out of the range of stray rockets and satellites in an outer universe.

It is perhaps clear that I have no religious faith, but I do love churches, and I am drawn to this one as a moth to a flame. The main attraction for me is the buildings, but there is also an appeal to being in places where people try to make sense, however irrationally, of why we are here and what it is all about. This building is late 19th century and of typical Orthodox Church design, having the dimensions almost of a cube instead of the long nave of western churches. It is oriented with the main entrance in the west and the altar to the east, the same as churches in England, which I have often used as convenient compasses, but a tradition that has become lost in New Zealand. Inside, as often seems to be the way with Orthodox churches, it looks smaller than it did from the outside. The main reason for this is the wonderful accumulation of clutter. A feast of statues of plaster and wood, crucifixes, one life sized and, as the walls and ceiling are full, framed pictures on stands and pedestals. The whole is embellished with gold and silver and imbued with the smell of incense. But dominating the scene is the iconostasis, the Orthodox equivalent of the rood screen, with its panoply of saints and angels, who all have a rather gaunt and severe appearance. It totally fills the east end of the church, blocking off the apse and is the other reason for the building appearing to be larger on the outside.

Visitors to the great cathedrals of Western Europe are struck by the awe inspiring grandeur of the stark grey columns and arches, but they would originally have been full of colour, with a similar profusion of statues and painting over the walls as is still seen in the Orthodox Church. The split, which occurred nearly a thousand years ago, was more to do with where power was held than with doctrine, and it may be that the inside of the Orthodox Church gives a truer impression of the way that Roman Christian churches were in the Middle Ages, than is gained by visiting those buildings today.

I wonder if the Catholic Church, particularly in Northern Europe, has deliberately scaled back on its decoration over the centuries as a response to Protestant charges of worshipping the 'graven images' of the pictures and statues rather than what they are meant to represent. From wandering around old parish churches it seems that the Anglican Church is pretty ambivalent about the issue, as it is about everything. It was an Elizabethan invention as a political compromise to try to displease as few people as possible and can now accommodate anyone who believes in anything. I'm not sure if it's still necessary to believe in God to be a member or even a bishop, but it does do an excellent job of preserving the cultural heritage of the country and should perhaps concentrate on this as its core business; it could amalgamate with the National Trust!

There is a tendency for many people who are brought up as Christians but who reject their faith when they start to think for themselves to become virulently anti-religion. I think that this must come at a great cost as so much of our culture is rooted in Christian beliefs. It may be that I am unable to appreciate the works of art, music and architecture as fully as someone for whom it has real meaning, but I still regard that heritage as being important to the history and identity of us all today.

I still have loads of time to spend in Atyrau and find what claims to be an Irish pub. This is a worldwide phenomenon and I have come across them, with names like Molly Malone's or Nelly Dee's, from New Zealand to China. They may even have them in Ireland. What they are trying to do is replicate the unique institution of the English pub, which is also found in Wales but not in Scotland or Ireland, other than as another attempt at a copy. It may be that they think calling something 'Irish' adds an extra layer of romanticism, or else the whole thing is an invention of Guinness marketing, which is quite a plausible explanation for the phenomena. It can never work of course because the English pub is a part of, and grows out of its environment. You might just as well dismantle London Bridge and rebuild it in a desert in Arizona (which for some unknown reason was actually done). The English country pub is something that I still have faith in and something that I miss in New Zealand, where they are just not quite the same.

It is just opening and I am handed a menu. The beer is so expensive that they can sell it for half price in Happy Hour, from 6 o'clock, and still no doubt make a good profit. It is 5.20 pm and the waitress seems to accept my suggestion that I stay sat outside reading until the prices become more reasonable. I wonder if this place explains the large number of banks in town as you would need to negotiate a personal loan every time you needed to raise funds to buy a pint of Guinness. At one minute past six I am at the bar, feeling very thirsty and ordering half a litre of their cheapest beer. They charge me full price. I object and they explain that while my watch shows the official time, and is correct for the train I need to catch, local time is an hour behind. I drink my beer and find my way back to the supermarket where I invest the remainder of my Kazakh Tenge in bread and cheese.

My ticket is for a bottom bunk but again I am asked to swap for an upper berth, which has very limited headroom. I don't really see why I should. They are a middle aged couple and if she doesn't want to clamber up to the top she could have his bunk. But then she starts to spread a meal out on the table. It is nearly 11 pm and I acquiesce so that I can go to bed.

I am pleased to be crossing into another country. It has taken 8 days to traverse Kazakhstan and 4 of those nights I have spent aboard trains. It would have been the same statistic in China (which is a much greater distance but with faster trains) but losing my passport caused me to have an extra night in a hotel. If one accepts the claim that this end of the country is in Europe, then Kazakhstan is what fills the gap between Europe and the Far East. Filling a gap, with the vast empty steppe is exactly what it feels like; there is little sense of anything that is uniquely Kazakh and although the bright blue flag can be seen flying throughout the country, the impression is that of lines drawn on a map rather than a coherent entity in its own right, and of course that is what it is. We are all woken at 3 am by the passport control but this is a soft border crossing and we don't even have to get off the train. I suspect that the next one from Russia to Georgia will not be as relaxed.

Part 3: The Caucasus

Chapter Nine: Big Brother

Astrakhan railway station feels clean and modern in contrast to those in Kazakhstan. According to the map I printed off the internet, it is not too far from the centre and, consulting my compass, I head south until I reach a canal. Other than The Radisson near the station, I have not seen a hotel and neither have I seen a public toilet, which I increasingly feel in need of. The toilets on these trains are not their best feature and I don't go near them unless I really have to, but I wish now that I had used the facilities before I got off.

Liz tells a story of when we were first in China in 1989 and nearly all the housing was single storey terraces with a communal toilet at the end of the street, as is still the case in the few areas that have not been flattened to make way for tower blocks. There is a strict division between the sexes but other than that privacy is an unknown concept in China, and the simple concrete structures provided holes at a slightly raised level to allow the excrement to then be shovelled into buckets as 'night soil' and taken into the countryside to fertilise the fields. On one occasion Liz was forced to use one of these facilities but of course was spotted by the local women, several of whom rushed in after her out of curiosity to see what a foreign woman's bottom looked like.

It is strange that some towns seem to have places to stay in every other doorway while in others you can search for hours looking for a room for the night. The difference, other than for the four and five star establishments, does not seem to be linked to any potential for tourism and it remains one of the mysteries of travel. Eventually I spot a sign and find a small hotel on the top floor of a commercial building. The cost for one night is more than the 4 nights I spent in, admittedly poor accommodation in Kazakhstan or the 5 nights I spent in Chinese hotels; it looks as if my Roubles may not stretch as far as Kazakh Tenge or Chinese

Renminbi (people's money), but I am really quite desperate to use the bathroom and the check in procedure is mercifully short. The room is pleasant but nothing out of the ordinary. Ideally for the money it would have English speaking channels on the TV, an electric kettle with tea and coffee and a toothbrush. The latter item is invariably provided in Chinese hotels and is something that I need as I realise that I have left my wash bag on the train.

One of the oddest places that I stayed at with Liz was when her company booked her into a hotel in Tianjin. On the outside it looked like a fairly new building but the decor inside suggested the faded opulence of a once smart establishment that was going through some difficult times. Old tapestries lined the walls and the style of furniture throughout the building suggested 18th century France.

Our room was actually a whole flat with the main area crammed with as much furniture as you would expect to find in a second-hand shop. As well as a three piece suite of overstuffed chairs and sofa, there was a writing desk and a bureau, dining table and chairs, coffee table, occasional tables a chest of drawers and a glass cabinet. Off this was a huge kitchen with worktops all round, cupboards, drawers and even a full oven, a rarity anywhere in China. But there was no cutlery or crockery, not even a teaspoon, so unless the guest was going to go out and equip the kitchen for their one or two nights stay it was totally useless. The bedroom in contrast was barely large enough to accommodate the bed, but the strangest thing about the hotel was the bathroom. Unlike many in China it didn't have sliding partitions or curtained windows into the bedroom area, the point of which is beyond me, but it was the first time that I had come across what claimed to be an intelligent toilet.

The very idea concerned me as intelligence suggests feelings and a prerequisite of a toilet is surely that it is insensible to the use to which it is put. More worryingly it implies an ability to offer criticism and I did not want my performance on it commented upon, or perhaps dietary advice given. However in the interests of research I had to try it out. I gingerly took my position and examined the control console which would not have looked out of place in a jet fighter. I touched the power button and looked in vain for a safety belt to buckle as sounds and vibrations of whirring and humming emanated from underneath me.

There appeared to be three main functions: I opted for 'hip cleaning' and a green light indicated 'water pressure for hip'. What on earth is hip cleaning? A helpful diagram on the button showed a UU shape which suggested that the use of the word 'hip' was extremely euphemistic, and this suspicion was confirmed as I experienced a well-directed jet of warm water. The second function is drying which is accomplished not by towel but with a targeted blast of air. The seat itself seemed to be getting hot and I noted that there was an indicator light for this although it had not come on. The third function was enigmatically described as 'for women'. There was a diagram on the button but it simply showed a stick figure of a female, identifiable as such by a triangular shape to indicate a skirt which also had an arrow pointed at it. I was unqualified to test this one, but having come so far; oh! It said 'for women' so it couldn't have been meant as a testicle washer.

The facilities in this hotel are far more conventional and I like the feel of Astrakhan. Walking the streets I find a low-rise city with the centre dominated by grand but crumbling stone buildings. I make my way to the Volga, which is the scale of river that really could divide continents and marks a clear limit to town development. Here there are floating restaurants and a musical fountain with its spurting jets failing to make sense of Tchaikovsky, but the attempt at tourism seems somehow half hearted. I catch a trolley bus, for no other reason than because it is there, and note the old lady next to me make the sign of the cross as we pass the Assumption Cathedral. It is situated inside the Kremlin which, when I eventually find my way in, is undergoing a complete make-over. A path for the faithful has been cordoned off from the building works and I gain access to the iced wedding cake of a building for another pungent dose of religious iconography.

For a relatively big town I am surprised that the traffic is so light and, after being in China for so long, I still haven't really got used to the novelty of cars stopping for pedestrians at zebra crossings. Away from what I take to be the immediate city centre the large stone edifices give way to chunky wooden dwellings made of thick slabs of timber and with heavy painted shutters. Few of the walls are still straight and many lean at dangerous looking angles. The impression is that it is the very weight and solidity of the construction that cannot be upheld rather than any flimsiness or lack of cohesion in the building.

Wood is different to any other building material as it comes from a living thing and seems to retain some impression of that life force. Liz and I lived for several years on an old wooden narrowboat in and around London before we had children, and I was delighted to find that the next part of our journey through South East Asia to China was to be on an old wooden boat not much bigger than our old home. The next stop on my itinerary would be Siem Reap, which is the nearest town to the ruins of Angkor Wat. Our hotel in Battambang had provided us with a packed breakfast as we had to leave early, and it was fortunate that backpacks were our only luggage as we were taken to the boat riding pillion on the back of a pair of motorcycles. There were just a few other foreign travellers, and I was pleased to see that the ferry clearly existed primarily as transport for locals, but of course authentic travel in the real world of developing nations comes at a price, and I was less thrilled with the prospect of several hours sat on a hard wooden bench.

In contrast to Thailand, Cambodia has had a long history of colonisation. Although at one time the Khmer Empire was the dominant force in the region, the country became a battleground and was fought over by its more powerful neighbours, Siam and Vietnam for a few hundred years until in the mid nineteenth century, inviting the wolf into granny's cottage, they asked France to give them protection. Cambodia finally freed itself from being a part of French Indo-China in 1953.

Colonialism and imperialism are now dirty words but it seems that the rich and powerful nations in the world continue to impose their culture and values on the rest, and have just found some more subtle ways of doing it than by annexing others' lands to themselves. I am afraid that travelling is a selfish pastime as sights and sounds and smells are absorbed and little or nothing given back in return. For the traveller the legacy of colonial influences, however reprehensible the original acts were, just adds another layer of interest. That the Central American republics are richer for their Spanish heritage is surely undeniable if you are sitting in the beautiful square in Antigua, Guatemala's old capital city. The richness of India is enhanced, not diluted by its British institutions and what Jamaican or Trinidadian would give up the game of cricket. Any culture that has the opportunity to borrow the good bits from another is going to be the better for it, as is demonstrated in the vibrant cosmopolitanism of London which, looking back to when I was a boy was frankly a dull old city. These were my thoughts when I unwrapped the breakfast we had been given and found a length of fresh French baguette stuffed with a tasty herb omelette.

The motor fired up and we were on our way, gliding through the milk chocolate water festooned with pockets of bright green vegetation. Fishermen bobbed up and down in narrow canoes but seemed to be enjoying less success than a nearby group of pelicans. Life on the water margins can be harsh but the fluidity of the environment seemed to smooth the rough edges and salve the abrasions. There is a harmony in the ebb and flow which creates a natural pace and dictates order, as surely as the rhythm of a boatman as we watched him unload cases of provisions, using the rocking motion of his craft to guide his movements.

We moored up next to him on a tiny eyot that had been enlarged by the addition of wonky piers of wooden slats lacing together a handful of buildings including a shop. Soon we were on our way again and plotting a zigzag course across the river to little bus-stop jetties; there was not much movement of people on and off the boat but plenty of activity along the banks where children, whose seemingly chameleon complexions reflected the colour of the river played and cattle drank, sucking the mud with their stilt legs which echoed the skinny stilts upon which the houses of the river folk were perched. The sacks of cargo on the fore-deck were gradually unloaded and a boy of about ten years of age took over the steering. He was clearly delighted with his promotion and raised his legs onto a ledge in imitation of his elders' relaxed posture. I suppose he shouldn't really have been piloting a passenger craft down a big river but, after all that the Cambodians have been through, to even think of health and safety rules seems churlish.

After four or five hours we came to Tonle Sap Lake, the body of water which in the rainy season acts as a massive storage reservoir for the Mekong River. To cope with the amount of water flowing down the Mekong, the size of the lake increases six fold to 16,000 square kilometres and the flow of the Tonle Sap River is reversed with the force of the inflow. Crossing its tip we entered a narrow channel lined with bright green vegetation and picked our way through a network of waterways to finally arrive at a cul-de-sac with no sign of habitation.

The boat dock is a little way out of Siem Reap but an enterprising hotel provided a bus to their door, where passengers could then decide to stay or to walk into town. After carrying out an inspection Liz pronounced that the hotel was probably as good as any other and we booked in. while she was doing that I was approached by a tall young man with a motorised rickshaw. I usually avoid these things like the plague, but I was aware that to visit Angkor Wat we would have to use tourist transport and I liked his mild manner and the fact that he could speak some English.

Polai was waiting for us as arranged the following morning, and we climbed aboard his carriage which was connected to an ordinary motorcycle. We were only half way to the ancient city before Liz started to argue that we should pay him more than he had asked for, because she felt that it was not enough for a day's employment. I finally mollified her with the suggestion that we could buy him lunch.

The ruins of Angkor are located amid forests and farmland to the north of the Tonle Sap and south of the modern-day city of Siem Reap. The temples of the Angkor area number over one thousand, ranging in scale from nondescript piles of brick rubble scattered through rice fields to the magnificent Angkor Wat, the world's largest single religious monument. 'Wat' is the local word for a temple and so Angkor Wat is only one part of Angkor as a whole, which is a region of Cambodia covering an area of almost 400 Square miles. It served as the seat of the Khmer Empire from around 800 AD, when the country was unified by the Hindu ruler Jayavarman 11 who declared himself a Universal Monarch and God King. The Empire flourished from the 9th to 15th centuries and stretched from the sea in the south all the way to the Chinese border.

It is impossible to be in Cambodia without seeing innumerable pictures of Angkor, which has established itself at the heart of the national identity, and as we approached there was a satisfaction in seeing those images becoming a recognisable reality. We allowed Polai to guide us where to be dropped and where to meet him in another vehicle park later in the day. The initial design and construction of the temple took place in the first half of the 12th century, during the reign of Suryavarman II and was dedicated to the Hindu god Vishnu. It was built as the king's state temple and capital city but in 1177, approximately 27 years after the death of Suryavarman II, Angkor was sacked by the Chams, the traditional enemies of the Khmer.

The scale of the place is hugely impressive and we wandered over a broad bridge to cross the 200 metre wide moat and entered the great knobbly expanse of stone ruins. The moat was clearly ineffective in repressing the Chams but has had some success against a far more persistent enemy; Angkor Wat is unusual among the Angkor temples in that, although it was somewhat neglected after the 16th century, it was never completely abandoned. Its preservation is due in large part to the fact that its moat also provided some protection from encroachment by the jungle. Elsewhere in Angkor banyan trees have taken root on top of the stones and their tentacles are relentless in their search for more footholds. The vegetation waits in the wings as a scavenger stalking a sick animal, ever alert for an opportunity to pounce and devour the remains.

There is an air of spaciousness about the site despite the crowds and a couple of hours passed before we reached our rendezvous point with Polai, but where was he? I had no doubt that he was there but so were dozens of other motorcycle chariots all looking remarkably similar. While other drivers rested, we eventually found him sitting in the back of his contraption reading a book about the site and he revealed an ambition to become an Angkor guide.

We climbed aboard to be taken to see the work of the greatest of the Khmer kings, Jayavarman VII. He came to power towards the end of the 12th century after the disastrous sacking and set about building something even grander. He established a new capital and state temple, Angkor Thom and the Bayon respectively, a few kilometres to the north. Unlike his Hindu predecessors, Jayavarman VII was a Buddhist and the religious practices that he established continue to the present day.

In 2007, an international team of researchers using satellite photographs and other modern techniques concluded that Angkor had been the largest preindustrial city in the world and that the local agriculture could have supported up to one million citizens. Only the gods had the right to live in stone buildings so all the housing, public buildings and even palaces were built of wood and have not survived the test of time. There is still an awful lot to see and as the decoration is carved into the walls and is not easily transportable much of it has survived, including the Terrace of Elephants. This is 350 metres of parading stone elephants in an elevated position where the king would have presided over ceremonies and displays, probably including colourful processions with real elephants.

One image from Angkor sticks in the mind to the exclusion of just about everything else it is so pervasive. The Bayon has 54 gherkin-shaped towers of the type that are emblematic of Angkor, each of which carries the same intent and enigmatic visage on all of its own four faces, making a total of 216. It is inescapable. Elevated above the humdrum of everyday life the giant faces watch and miss nothing. It is a Buddhist bodhisattva, one who despite having achieved enlightenment is willing to hang around on earth and help lesser mortals. Religion is used throughout the world as a means of social control but rarely as blatantly as it was deployed here. The image may be caring and compassionate but it is also supremely powerful. It is the good shepherd watching over his flock, but woe betides any who plan to stray. But that is only half the story; it is believed that the model for the features is none other than Jayavarman VII himself. George Orwell needn't have gone into the future to reach 1984; Big Brother has been here all the time.

Polai is going out the back of the restaurant to eat but, having established that he is not fed for free in return for bringing us here, he gratefully accepts our invitation to join us for lunch. We take the opportunity to learn more about him and the country. I doubt that there is anyone in Cambodia who did not suffer the loss of a relative under the Khmer Rouge regime and it is estimated that during their short rule (from 1975 to 1979) a quarter of the population died from starvation, disease or execution. This was a Cultural Revolution on speed; even poor eyesight requiring glasses could be enough to label a person as an intellectual and sentence them to death. Polai tells us with sadness but not anger or even bitterness, that his father was one of those killed.

It seems extraordinary that a nation of such gentle mild-mannered people produced such an evil inhumane system of government, and there is a kind of resigned cynicism to the notion that many of the perpetrators still wield power in the political system today. The regime was finally driven out by Vietnamese forces but continued to have influence in the western part of the country and, to our shame, was supported by the governments of western nations. The Khmer Rouge survived in some form until the late 1990's and Pol Pot himself died in 1998. The infamous head of torture known as Duch operated from a converted school in Phnom Penh, now turned into a museum of sickening torture apparatus which I saw with my daughter on my previous visit to the country. Incredibly he was allowed to remain a free man until 2010, when he was finally convicted and imprisoned, more than 30 years after his crimes against humanity. The apparent ability of the Cambodian people to put the past behind them is admirable, but surely there should be justice as well.

Curiously for a Communist regime the Khmer Rouge came to power in alliance with Prince Sihanouk. He was an extraordinary maverick who, as the country's king became head of state on independence from France in 1953. He later renounced the throne and ruled as prime minister until displaced by a coup in 1970 when he became an exile in Beijing. The Guinness Book of Records identifies him as the politician who has served the world's greatest variety of political offices. These included two terms as King (the second from 1993 to 2004), two as Sovereign Prince, one as President, two as Prime Minister, as well as numerous positions as leader of various governments in exile, and he served as puppet head of state for the Khmer Rouge government in 1975–1976. Sihanouk kept strong links with China and I watched various news items about him on Chinese television following his death in 2012, a fortnight before his 90th birthday.

Despite its extreme Maoist policies the Khmer Rouge was first and foremost a nationalist party and the support of Sihanouk swelled its numbers enormously. Ethnic cleansing was high on the agenda and Angkor was an important symbol of Khmer purity with the iconic towers even appearing on the flag of Democratic Kampuchea, as the country was then called. Polai tells us that part of the deal for the Vietnamese army ousting the Khmer Rouge was that they took control of Angkor. This seems an extraordinary claim to me; that a foreign power would mount a military invasion of another country in return for control over a tourist attraction. Whatever the truth, Polai is convinced and the importance of Angkor cannot be overstated. Not only is it at the heart and soul of the people but, in a poor country it is also a huge money earner and the basis of Cambodia's emerging tourism industry.

According to Douglas Adams the answer to Life, The Universe and Everything is 42, but Jayavarman VII clearly believed that it was 54. We leave the 54 towers of Angkor Thom and stop at the massive North Gate. Polai says that the other four gates (two in the east) are built to the same pattern, with the statues of 54 gods on one side and 54 demons on the other. But all these gods and demons are overshadowed by that face again on all four sides of a tower crowning the gateway and ever alert to the toing's and froing's of the people. Customs posts and immigration officials become superfluous when a visage like that is guarding the gateways.

The girl on reception at the hotel in Astrakhan tells me that buses run regularly to Elista, the capital of the Russian Republic of Kalmykia, but I decide to visit the bus station to check. Communication is not easy but my understanding is that there are just four a day. The first is too early as I am not prepared to miss the breakfast that comes with this expensive room, and so I won't be able to leave until one o'clock, later than I had intended. I consider trying to get a ticket now but decide to keep my options open in case I have not properly understood. Back at the hotel the girl on reception admits that she has no real idea about buses and I therefore assume that the information I got is correct. I am planning to couch-surf in Elista, something that I have done before but not recently as I got fed up with people, both those hosting and those surfing, not keeping to arrangements made or communicating changes. In light of this rather superior attitude of mine, I am anxious to keep my host informed and I send an e-mail to say that my arrival will not be until early evening tomorrow.

By now it is dinner time and I head back out into the surprisingly quiet streets to look for somewhere to eat. I can't find anywhere. Again, having grown used to China where food vendors are everywhere this strikes me as being extraordinary. I know that if I make my way to the river or back to the train station there are places to eat, but this is the centre of town, surely something should be open. I am distracted by singing and find an outdoor performance in a small square with an audience of a few dozen people sat on park benches. The operatic voices sound a little over the top and, to my ears only just fall short of being a comical send up. But the reason I can't stay and listen is the same as why I can't sit on any of the many outdoor benches in town; Astrakhan is plagued with little white flying insects. They don't bite but as soon as you stop they are in your face and become unbearably annoying. Towards the Caspian Sea is the Volga Delta, a great nature reserve but, I suspect also a great breeding ground for these midges. I've had enough. I ought to use my pleasant hotel room to get my money's worth and I still have some bread and cheese left that I bought with my last Tenge in Atyrau. That will do for tonight.

A leisurely start this morning and I catch the marshtruka to the bus station in good time. Disaster- the bus I intended to catch is sold out; the next one is not until 16.45 and doesn't arrive until 22.45. I am kicking myself that I didn't get the ticket when I was here yesterday. But then yesterday I was kicking myself for being so disorganised as to leave my wash bag on the train. I'm not going to enjoy this trip if I'm forever blaming myself for making the wrong decisions, and with the benefit of hindsight there will always be things that I would have done differently. I need a more philosophical attitude- but first of all I need to find somewhere with internet access. I rather cheekily tell reception at the Radisson Hotel that I don't want to stay there but would like to use their WI-FI. They appear unperturbed and inform me that it is available throughout the building and I fire off another e-mail to Elista.

Finally I am on my way in a Mercedes minibus, which I take as being a class up from the Russian Ford Transit lookalikes which dominate the bus station. The landscape of still, reflective areas of water and richly green marginal plants slowly gives way to something like moorland. The ground looks flat on both sides but the view of the road ahead suggests that we are making a steady ascent. After we have been travelling for an hour and a half it occurs to me that we have not seen another building since clearing Astrakhan, and when we finally come to a village it is just a few scattered houses around a road junction.

This feels very different to the Russia I have been to before, which I remember as being a cold grey country with severe humourless people. A problem with travelling is that one only ever skims the surface, which can feed stereotypical assumptions and generalisations, and I need to keep an open mind. This part of the country, squeezed between the Caspian and the Black Sea, is far from the big industrial areas and any tourist routes but it has a fascinating chequered history and I am eager to explore.

Thinking back to Cambodia, I am pleased that I visited Angkor and for once appreciated a world class tourist attraction. It does seem remiss that we missed it when passing through the country before (I blame Emily's need for clothes shopping), but it would have been a far greater crime to have come to Cambodia and not experienced the charm and warmth of the people. Travel essentially comes down to briefly sharing in the life of others in the world, and I wonder what adventures may be in store as I delve into a new region.

Chapter Ten: Conquering the World

I abandoned my original plan to catch a ferry across the Caspian to Azerbaijan because it was reported as being too unreliable. The absurdly small scale map in the Thomas Cook International Timetable indicated a train through to Volgograd as the alternative, but this would take me further north than I needed to be. A more direct route to the Georgian border through Dagestan and Chechnya was felt to be inadvisable because of on-going unrest in the region and it looked as if trains were not even running right through those republics. But in the middle of the stretch of land between Astrakhan on the Caspian and the top of the Black Sea, is the Republic of Kalmykia. I had never heard of it before, but the more I read the more intrigued I became.

The area, which is in the Volga region, was settled by Buddhist nomadic peoples, who had journeyed all the way from Mongolia some centuries ago, and the present day inhabitants are largely their descendants. They initially had a good relationship with the Russian authorities as they protected the country's southern border, but a repressive regime in the 18th century forced most of the settlers to leave. Those to the west of the Volga were unable to get across the river and, as events turned out, fared better by remaining. But this was not the last attempt at their expulsion; the area was under German occupation in the Second World War and, rightly or wrongly, Stalin believed that the people had collaborated with the Nazis. His response in 1943 was to load the entire population, together with many others from neighbouring republics, into cattle trucks and send them all to Siberia. There they remained until the sentence was rescinded in 1957, after Stalin's death, and most of the surviving Kalmykians returned to their homeland.

So we have a twice displaced population of Buddhist Mongols living peaceably in a quiet corner of Europe. But wait-there's more; while Kalmykia remains part of Russia, in 1993 elections were allowed for a president of the Republic. The people chose a local young billionaire, whose parents were amongst those exiled by Stalin, and he remained in power for nearly 20 years, campaigning on platforms such as free mobile phones for every shepherd. Kirsan Ilyumzhinov is a larger-than-life figure who, although voted out of office in Kalmykia, remains a controversial president of the World Chess Federation and made the Republic the only place in the world where chess is an obligatory school subject. Although he is undoubtedly hugely successful he sounds more than a little out of touch with reality, and claims to have been taken on a whistle stop tour of the galaxy in 1997 in an alien spaceship.

Can it get more bizarre? Yes it can; he is also a fan of an early 20th century Russian satirical novel, The Twelve Chairs, which has the con-man character of Ostap Bender as its central figure. He dreams, amongst other things, of building a chess city, although it turns out that he has no idea even how to play the game. Ilyumzhinov decided to turn fiction into concrete, bricks and mortar; Chess City now exists in the Kalmykian capital of Elista.

I love it when fantasy and reality become muddled and pure imagination takes a solid form. It is like Doctor Who finding a hole in the space time continuum and, as bits from another universe seep through, all the natural laws of physics become challenged. In a way this can be the attraction of ancient sites, as the lives of people living hundreds of years ago only really exist for us in our imaginations, maybe fuelled by colourful images from history books. When we come across the solid structures that they used to live or worship in, it provides that clash of storybook and harsh reality which can cause a frisson of excitement. In Angkor Thom that process was undoubtedly helped by the ubiquitous chillingly controlling face of the creator and ruler of the city.

The day after our visit to Angkor Wat we left Siem Reap by bus to Kampong Cham, on the Mekong proper, but the Chinese had beaten us there. I had hoped to be able to catch ferries to take us north up the river in an exotic and leisurely fashion, but we found that the great river highway has been replaced with slick black and utterly boring tarmac. It seems that, as the United States views the Central American republics as its backyard, the rising superpower of China has appropriated South East Asia to its sphere of influence.

The infrastructure of Laos and Cambodia has certainly benefitted from new roads which has also enabled goods to be transported far more easily north of their borders. Eastern China, where most of the population is, has always suffered from a shortage of wood, which is a main reason for the way that the cuisine has developed; cutting food into small pieces which can be cooked quickly over a high heat using a relatively small amount of fuel. Today's China needs timber for more than cooking dinner and regards Laos in particular as a prime source. Yunnan and other areas of China may have an equally rich supply but, in the true tradition of colonialism, there is no reason to deplete one's own resources when there is the alternative of deforesting one's poorer neighbours.

Having had an average of one US bomber load of bombs being dropped every eight minutes 24 hours a day from 1964 to 1973 it is perhaps remarkable that there is any vegetation left in the region at all. The carpet bombing, the full extent of which was only revealed in the year 2000, was of course restricted to a specific area along the Vietnam border and targeting the Ho Chi Minh Trail. It did earn Laos the title of the world's most bombed country and there is still danger in the countryside from unexploded cluster bombs.

All of which history made me feel a bit mean that my major concern was the absence of a ferry to give me a more atmospheric trip along the river. We found an old boat station in Kampong Cham but it was deserted and fast becoming derelict and we were forced to take another bus to Stung Treng. Here I found a magnificent multi-storey vessel with polished brass and teak woodwork. It would have looked more at home on the Mississippi than the Mekong but I negotiated the gangplank and spoke to a smartly uniformed officer who told me that when they sailed it would be downriver towards Phnom Penh, the opposite direction to where we wanted to go. I was determined to get onto the water and to this end we tracked down Mr T. to his office base; a table in a riverside café. He is the local ticket king and arranged that the next day we would be taken in a proper Mekong canoe down to the Laos border and would hopefully get to see the very rare freshwater dolphins which are peculiar to this stretch of the river.

We didn't get to see any dolphins and the boat ride was over far too quickly but it was good while it lasted. We were in a red and yellow painted wooden canoe-style craft known locally as a long-tailed boat. The name seems to come from a reluctance on the part of the builders to finish the stern, which just continues as two sides and a bottom, but is raised to a good height above the water. I sat on a wooden slat in front of Liz at about water level with maybe a foot of freeboard, and we screeched up the river. I don't know where the dolphins were that day, it would have been nice to have seen them, but that would have been a bonus rather than the raison d'etre. Wildlife I consider to be an interesting added piece of colour. I can understand why some people make it a focus of their travelling, but for me there also has to be a human element or at least some context.

Of course the bus would have been cheaper, faster and more comfortable but not as close to the environment that we were travelling through. I could feel the battered woodwork of the boat and trail my hand in the murky Mekong and there is a need to be able to feel and touch, not just view through a window. As technology becomes more and more able to simulate experiences, I for one want to hang onto my real reality and not settle for the virtual.

When we got to the border I realised that we were already in Laos and had to walk back through in order to exit Cambodia. We were the only customers and the whole place looked like a folly, as if the border posts had been constructed in the expectation of a road which ended up taking a different route. Wooden cabins housed the respective border guards and it was far from obvious which were Cambodian and which Laotian. Both expected some form of tip, explained as an immigration or emigration fee, and I guessed that their dour countenances were due to their misfortune at being given such a quiet posting. Some people in uniform assume a similar expression as a reflection of what they perceive as the importance of the role they perform, but these guys had no such pretensions; they were simply money grubbers.

There is an argument that travellers should refuse to pay these bribes and demand to be allowed free passage. I take the view that as a visitor to a foreign land one should be tolerant of the different ways in which societies operate and not try to impose cultural beliefs and values on others. There is really little difference between this and the system of baksheesh in India, where a little extra is expected to get any service performed or indeed tipping at restaurants in America, and to a lesser extent Britain (but thankfully not New Zealand), where staff wages are kept low in the expectation that they will be made up in tips. I did however draw the line when a particularly youthful guard requested more money because it was the week-end. I couldn't help laughing and he sullenly returned our passports avoiding eye contact.

I had been to Laos before and loved it. On our way to New Zealand Henry and I entered the country from China and spent 2 days travelling by motorised canoe down the remote River Namtha, staying overnight in the boatman's village. It was the highlight of the whole journey and the 11 year old Henry spotted toucans in the dense forest that the river carved our way through. I did wonder about his skill as a twitcher when, a couple of weeks later, we reached Penang and he pointed to a rather shabby breed of pigeon on a street corner in Georgetown and said *"look a kiwi"*. I'm far from sure that toucans really belong in South East Asia anyway.

Emily and I entered Laos from Vietnam and explored Vientiane, the quietest capital city I've been to, where we could saunter down the middle of the road with no fear of being run over and enjoy French cuisine for transport café prices. We then travelled south to on an island in the middle of the mighty Mekong where we stayed in little huts like individual bedrooms by the river which cost US$1 per night each.

When I returned to Si Phan Don with Liz we looked for more upmarket accommodation. It's an unusual place; walking around the island there is typical farming activity and rural folk going about their business but the small town is a little tourist trap. The main street, which is just wide enough for a vehicle for a short distance before it becomes a beaten earth path, is lined with cafes and guesthouses and most of the clientele are young foreigners. On my previous visit there was a distinct hippie atmosphere and the menu for the restaurant attached to our cabins proudly announced that for a small surcharge any order could be made a 'happy meal'. This was clearly not in the McDonalds sense of the phrase and I looked wistfully at the menu as I would have liked to have tried it, but felt that this would not have been a very responsible act while accompanying my 13 year old daughter. I've never been much of a drug user and, since giving up rolling my own cigarettes over a quarter of a century ago, haven't dared to smoke anything in fear of getting hooked on tobacco again. The town had cleaned up its act by the time Liz and I arrived so I had sadly missed my chance for that culinary experience.

Liz liked the place and complained that she was tired of travelling every day and that she wanted to stay there a second night. I said that we hadn't travelled every day as we had stayed for 2 nights in Koh Tao in Thailand and again at Siem Reap, in order to have a whole day at Angkor Wat. This didn't seem to impress her so I pointed out that she wouldn't want to sit in a hotel room all day so we would be travelling around to look at things, why not turn that energy into making progress along our route, and that if we didn't keep moving we would be in a rush to get to China at the agreed time for her to start work. She said that we could fly part of the way.

This was below the belt. She knew that the idea of taking to the air was anathema to me but that I couldn't properly explain why. I have nothing against flying but not as part of an overland trip. Is this an obsessive/compulsive trait coming out again- that I can't bear to mar the purity of surface travel or regard it as cheating on a challenge? I think it may be more than that. Travel in an aeroplane is like using a secret passage to magically pop up on another part of the globe, but by travelling a great distance overland a proper understanding of the size and scale of things can be gained. This gives some insight into where one fits into the order of things. In a sense it is a means to conquer the world; to master the enormity of it and truly know where you belong. The paradox is that if you could succeed in this, the world would suddenly cease to be overwhelmingly large and become frighteningly small, but that doesn't stop the need to try.

So the next morning we caught a bus to Pakse and from there headed to the Bolaven Plateau. I had not been to this part of the country before and I was looking forward to travelling through lush rural landscapes and seeing the area which is inhabited by several minority groups, well away from the Chinese laid tarmac along the Mekong. I had also identified a little used border crossing into Vietnam which would keep us well away from any major routes. This is the major coffee growing area planted by the French and we had a tour of a plantation in the little town of Paksong, but then the weather closed in. It was cold on the plateau and drizzling with rain. Liz was not happy. The only accommodation we could find provided a bare room with a lumpy bed and plaster peeling off the walls. Liz was not at all happy. There was nowhere to eat and it started raining hard. I was well and truly in the dog house.

The next morning we were both eager to move on but no-one seemed very sure about when a bus would pass through. A little café had opened up next door so we ordered breakfast, but before it came a bus arrived. We quickly cancelled the order and I frantically signalled to the driver to give us two minutes. We ran up the stairs to our room grabbed our bags and bundled into the empty vehicle which appeared to be in no hurry at all and just pleased to have found a reason for its existence. We lumbered slowly through the countryside and it was nice to be moving again. The bus collected a few more passengers before it eventually broke down and we were transferred to a pick-up truck. These sawngthaew, meaning two benches are the principal form of public transport in Laos and a succession of them took Emily and me across the country. I remember that she formed the view that to be a real local necessitated acquiring a chicken, as we invariably had a travelling companion with a favourite hen clucking contentedly on their lap.

We reached the slightly larger town of Attapeu and finally found something to eat. After exploring every corner of the dusty little town, we discovered a bus company tucked away in a side street who sold us tickets to Vietnam, 100 odd km. away across the Annamite range, leaving early the next morning. The accommodation available was simple but just acceptable to Liz and, with the prospect of a new country, travel seemed good again.

When it arrived we boarded, not the full sized vehicle in the picture at the company's office, but a dreaded minibus. It didn't matter as we were the only passengers; at first. By the time we left town the vehicle was packed but we still collected more people en-route through every village. They somehow squeezed in and became absorbed until we felt like one huge being rather than a collection of individuals. We also developed a shared identity; this was not a usual commuter trip but something special for most of the passengers, and there was a kind of holiday atmosphere and feeling of belonging to a shared experience which it felt good to be a part of. This was especially noticeable at the border. From Laos to Vietnam is not an especially sensitive crossing but inevitably we had to go through all the motions and, as the customs officials were clearly not used to travellers from out of the region, they took a bit longer to process our documents. We were watched over by our fellow passengers as part of the pack and although we didn't really need any help, it was nice to have that sense of belonging. By the time that the bus dropped us all at the first small town in Vietnam we were fully adopted into a family group and all sat together at a pavement café drinking tea and waiting for the right bus to continue our journey.

We were heading for Hoi An and I would have boarded a bus bound for Hanoi, which I thought was the right direction but our new family said to wait. Several big buses signed Hanoi went past but we stayed with the group and eventually what they were waiting for arrived. If I thought that the little bus we had just got off was crowded, it was nothing compared to this. The family complete with baggage somehow squeezed into the overladen minibus and expected us to join the scrum. No way was I getting in there and ignoring their gesticulations we waved them goodbye.

On the minibus from Astrakhan to Elista, which is mercifully not overcrowded, I look at my fellow passengers and, sure enough, at least half of them have the facial characteristics of people from the far east of Asia which fits with their historical migration from Mongolia. The arrival time on the ticket is unduly pessimistic and I suspect that the road has been improved, because it is just 9 o'clock when we pull into a dusty and deserted compound which I take to be the bus station. I know the number of the marshrutka I need to take but it all looks very quiet and, as I get off I show the driver details of where I need to go. He rings my couch-surfing host and tells me to get back into his bus. We go a mile or so before he pulls up in front of a marshtruka and we both get out. He asks me for money and I try to establish how much he wants, but there is urgency to board the bus and he is giving the conductor instructions about where to take me. I offer him a note but realise that he was telling me that I needed money for the bus and is not asking for any payment for himself.

It seems like a long journey but I'm sure that I'll be told when we reach my stop. I am finally told to get off and my host is there on the pavement to meet me. My faith in couch-surfing is restored. Ana and her 13 year old son are welcoming, generous and delightful and on the strength of this I send a request through to someone in Vladikavkaz, where it would be very useful to have some local information about how to get to the nearby Georgian border. In the morning we visit the central square of the city which is richly endowed with sculptures, although I am told that the statue of Lenin has been demoted from the central spot it once held. Around the perimeter we study scenes of blown up old photographs from the Republic's history. Ana says that the city is like a big village with a good sense of community but it is very spread out and covers a large area.

Fortunately there are regular marshrutkas and we next go to an enormous temple which I had noticed from the bus yesterday.

This is another of the ex-presidents grandiose schemes and we do a proper visit. First we walk clockwise around the grounds passing gold painted statues before going up a level, past water cascading down marble steps, for another circumnavigation, this time spinning prayer wheels as we go. Finally we enter the magnificent square building and remove our shoes to walk on the rich red carpet. Inside is full of colour but in smaller and more intricate patterns than the Orthodox churches. My first inclination is to appreciate the splendour of the building, but to give it only passing interest as it is clearly very recent and has no historical value. But even though it has no past it may well have a future. It appears to have been constructed regardless of cost, perhaps a thousand years from now it will be an historical monument visited by our ancestors, who will marvel at such a place was built for worship. Would I have dismissed York Minster as being of only passing interest if I had been there when it was new? And this building is for worship, not a museum or a Chinese reconstruction, as is evidenced by the young man prostrating himself on the floor. With these thoughts I see the place in a new light and with renewed interest. The solemnity of the temple is only marginally dented when I come across a line of grinning demons that immediately bring to my mind the Simpsons cartoon character- Krusty the Clown.

I still want to see Chess City, the ex-presidents finest folly and a wonderful example of the way in which fiction and reality intertwine and affect one another. For me this was most starkly demonstrated when I had the opportunity to work on Pitcairn Island, isolated in the middle of the Pacific Ocean with a population of 40-50 inhabitants all of whom are descendants from the mutiny on the Bounty. Before I went there I had not even been certain that the mutiny had been a real event and not an invention of Hollywood.

First we see a statue of Ostap Bender in front of the eponymous twelve chairs. He is a cocky looking character and I wonder how much Kirsan Ilyumzhinov sees of himself in the figure. One big difference between them, apart from the ability to play chess, is that the fictional character only had dreams while the real man made both their dreams come true. The reality of their dream is pleasant enough, there are some nice expensive looking buildings that seem to be occupied and the main complex is an imaginative piece of architecture, but now empty and redundant. The glory days of world chess championships played here is just a faded memory; it has had its day and is now exposed as a true folly. Outside, with the metal frameworks representing bishops and rooks, is a large poster of the republic's new president and his family. That is really rubbing salt into the wounds.

Next stop is the Caucasus and my plan is to catch a bus to Mineralnye Vody. My host kindly rings the bus station but the times are horrendous, leaving late in the evening or after midnight and arriving far too early in the morning. I consult the map and ask about buses to Stavropol, which is part of the way. This seems more promising but Ana says that as the bus only passes through Elista, I cannot get a ticket in advance and must just hope that there is a seat available.

Chapter Eleven: The Great Game

This is a proper bus, not a minivan, it is painted in orange and blue and sign written 'La Conception' in Latin script. It's certainly not an immaculate conception but, maybe 30 years ago it would have been a fine vehicle. Leaving Elista we are again in empty steppe, but it soon turns to greener grassland with grazing stock and horses. The countryside becomes pleasantly undulating and fields of crops begin to appear. As we travel south, the agriculture becomes more intense and I assume that we have now left Kalmykia and the descendants of Mongol herdsman behind, as the landscape turns golden with vast expanses of ripe wheat and barley.

In Vietnam we were also waiting for a proper full-sized bus and, having foolishly let so many go, I was very eager, not to say impatient to get on board one. But the beauty of travel is that you can never be sure what is around the next corner. Consequently you can never really know if you've made the best decision or a disastrous one, and a foolish act, or what seems to be a misfortune, can often turn out to be just what you want. If you can get mind and body attuned to this approach to travel it can bring the kind of serenity manifested in Buddhist statues, as you become elevated above the normal trivia of daily life. Instead of suffering frustration when a bus doesn't come or becoming irritated when things don't go according to plan, it can all be accepted with that hint of a smile that Bodhisattvas invariably wear.

Travel is a great game; you roll the dice and move that many squares on the board. Sometimes you land on 'delightful wooden boat trip' and at others you get 'lost passport go back to Turpan'. It is a game but it is also when I feel most alive. What does that say about the reality in which I live? Of course it's still annoying when you make a stupid mistake in your play, like watching buses you should have caught go sailing by, but once the correct frame of mind has been established, even this can be taken philosophically as it may all turn out for the best anyway. And so it was. When a bus bound for Hanoi finally arrived, the driver issued orders that the crew clear their stuff off the front two seats for us and, from the comfort of our prime position, for the next few hours we were entertained to a splendid panorama through glorious mountain scenery dotted with pretty little villages.

Vietnam: a place full of exotic images, global political power play and horrendous deeds. It was a huge name for my generation and a place that ultimately helped to define us. Although the Labour Government in Britain had the good sense to stay out of that American adventure, that did not stop us from indulging in the cultural orgy of anti-imperialism which swept the western world. Maybe all emerging generations need to challenge the existing order, but we did it as no other. 'Make love not war' was a slogan created by the conflict in Vietnam, and with Flower Power and transistor radios we wrested control from the Establishment and never looked back. Even today music from the sixties and seventies rules the radio waves; music which from Bob Dylan to The Beatles was typically written by the performers and not spoon fed them by corporate institutions concerned only with making money. With the body bags returning to America it was there that the main protest movement was generated. But it wasn't just an injured cry for change; it was also a seizing of power by the sheer force of adolescent hormones erupting in a very different cultural revolution to that getting underway in China. The penetrating discordant nasal tones of Dylan spelt it out:

Come mothers and fathers throughout the land
And don't criticize what you can't understand
Your sons and your daughters are beyond your command
Your old road is rapidly agin'
Please get out of the new one if you can't lend a hand
For the times they are a-changin'

When the Americans ignominiously fled Saigon it was not just a victory for the Vietcong, it was the victory of my generation over what we saw as an old fashioned and narrow minded view of the world. But of course over the years we've gone soft; our idealism has been worn away with mortgages and television soap operas, and so to our shame we allowed the British Labour Party to abandon its principles, stood idly by while money and greed re-established their dominance and let the invasion of Iraq happen.

The Vietnamese have moved on. There is no hint of resentment against Americans or any other foreigners and the country, much more densely populated than Laos, is a hive of activity. I would have liked to have visited the tunnels that the Vietcong built to escape the American bombing and from which they launched their offences, but Liz wasn't keen. Significantly these are not now monuments or war memorials but money making tourist attractions; the Vietnamese are nothing if not pragmatic. All of which heightens the sense of senselessness about what they call the American War. The people are living peaceably, developing a tourist industry which welcomes visitors from all over the world and are generally content with their government. What on earth was it all about?

To defeat the Americans the Vietcong were supplied with arms by China, but they upset their big neighbour when they kicked the Maoist Khmer Rouge out of Cambodia in 1978, and China thought to teach them a lesson. Mobilising more than half a million troops they invaded the country only to be given a bloody nose by the Vietnamese forces, reprising their guerrilla war tactics, and made to retreat with their tail between their legs. So in my lifetime the Vietnamese have fought and defeated both the Americans and the Chinese: how tough are these people? The Chinese invasion was part of a much bigger power game between China and the Soviet Union who were supporting Vietnam. Ten years later we crossed by train from the USSR to North East China and tensions were still high. Over the border at Manzhouli the railway was lined, seemingly for miles, with the Peoples Liberation Army. I vividly remember that the effect of a belligerent force was completely destroyed by one ill-disciplined soldier who, standing in line on that freezing February day, raised his hand just to shoulder height and gave a little child-like wave to the train.

Walking the winding lanes in the coastal town of Hoi An I found it difficult to imagine the conflict the country has suffered. The town was built on the spice trade and prospered for centuries as a port of call for the Portuguese and Dutch as well as the Chinese and Japanese. It still feels prosperous although its market has changed; the port silted up in the nineteenth century but Hoi An is now recognised as a UNESCO world heritage site and plies its trade in tourism.

We naturally gravitated to the river where an armada of craft were available for tourists, but none were being used. I would have thought that August would be high season but the town seemed set up for a party that no one had come to. The riverside restaurants vied for our custom; they were all pretty much the same but it was pleasant to sit and watch the world go by and observe the traffic on the water. In the end I couldn't resist it and we negotiated a fair price for a trip up the river on a good size wooden boat that could have seated a dozen or more. The skipper was cheerful and pleased to have any custom while Liz and I just enjoyed being afloat. Travel for me in some way heightens the sense of being alive and the quintessence of that feeling is to be moving on the water. Whether it is sailing a yacht, catching a Thai island ferry or cresting the waves on a ship in the open ocean, there is always something thrilling about being afloat. Perhaps it is because the surface is alive with movement that the traveller becomes part of a larger life force, maybe it's a regression to being cocooned in amniotic fluid, or it could just be the added dimension of the pitch and roll of the vessel which stimulates the senses.

A fisherman in a traditional conical hat cast his net from his wobbly canoe with a great flourish and grinned at us while Liz took a photo. Our skipper then indicated that we should give him a few Dong and I realised that it wasn't fish he was catching but, like the rest of the townsfolk, he had joined the tourist industry. On the way back I was surprised and delighted that I was allowed to take the wheel. Having lived for several years on an old narrowboat in England handling the steering came as second nature to me and I quickly felt where the boat was balanced, managed to avoid the other craft on the river and lined up the bridges successfully. Another boat tried to force us off course as its skipper thought it hugely amusing to see a tourist at the helm, but our man kept faith in me and we played nip and tuck back to the wharf, where he even allowed me to bring the boat to its mooring. That was great fun and put a big smile on my face. In the game of travel I would count that boat trip as a winning move.

It is pleasing that our old boat has now been restored to original working condition and won the 2013 Historic Narrowboat Society Keay Award for the most improved wooden boat. At the time that we had the boat I just thought it interesting to live on the canal and avoid being saddled with responsibilities like a mortgage, but I wonder now if that way of life was fulfilling the need for travelling. We were always on our way to somewhere. There would be a gathering at a different venue each year for Christmas and it would usually take several weeks to get there, moving at the week-end and commuting back to London from various points from Monday to Friday. There could be long days of winter boating in the holiday after Christmas to get back and typically we would aim to be at the pub at Cowley Lock in West London for New Years Eve. New Years Day we would take our hangovers up the Paddington Arm and a collection of boats would moor for most of January in Little Venice, some years we would get iced in. We might then spend a few weeks at our mooring near Kings Cross but I would be planning the next journey; maybe up the Lee and Stort or the Thames and Wey or another trip along the Grand Union and perhaps the Aylesbury Arm. We commuted back to work from every point of the compass.

We moved at a snail's pace but that didn't seem to matter, the draw was the ever changing scenery and not having to be tied to one spot. This gave an impression of freedom, although we were always aware of the chain of work that tugged us back when we went beyond commutable distance. What fed the travel bug was the chameleon like ability to change surroundings and the illusion that by some paradox, living in a world of constant change could arrest the natural and inevitable march of time. This was a subconscious idea that change is a constant force and that if everything around you is changing then you can stand still and resist moving on to the next stage of life. Whether this was to savour and get the most out of a good period of life or to tread water in an attempt to compensate for a disabling immaturity, I am not entirely sure. But eventually it wasn't enough. There was too much of the world that we were not getting to, and so we left our jobs and caught the train from Liverpool St. to China.

At Stavropol bus terminal I have my travelling priorities in order and buy a ticket for Mineralnye Vody, leaving early tomorrow morning, before going in search of a hotel. Stavropol, a little to my surprise, is an attractive city. The centre is dominated by a huge square with some fine old civic buildings, in much better condition than those in Astrakhan, and the whole place gives an impression of tidiness and order. On my previous visits to Russia and the USSR I had found it to be a dull grey country with grimy cities and leaden skies, but this region, despite being poor, is really quite pleasant and the drama of the Caucasus Mountains is still to come.

The populace of Stavropol, unlike the other republics in the region, is overwhelmingly of Russian ethnicity. While the Soviet Union was a huge amalgam of different peoples, with its break up and the splitting off of some parts but not others, the country is left with a confused identity. There is a lot of support for the idea of 'Russia for the Russians' and Stavropol finds itself effectively on the front line of Russianness. Further south, in predominantly Muslim Dagestan and Chechnya only 4% of the population identify themselves as being of Russian ethnicity, even in predominantly Christian North Ossetia most of the people are ethnically Alans as opposed to being Russian, and the whole area has been in turmoil since the collapse of the USSR in 1991.

The region was brought into the Russian Empire by Peter the Great and his Cossack army in the early 18th century but many of the republics remained opposed to their amalgamation and, as in Kalmykia, the populations of Chechnya, Dagestan and Ingushetia were exiled by Stalin (himself of course from nearby Georgia), for allegedly collaborating with the occupying Germans. Today tensions are exacerbated by the need for central government to make large subsidies to the region to maintain the economies of the republics, and in a 2012 poll a majority of Russians said that they agreed with the slogan "Stop Feeding the Caucasus". It seems that with the end of the Soviet Union the country's borders became frayed. Georgia has clearly become a separate country but its regions of South Ossetia and Abkhazia are still unsettled and the Ukraine now appears to be an unsolvable mess.

It seems astonishing that Russia allowed its best ice-free seaport and major naval base to be located in a foreign country when the USSR collapsed, particularly as The Crimea was only made a part of Ukraine by drawing a line on a map rather than by any cultural associations. Of course the idea of part of a country voting to join another much more powerful neighbour has a parallel in Northern Ireland. The major difference is that in that instance Britain didn't have the excuse that the 'donor' country had never had clear boundaries, as clearly the island of Ireland is a natural entity. The territory of the Ukraine has been divided between other powers for most of its history and the borders of the country were an invention of politicians and cartographers. The Crimea was added to the Republic in 1954 when Khrushchev, who had been head of the Communist Party in Ukraine, was coming to power, and just 60 years before it voted to return to Russia.

The man whose policies led to the collapse of the USSR was himself from Stavropol Krai. Mikhail Gorbachev was born and grew up in a local village where his father was a peasant farmer and, after collectivisation, a tractor driver. Mikhail Gorbachev rose to the highest position of First Secretary in Stavropol before entering national politics. Recognised throughout the world as the person who more than any other brought an end to the Cold

War and enabled us all to sleep easier in our beds, in Russia he was cast aside for that buffoon Boris Yeltsin. Boris of course is a particularly good name for a clown as has been eminently demonstrated by the Mayor of London.

Leaving Stavropol I am the last to push onto the marshtruka and have to take the rear seat. I have lots of legroom but am raised up so that I can't see out of the window beyond the edge of the road. The driver is curtained off so there is no view to the front, it is too dark to read a book and the bumpiness of the road makes writing impossible. I find it very frustrating not being able to see where we are going and I am reduced to watching the entertainment provided on a big TV screen; an improbably glossy Russian soap opera where a large moustachioed restaurant owner presides over all his staff falling into bed with each other- regardless of gender.

I am undecided what to do next: I could stay and explore Mineralnye Vody or try to push on to Vladikavkaz. I have heard back from Regina, with whom I hope to couch-surf, but have not yet confirmed any arrangements with her. Despairing of the soap opera, I attempt to look at information which I have downloaded onto my computer about this region. Another possibility presents itself; on my route is the town of Nalchik, which is the capital of the Republic of kabardino-Balkaria (I had never heard of it either). From here I would have the option of making a side trip to Mount Elbrus, Europe's highest mountain. Mont Blanc, which I had thought was the top of the tops, is apparently only a miserable 16th behind the peaks of the Caucasus. These are serious mountains. On arrival at Mineralnye Vody I go straight to the ticket window in the bus station and ask for Nalchik. I am in luck, there is a bus leaving in a few minutes and, although it might be interesting to see the mineral waters which give the town its name, there is nothing very special to detain me here. I go back outside and a woman in a smart blue and white uniform checks my ticket and invites me to board- the same blooming minibus I have just escaped from. But now the rear seat with leg room has been taken and I am obliged to squeeze next to a man who, although not as tall as me, has to angle his knees to fit behind the seat in front forcing my lower limbs into the passageway. It's only another two hours.

Nalchik is another really quite pleasant town. Walking along Lenin, the tree shaded main street, I can almost imagine being in Tunbridge Wells! Except of course Kentish men don't generally throw bombs about. In the park fashionably clad young women hobble along on stiletto heels and primary coloured young families enjoy the surroundings as if they were in a washing powder commercial. It is hard to reconcile these images with the recent history of violence. In 2005 government buildings in the town were taken over by armed insurgents and by the time they were subdued scores of people, including many civilians, were dead. In 2011 the ski field at Mount Elbrus was attacked with considerable damage to the cable cars, disrupting the Republic's major tourist attraction and seen by the Russian authorities as a threat to the 2014 winter Olympics in nearby Sochi. This area is reported to be struggling economically with very high levels of unemployment, but it is not noticeable to me on the streets where the populace looks quite prosperous, well fed and well clothed. Perhaps I am only seeing the fortunate few with jobs while the rest languish at home in front of more Russian soap operas.

I have decided that it is too much of a detour to get to Mount Elbrus as it would effectively mean a day travelling in each direction plus time spent there, and I have indicated that I will be with Regina earlier than that. Fortunately I'm staying in a pleasant hotel in the centre of town and only a 10 minute walk away from the railway station. Unfortunately they won't sell me a ticket. Yesterday I thought that I was told to come back today, but when I ask for Vladikavkaz I still get a 'niet', the Russian equivalent of 'meiyou'. I wrote down the train number and the time it is due to leave but all to no avail. Communication is difficult as I know very few Russian words and nothing of any local language. Trying to make myself understood I am forced to say something, even though no one can follow a word I utter. But I feel uncomfortable speaking English as it suggests that to me that they should understand my language even though it is me who is the visitor. It is perhaps the stereotypical arrogant Englishman abroad that I am conscious of and eager to avoid, which I do by reverting to Mandarin. This may be silly but it makes me feel better as it is a struggle for me to communicate in Chinese, which means that I can think that I am at least making some effort, and it makes no difference to the listeners as either language is completely incomprehensible to them.

I just hope that there isn't a flare up in terrorist activity which has closed the place down. Vladikavkaz has been the target of bombings in recent years including the appalling tragedy of the siege at nearby Beslan School which made the headlines around the world, and in 2008 the mayor, and the following month his successor, were both assassinated. I am not aware of any clear call for independence for these republics, but Chechnya is only next door and it seems that the violence is simply in the air as the region continues to be in turmoil.

The border crossing beyond Vladikavkaz is the only overland route between Russia and Georgia. It has only re-opened in recent years and being in such a volatile region it is always going to be susceptible to closure if the security situation changes. If I cannot cross there I will have to go all the way around the Black Sea, unless I can catch a ferry across it from Sochi to Trabzon. My son and I travelled on this boat in the opposite direction, from Turkey to Russia, on our way to New Zealand in 2002. It only just seemed to be operating then, and certainly not to any clear schedule. There were only a few passengers and I remember that we had to wait 24 hours for it to sail, presumably as the operators were hoping that more cargo would arrive.

I don't know why I couldn't catch the train but the marshtruka are running and I'm on my way, and with a clear view out of the window. The Caucasus Mountains seem to be taunting me. I know that they're not far away but I can't quite see them, but then this morning they were there in snow covered glory to the south of Nalchik. Where were they yesterday when I walked down the same road? It was a dry and sunny day. I expect them to rise up any minute, and we are at last coming to some undulating countryside. I look again and it is as flat as a pancake ahead and on both sides. Out of the rear window the hills are as sizeable as the South Downs.

Chapter Twelve: Fiction Trumps Reality

I find the address I have in Vladikavkaz and wait in an up-market woman's shoe shop next door for my couch-surfing host. They are very friendly and bring me a coffee, but really it looks like a great job. They are a team of four young women and the shop is equipped with comfortable seating and a large flat screen television, but in the 30-40 minutes that they entertain me, there is not so much as a suggestion of a customer. Before I leave they take photos of me with them, I don't know why- very little must ever happen in this shop.

I take to Regina as soon as we meet. She is a busy, bubbly person and we are off in a taxi to- I'm not sure where- but after buying sweets and cake we meet Alexander on the 15th floor of a decaying apartment block. I'm struck by this year's calendar with a picture of a youthful Stalin and am told that he is still a popular figure and recognised as being a strong man. I say that his reputation in other countries is not so great, and get an acknowledgment of his ruthless cruelty, but this is clearly outweighed by his estimable toughness. Regina says that the plan is to now go to her office where she works doing land measurement, but then changes her mind and says that we should eat some Ossetian pie.

We find a restaurant and get a plate piled with so much pie that we could never get through half of it. It is very good; the pastry is a bit like pizza dough and the cheese filling does nothing to dispel the comparison. Most of it is put in a plastic bag for us to take away. Now we find another taxi and are going to her place of work. She tells me that her father, mother and husband are all in the same company which is contracted by the government to do land surveys.

We are only there for a few minutes before we are on the move again. Walking through town Regina points out a spot where a bomb went off when she was in the vicinity and another place where a suicide bomber blew up a marshtruka and its occupants. I want to know what these people were hoping to achieve, but she says that nobody knows, which surely makes the actions totally pointless. The belief in North Ossetia is that it is not directly to do with them and that the violence always involves Chechens. We next visit a food shop, she wants to know what I like to eat and I say whatever you have, but she gets into a long conversation with the shop assistant and another customer about beer and comes away with a selection of bottles. Finally we are back at her apartment and have dinner- a little before 10 pm. Regina lights up a cigarette before telling me that it is illegal to smoke in the street- for women- men can do as they like. I shudder at the thought of Liz's reaction to this conversation. We talk a little of expectations of male and female responsibilities, and it is clear that changes in attitudes in gender roles over the last 100 years in my culture have yet to permeate society here.

Regina has negotiated with her boss, who is also her husband, to take the day off so that she and her father can take me into the hills. In the event her sister-in-law drives us in a new Jeep. Regina, her father and her husband, who are all quite broad, squeeze into the back and they insist that I have pride of place in the front passenger seat. Presumably the firm can manage for a day without its principal players. Part of the attraction for Regina of hosting couch-surfers is the opportunity to develop her English, but as the nominated bi-linguist she is beginning to get tired of translating everything that her family, particularly her father, wants to know. It is good to be in the hills and we stop at various sites before finding a restaurant where we have a table in a cabin built on a rock in the middle of the river. Ossettian pie arrives, but three layers of it for five people I think is almost manageable, yesterday Regina ordered two for two. But then the main course arrives. We have only been issued with what I consider to be side plates, and mine is full of pie before a sizeable proportion of a pig is balanced on top.

Leonid, Regina's father, produces a bottle of spirit and toasts are made prior to glasses being drained. I am not very capable at many aspects of male machismo, especially those involving hand to eye co-ordination, as anyone who has seen me try to play golf will testify, but I am tolerably good at drinking alcohol. Fortunately this seems to be the most important task that the North Ossetian male must fulfil. While Regina's husband wields the bottle, and short changes his own glass, Leonid and I, of a similar generation but unable to communicate with speech, forge a new Anglo/Russian alliance with clinking glasses, proud speeches and silly grins. The women have sweet coloured water to drink. I had intended to move through North Ossetia, a Russian republic without the very real dangers of Chechnya, but nevertheless an area that has been plagued with violence and one that it is strongly advised to avoid, as quickly and quietly as possible. I have now accepted an invitation to attend a wedding tomorrow and will therefore spend three nights here, longer than I have stopped anywhere else. But then this is what travelling is about. This is what provides the edge; being in a situation where almost anything can happen, expecting the unexpected and accepting ones fate with wonder, as it is rolled out like a red carpet.

Three nights is also longer than Liz and I stayed in any one place on our way to China. When we left Hoi An a bus ride north to Datong got us to the railway and an overnight train to Hanoi. The line was spectacular at first as it hugged the coast and I was glued to the window. We had a compartment to ourselves, or so I thought but my eye kept being caught by something on the floor. Eventually I saw it; a little grey mouse. This train lacked the clinical cleanliness of the last one we had caught in Thailand and Liz was even less impressed when our compartment filled up in the middle of the night with a group of very noisy passengers who had no consideration at all for those already in bed and trying to rest.

We found a small hotel in old Hanoi and Liz declared her intention to catch up on lost sleep. I had been puzzling over the next part of the journey. The obvious route was to catch the bi-weekly train into China's Yunnan province, but I had read of a boat going up the coast to the border crossing at Mong Cai, and a chance of boat travel trumped the train. Information was very sketchy but one website I found claimed that there was a daily hydrofoil operating between Bai Chay in Halong City and Dan Tien, just 15 km from China.

The old town of Hanoi is ruled by the two-stroke. The roads are dominated by buzzing little motorbikes, their engines revving ecstatically, and the pavements are chocker with the same at rest so that pedestrians have to take their chances walking in the road with the stampede of two-wheeled machines. While Liz rested I explored and was encouraged to find a number of travel agents advertising tours to the local attractions. I visited all of them that I came across but not one had heard of a boat to Mong Cai. They wanted to sell me a trip on a boat around Halong Bay and in the end I capitulated. Staying overnight on the water is always a treat, (except perhaps when sharing a small cabin in Thailand with 40 others) and these trips which include all meals are good value. I said that we did not need the return bus to Hanoi and hoped to find the elusive ferry in Halong.

I think at times I may be guilty of a kind of snobbishness in avoiding tourist attractions, liking to think perhaps that real travellers find their own places of interest rather than following the herd. Sometimes an area becomes a tourist attraction because it has so much to offer the visitor and Halong Bay is one of these. It has a huge industry in ferrying sightseers on fake traditional craft, but the landscape is stunningly beautiful and deserves its World Heritage Site designation. Everywhere on our boat was polished wood and we had our own cabin with fresh linen, the food was good and the karst scenery of about 3,000 islands spectacular. I was less impressed with the cave we were taken to which was garishly illuminated with multi coloured lights and in which the tour guides had further cheapened the experience by trying to match the natural rock, stalagmite and stalactite formations with animals they thought they resembled. When we anchored for the night Liz and I took canoes around the little bay in which we were sheltered and even managed to buy a couple of beers from a floating shop. These we drank as we drifted lazily back to the boat feeling pleasantly naughty, as we were expected to pay the inflated prices at the bar on board.

But in Halong as in Hanoi nobody would admit to knowledge of a ferry going up the coast. I decided that even if it still existed I certainly wasn't going to find it and, having got this far, reluctantly found the bus station for Mong Cai. Really I would have preferred the train from Hanoi but it was too late to go back there.

Mong Cai was a hole; a seedy neglected frontier town which probably lived off some kind of dodgy cross-border dealing. We booked into a drab hotel and I went for a wander around noting a very large dead rat near the market, and checking where we would need to walk to get to the border in the morning. Mong Cai in Vietnam and Dongxing in China are really two parts of the same town. No-man's land is a bridge over the river going directly into the Chinese immigration area, so that curiously we arrived in China on the upper floor of a building looking down into the street. I don't know what I expected but it seemed a bit of an anti-climax.

But it had been a great trip. South East Asia is a delightful part of the world to travel in and for Liz and me it marked a change in the stage we were at in our lives; from being parents with dependent children to having the freedom to go and do whatever we wanted. And what I wanted was to travel more. With a move to Nanjing and Liz's job taking her all over the country the opportunities were mouth-watering. Not only could I chase my wife all around China as she went about her business, but in the spring break we would go back to New Zealand and I would stop over in Fiji, Sydney, Kuala Lumpur and Singapore. In the summer we would head to Europe and, travelling overland I would find myself, quite improbably, at a wedding in North Ossetia.

In fact the wedding in Beslan, near Vladikavkaz is not for another two months but today the proposal is to be put to the families. We set off but don't get very far before we need to stop for lunch. Before we get to Regina's parents I am taken to see Beslan Number One School. It was the first day of the academic year in 2004 when Chechen terrorists occupied the school and held hostages in the gymnasium. The siege lasted for three days before security forces brought it to a bloody end. Today it is kept as a monument to the 331 victims, most of whom were children, and whose photographs line the charred remains of the building. How anyone can believe that their 'cause' is worth so much suffering is inconceivable. We then take flowers to the cemetery with its 331 near identical graves. Each bears a picture of its occupant whose life was taken so meaninglessly. It is quiet and peaceful, but then from the far end comes the sound of wailing; a grief stricken woman for whom the wounds won't heal.

Regina's parents live in a large stone house which overflows into an outside covered living area, in a manner which is also popular in New Zealand. My explanation that I'm not hungry as we've already had lunch is waved aside, although it is now mid-afternoon as we tuck into Ossetian pie and home-made wine. I am told that we are going to the house of the groom's parents, but I am accompanied only by Leonid and his granddaughter who is my interpreter. A table is set outside where we drink arak and eat yet more Ossetian pie. But we are on the move again and squeeze into a four wheel drive to go to the house of the groom's parents. Hang on; I thought that that was where we were. Oh well. When we arrive, there is a gathering of men outside and much shaking of hands before we go into a cramped apartment. There is a table which is groaning with the amount of food on it and I take my place beside a plate piled with Ossetian pie! I really don't think I can eat another thing. By no means is everyone at the table and it appears that I am honoured to be with the elders. My interpreter is banished to the kitchen with the other women.

The proceedings are very formal and start with a toast to St. George. He seems to be very important here, although the Catholic Church demoted him on the grounds that many of the tales about St. George were 'beyond belief'; a dangerous precedent I would have thought for any faith, as there would be little left to believe in if all the fairy tales were removed. Then someone takes a bite of Ossetian pie and passes round a bowl of liquid which I manage to avoid. Two large slices of pie are put on my plate, but I'm more worried about the sheep's head, which is lacking wool but otherwise complete and which I really don't want to taste.

Toasts are made and I copy Leonid, but I'm getting caught out; he and the two men next to him drain their glasses first and then those next to me clink glasses, but as I've copied him, mine is now empty and has to be refilled, so I'm getting through twice as much as everyone else. Opposite me is a bald headed man the top of whose head is beaded with sweat and getting redder and redder. I hope he lasts the evening. *"Don't stop"* he tells me, indicating the vodka bottle. I think it is the only English he knows. There is more food than we can possibly eat but it keeps arriving. Consequently, instead of eating the food, it is being constantly moved around to make room for the latest offerings from the kitchen. I am informed that the marriage proposals have been accepted. To celebrate, more plates of Ossetian pie are squeezed onto the table.

What a memorable evening- except that I can't actually remember the end of it. I recall that we left the apartment but that some returned to the kitchen. Correctly guessing what was happening, I followed and copied Leonid in draining another drink and returning the glass with a bank note in it, as a wedding present. Staying with this family I have managed to spend so little money that I have roubles to spare. I think that it is a shame that we have discarded so many customs and formalities, but perhaps they're more important for the North Ossetians to hang onto; the unique culture of their little republic in a quiet corner of the Caucasus could easily become lost in the vastness of Russia.

I have done well with wedding celebrations this year as we were invited to that of a Swedish colleague of Liz's who married a girl from Inner Mongolia, and we travelled there for the reception. The bride had instructed the groom to have me fitted for a suit and Liz told the tailor to make me a shirt as well. I bought a tie in the Beijing silk market and I think that (for once) I looked very smart, as did Liz who also had an outfit made for the occasion.

The wedding day starts with the groom and the groomsmen being collected from his home. In our case 'home' was the hotel we were all staying in and the groomsmen were his parents and us. At the last minute we were told that we were not to go down to the lobby because the video group wanted to start filming in the hotel room. It seems that obtaining a film is the main reason for having a ceremony and that holding the camera bestows the right to dictate the proceedings. I believe that this is a dangerous attitude and that in its most extreme form it can lead to a complete neglect of living in the present, other than to provide a film track of the past to look at in the future.

What is recorded may have some interest tomorrow, but nobody is ever likely to want to see it after that. I remember that when both my parents had died and we had to sort through their personal possessions there were several hundred photographic slides taken on holidays which hadn't been looked at for years. Taking pictures of what you are doing can easily become more important than actually doing it, and I am wary of travelling with a camera, although I do occasionally point my phone at something and click the button. As I am rarely able to see properly on the screen what I am snapping, the image usually gets deleted anyway.

This is the brilliance of digital cameras, but I do feel that my children have missed out on the excitement of going to the chemists to collect their prints from the film taken there the previous week. To be honest a couple of mine were always close-ups of my finger and I did have a tendency to behead subjects, particularly with my first camera which was operated at waist level. But I was as pleased with the ones that came out as anybody now is with so many megapixels of realism. We continue to make things better and better but our emotional capacity for appreciation stays the same. Watching some of the poorer children in China playing in the street; they are totally engrossed with their bits of sticks and leaves and, using their imaginations they get as much pleasure as any child with any high-tech toy. Similarly, I know that wine buffs will disagree, but I am sure that I used to get as much pleasure from drinking the cheapest plonk from a day trip to Calais, which I now find unpalatable, as today I get from a half-decent bottle of Aussie Shiraz. We constantly up the ante to fulfil the same need. This ramble does have some relevance because the urge to travel is also meeting some basic desire. It is the fulfilment of a need to explore, which for a young child may only extend to seeing what is in the next room, but becomes more challenging to satisfy as the bar for finding new things to see is constantly raised.

In China people take pictures of anything and everything, but I recently read of a company which has been set up to take wedding photography, which is already big business, one step further. They don't just film the wedding but help the happy couple to write a drama, which may or may not be based on the history of their own romance, and then dress them up to play the lead roles. They end up with their own extreme low budget, badly acted and poorly scripted movie with which they bore the pants off any friends they still have left. No doubt they think that their grandchildren will treasure such a piece of family history, but the reality is that they will be more concerned about getting their own present lives recorded for posterity and will consider themselves too sophisticated to look at blurry out-of-date technology anyway.

But back to the wedding- when we did leave there were three Rolls Royce Phantoms lined up in front of two Bentleys waiting outside the plate glass doors of the lobby. I looked at Stefan who shrugged; he had already told me that I knew as much as he did about what was going to happen. In fact I knew a little bit more about the next part than he did, but not about the cars and of course this was a convoy for someone else's wedding. It was also another example of the amount of money available in modern China, even in the back of beyond of Inner Mongolia. Lynne (as she has chosen to call herself for the benefit of English speakers) and Stefan were transported in a Mercedes, ahead of his parents in a BMW and Liz and I joined two cousins in a Chevrolet. Communication in English, Swedish and Chinese had become quite complicated and didn't seem to get any easier:

Liz *"I expect that you've been busy"*

Brides cousin *"Yes I am going to have a baby"*

The fourth car contained the film crew and was a four-wheel drive, which reflected the adventurous go-getting nature of the role of its occupants. The front seat passenger leaned out of the window like a trapezing yachtsman with his camera to capture for posterity the manner in which our driver negotiated a roundabout.

We arrived at the Brides home and then the fun started. This is the opportunity that the bride's family have to check the suitability of the groom, and traditionally they have used it to try to humiliate him. In the past this may have been by demanding that he prove that he is strong enough to care for the bride by breaking a sheep's neck into which, unbeknown to the groom, has been inserted an iron bar. Lynne had told us what was in store for Stefan but he was blissfully ignorant of his fate. Wedding parties are invariably announced, as ours was, with as much noise as possible and the smoke and sparks of exploding firecrackers. There are so many of these events happening all over the country, particularly at week-ends, that little notice is generally taken, which probably just encourages each party to try to be even noisier. A bit like the DJ who, because nobody is taking any notice of his music, probably because they would actually like to be able to speak to the person next to them, keeps cranking up the volume to make his unwanted presence felt.

This wedding however was not a commonplace event; we had a foreigner in a leading part and the neighbourhood had turned out to gape. As well as a crowd in the street every window in the surrounding tower blocks featured a face, as a cousin used a red sash to tie a broom around Stefan's waist and he was given his instructions. He took it all in good part and I think that his Chinese was just about comprehensible to the assembled crowd as he shouted out to his mother-in-law, several floors up, the words he had been given, which translated that he had come to sweep her steps. I have no doubt that the dumbfounded neighbours are going to be talking about this for many years to come.

We were in an area of new apartment buildings and were given refreshments in Lynne's parents bright modern flat. From the window I could see a small squat brick building with a crooked chimney which was clearly much older than the surrounding buildings and I was told that the resident refused to move when they were developing the area, and so they built around him. I recall a similar incident that reached world news when an old house that the occupant refused to vacate ended up in the middle of a traffic island.

I think that this story is interesting for several reasons; the Chinese do as they are told and they all do the same thing. A sweeping generalisation, but it is the legacy of Confucianism that authority and power structures are respected and obeyed. So it is notable that one person displayed some individualism of character and took a stand. It is also noteworthy that he wasn't carted off, as I am sure that an authoritarian state could easily make a case that someone acting so much outside behavioural norms must clearly be of unsound mind. It could be argued that the developers rode roughshod over him, and it must have been a nightmare to have lived in that little cottage while skyscrapers were going up all around, but really it seems to me that both sides displayed passive resistance; he refused to move and the developers refused to stop building. If they both now believe that they have won then it must be a good outcome and they have all avoided the taboo of confrontation.

Back in the cars we left a trail of firecrackers and headed for the reception. Marriage in China is a three part affair and the official ceremony was performed in the equivalent of a registry office some months before. The second, and most important part, is the photo-shoot. This involves the hiring of several sets of costume and employing professional photographers to create artistic images of the happy couple in various romantic scenic spots. The result is a collection of film star type poses with, after severe air-brushing, the subjects still just about recognisable as the couple known and loved. The pictures must precede the reception, as the enhanced images have to be displayed on posters and giant screens all around the room.

In our case the room was a Mongolian yurt, the round tents used by both shepherds in the grasslands and the armies of Genghis Khan. It wasn't of course. It was a part of a huge solid brick and concrete complex built in those traditional shapes and ruled over by richly coloured silk-clad staff. Inside, a floral archway led to a runway festooned with silver and guarded by theatre lights, with large round tables for guests in a horseshoe around it. The start of proceedings was signalled by the deafening detonation of a line of cannons just outside the door, and the noise level was maintained by a professional Mistress of Ceremonies who shouted at full volume down a microphone as the video crew continued to ensure that nothing would go unrecorded. The lighting men wouldn't be left out and each time, which was very often, that the girls voice reached a momentous climax the lights fluttered in epileptic inducing ecstasy. It was all quite splendid.

The groom's side consisted just of his parents and us, but there was a proper divide between the families of the bride's mother and the relatives of her father. Invitation I was told is dependant, at least in part, on past performance. There are no wedding presents other than gifts of money. These are traditionally presented in red envelopes but there is no confidentiality about the amount donated and I can't really think of anything in Chinese culture which is regarded as private to the individual, even personal space is an alien concept. What each person or family gives is carefully logged and previous family records are referred to when a wedding invitation list is being drawn up. This can influence who to invite and also how much to give when that family are on the receiving end, so presumably the most generous people are those who love weddings and families who have lots of daughters.

A large brass bowl with flames licking at the base to keep the liquid inside bubbling was placed on each table and I told Stefan's mother that it was a Mongolian fire pot and that we would get raw meat and vegetables to cook in it. It turned out that I was wrong and a small bowl of green tea that I had been drinking was removed and replaced with a ladleful of the broth, which actually turned out to be Mongolian milk tea. It was very rich and quite sickly, and there were solid squares of extra milk on the table to make it more so, although it already contained strips of skin from the scalded milk and little beads of some sort of reconstituted nut.

I tried to ignore my bowl of milk tea as plates and plates of food started to come out at seemingly ever increasing speed and variety and placed on the revolving glass table top. I just helped myself to whatever I liked the look of when it came round and particularly enjoyed the lamb dishes, which are a rarity in Eastern China. More and more toasts were made with the fearsome distilled rice alcohol that flowed freely and, being of better quality than most, was beginning to taste almost drinkable by the end. The most basic stuff is cheaper by volume than beer and can be accurately described as white spirit. Various pseudo Mongolian entertainments took to the stage and then a decorated bier borne by pall bearers and displaying the golden brown roasted body of a whole sheep, horns and all, was ceremoniously paraded.

I am often intrigued by the interface of reality and fantasy, and I suppose that this could be described as a theme restaurant, taking some fundamentals of historical Mongolia and then letting the imagination of the designers run riot. But it occurs to me that there is a curious irony here; from the perspective of the Chinese family and guests the whole thing was a romantic escape into grossly inaccurate images of the past muddled together with other bits of tradition and the latest technology. Our reality was totally different, as from a foreigner's point of view there was nothing false or contrived because, as outsiders looking in, we were getting a completely authentic experience of a modern wedding in China.

Stefan and Lynne, who had now changed from a gorgeous red silk Chinese costume into what I would recognise as a traditional wedding dress, came through the floral arch as Mendelsohn's Wedding March was belted out. The proceedings were nothing if not eclectic. Liz and I had walk-on parts (probably why I needed a suit) to hand them rings which they then exchanged.

Next we had to follow them going round all the tables and drinking toasts by downing a small glass of rice spirit with each group of guests. Liz carrying the bottle to refill the glasses reminded me of an altar-boy waiting to serve the priest with wine and water. I noticed one of Stefan's new in-laws, who had plied him with drink the night before in the vain hope of getting him drunk, watching in awe as he continued to knock the stuff back with ease. Despite the availability of cheap booze the Chinese aren't great drinkers, and they could never be a match for a Swede!

Part 4: Georgia

Chapter Thirteen: Expecting the Unexpected

To my surprise people in Vladikavkaz have little knowledge of the border with Georgia, which was closed for many years due to hostilities between the two countries, but I would have thought should now have transformed the city from occupying a remote corner leading nowhere to being on an important international trade route. Nobody even has any idea where to catch a bus from, and Regina has made several enquiries. Eventually, with the aid of the internet we track down the appropriate bus stop and I am heading for another country. I am the only passenger left on board when we cruise past the line of heavy goods vehicles and come to the last stop at a barrier, through which nothing appears to be allowed to move.

A uniformed official eyes me suspiciously but doesn't ask to see my passport so I start to walk. He calls me back and says that I must have a car. Not this again. Why is it that only motorists can be allowed to travel from one country to another without boarding an aeroplane? And why does the bus drive right up to the border if its passengers aren't allowed through it? I point out, what I had thought to be fairly obvious, that I don't have a car with me. I turn out my pockets to demonstrate that I am not concealing a car about my person. He is not amused and seems to think that I should walk the 30 km back to Vladikavkaz to buy a car so that I can cross his barrier in the correct fashion. I set off again towards Georgia, ignore his first call and only slowly return when he is getting frantic. Finally he asks for my passport.

Having eventually realised that he is not going to get rid of me, the guard tells me to get in an old Volga driven by a Chechen, with his aged mother in the back. There are times when you just need to be a little bit obstinate. I suspect that the car has a colourful history; the lock in the driver's door has been removed and there is an arrangement of loose wires under the steering wheel used to start the engine- but I would not be surprised if this is usual in Chechnya. As I sit to his right he constantly knocks my left arm to ask me all sorts of questions which I don't understand, but I don't complain as he agrees to give me a lift through to the first settlement in Georgia, Kazbegi, which is where I want to stop.

The border is set in a beautiful narrow gorge which, in some parts is not even wide enough for a road and has to resort to tunnelling through sections of the mountain. This is the Georgian Military Highway, built by the Russians in the 19th century. Although this path through the Caucasus has been used since ancient times, I am now definitely off the main Asia to Europe trading routes referred to as the Silk Road, which would either of sailed across the Caspian (as I originally planned to do) or kept to the south of it, through present day Iran. Once we have finished the formalities it is a short drive to Kazbegi (now officially known as Stepsantsminda) and I thank the cheery Chechen and his mother, who have actually saved me a lot of bother as no public transport appears to exist on this side of the frontier. I find a simple guesthouse to stay at and go for a wander. Mount Kazbegi, which gives its name to the area, is on the other side of the valley but walking uphill on this side I am towered over by a curtain of craggy snow covered peaks.

The dusty pot-holed roads are home to a variety of domestic animals. Packs of brown dogs of various sizes police the streets while dairy cows seem to be searching for something as, in twos and threes, they slowly take a few steps, stop and look around before deliberately moving off again. There are also black and white pigs who, unlike the others, give the appearance of having a destination in mind, and chickens that mainly go round in circles. As I climb I enter a bright green meadow full of buttercups and find a sunny spot to sit and read a book, looking up between pages to drink in the picture postcard scenery. Why the animals don't come up here is a mystery to me.

For the first time since visiting the terracotta army at Xian, which was the first day of my journey, I am with other foreigners. I share the guesthouse with a young mountain climber from Poland and a pair of adventurers from Croatia. They have come through the country from the south and express surprise that I was able to cross the border from Russia as they thought that they were at a dead end. The draw is the mighty mountain, which is higher than anything that the Alps can offer, and looms menacingly from across the narrow valley. This is where poor old Prometheus was chained and had his liver daily pecked by birds, as punishment for giving fire to humans. The Croats and the Pole are planning an assault and have rented equipment from the village, including crampons and ice axes. I wonder if they will continue to chain smoke all the way up. There is also a young Filipino couple who, like me, don't plan to do anything nearly as strenuous. Perched on a grassy hilltop 500 metres up is the attraction for the less adventurous, the pretty little church of Tsminda Sameba, and that looks much better suited to my needs than serious mountaineering.

On the way up I meet a straggle of people from England who are on an organised walking holiday. They are a pleasant group of individuals of assorted ages, some of whom are very well travelled, and I tag along with them for a while, but they have instructions to meet at a certain point and I carry on to the church alone. The first thing that strikes me is the crudity of its construction, the blocks of stone are of a variety of colours and just sit on top of each other in an almost haphazard fashion. It was built in the 14th century but the design seems older. Someone in the walking group told me that hilltop churches in Georgia are usually built on the site of older pagan places of worship and I wonder if some of the building material was recycled. The main west doorway is square with an ill-fitting lintel and the windows are simple rounded arches. There are many designs and patterns on the outside of the building, but they are not all complete or properly match up. It actually looks as if someone has taken the whole church apart and tried to put it back together as a jigsaw puzzle, but has got fed up with it and forced the last few pieces in where they don't belong. None of this really matters as it does nothing to detract from the centuries of religious worship that seems to be steeped into the very walls, creating an atmosphere which is enhanced by some singing practice going on in a corner as I enter the tiny building. In times of trouble this little church was used to store precious and sacred items, presumably with the idea that any prospective looters would be put off by the climb up here.

Back in the valley, I need some money but I can't find a machine to dispense it. Again I am surprised that not more notice is taken of the international border just down the road, I would have thought that a means to get currency would be one of the first things to be put in place. I was told that there is an ATM at a hotel and I have been sent to an area where the main road widens into a car and bus park and which I think of as being the centre of town, but no money is available here. I ask and am waved down the road, but this is clearly getting nowhere, and the next person I ask points me back in the direction I have come. Finally it is explained to me that I need to take the little roads up the side of the valley to a big new hotel. I think that I saw it in the distance, a massive brown building, while I was coming down from the church.

It is a good climb before I come to a long solid wooden fence and try to find a way in. There is no sweeping driveway here, just a pair of metal gates at the end of a dusty road. The building is totally clad in wood and with no signs or colour of any kind it gives more the appearance of an institution than a hotel. Inside the bare wooden floors look newly laid but are distressed and even have great gouges taken out of them in places. In contrast, a very smart uniformed young woman sits behind a reception desk and points me in the direction of the money machine. Running across the width of what could be thought of as the lobby, are rows of utility metal shelving holding a variety of books and giving the appearance of a half stocked public library. Outside and for the entire long length of the building is a veranda full of cane furniture and two people who I assume are guests. The seats are uncomfortable because the cushions for them are still piled up inside, but the views across to Mount Kazbegi and both up and down the valley are quite stunning. Before I leave I have a look through another door and find myself in a casino with an attractive young woman inviting me to play cards. The offer is tempting but I am addicted to travelling not gambling and I need to hang on to my money. What a very peculiar hotel.

Since arriving in China I have got used to staying in more up-market hotels as I trail behind Liz. Typically she will catch a plane or bullet train to another city and I will get a ticket for the ordinary train. Sometimes I will leave the day before and travel overnight, or maybe stop somewhere en-route and book into a cheap hotel before catching up with her in some fancy place that her company has booked her into. The first of these forays was way out west to Chengdu in Sichuan Province.

At Nanjing station I joined a queue to find my way to the appropriate waiting room for train K722 to Chengdu. As at an airport all bags have to be put through an x-ray machine and passengers checked with an electronic baton. The difference is that while the devices constantly bleep in alarm nobody is ever asked to open their bags or remove keys from their pockets. The system seems to serve the purposes of restricting the flow of passengers into the building by keeping the bottleneck outside in the fresh air, and of providing a role for a few more people in China's apparently limitless supply of labour. This is evident everywhere as whole armies of personnel maintain the grounds around each apartment block and uniformed security guards stand outside any significant building or entranceway. All in a country where people won't even raise their voices, let alone break into someone else's home. Clearly while labour is used so freely a realistic minimum wage could never be achieved and the divide between the 'haves' and the 'have not's' will only continue to deepen.

Crowds are a permanent and inescapable reality in Eastern China; I find that I am constantly bumping into people and I get fed up with always having to be the one who gives way. But the Chinese manage to avoid each other as they navigate the streets so I must be doing something wrong. It doesn't help that I am invariably moving at a different pace. Even in the bustling cities I am constantly trying to get past pedestrians who move so painfully slowly that I could never adjust to that tempo. I do believe that this is linked to the mindset of there being such an abundance of labour that time, rather than being a valuable commodity, is actually something that needs to be used up and wasted in whatever way it can be. If I'm correct this is really very sad and degrades the value of life itself.

A nice example that I saw involved a person who was employed to put flyers for a new apartment block under the windscreen wipers of parked cars. This was probably a good piece of marketing as car owners would likely be able to afford their own home. The cleaner for that street realised that most of the leaflets would be tossed on the ground for her to pick up and, as it was much easier for her to collect them at car bonnet level, she was following a few cars behind and undoing all the other persons work. What struck me as odd was that they were clearly both happy with the situation; they both had jobs to do and they were doing them. That the whole exercise was a complete waste of their labour was of no concern to them, on the contrary it created work which mopped up a certain amount of time.

But that doesn't explain why it is always me who has to dodge around everyone else on crowded streets. I developed a theory about this and found a bench to sit on in a busy Shanghai park one day to observe and test out my suspicions. Next to me two lines of middle aged women synchronised their exercise to the orders of a little radio placed in front of them, but I was watching the busy path behind them. People went in both directions without colliding so who was giving way to whom? My results are far from being scientific, but it seemed to me that individuals gave way to couples, who in turn took responsibility for avoiding larger groups. A coachload with a leader holding a flag at its head just steamrollered through. The basic rule is that might is right. There is nothing threatening or aggressive about the behaviour, and having a child or a frail elderly person is a bonus rather than a handicap to ease of progression through the crowd, but where in my culture a group would single out to enable everyone to continue unhindered, in China it seems that the weaker in number have to bow to the strength of any larger group, and as I am usually alone, I am bottom of the street pecking order.

Does any of this matter? I actually think that it does. It is a manifestation of what I view as being a basic flaw in the way that Chinese society is organised. There is a lot that is praiseworthy in the way in which people manage themselves. Despite considerable poverty there is little crime, not because of fear of punishment, but because nearly everyone supports an orderly and well structured society. Similarly there is no graffiti on the walls and life is lived generally in an atmosphere of peace and harmony, observing the rules as laid down by Confucius. But within that structure there is no sense of there being a wider society. The individual, the family unit or whatever larger group is formed cares not a jot for everything and everyone outside that sense of identity.

I had thought that the unsettling impersonal character of the country was just due to everything in China being on such a large inhuman scale. Interactions are very businesslike. Nobody bothers to smile or say thank you in everyday transactions, it just doesn't occur to people to take any notice of those who are strangers to them. But maybe it's more deep rooted than that; there is a fundamental lack of empathy or consideration for fellow beings who are 'them' rather than 'us'. This is not to say that individuals are unfeeling; if I am stuck there is always a Chinese person who will come to my rescue. But the society as a whole is ruled by a kind of passive aggression which is constantly trying to promote the needs of its own against the rest. This is the explanation for why people try to get in the lift before you have a chance to get out, why a group of friends stop for a conversation in the middle of a busy street rather than moving to the side and why nobody will get out of my way.

This attitude has more serious consequences than me bumping into people. I read in the China Daily (the English language Chinese newspaper) a letter written by a doctor complaining that his prospective patients were turning up dead. The reason he cited was that it was taking too long to get them to hospital, as the other traffic would not get out of the way of the ambulances. My initial reaction was to be appalled that people could act so selfishly, but the truth is that we hear every day on the news of people dying from all kinds of accidents, natural disasters or deliberate acts of evil, and we don't really care. We may think it sad or wrong or that someone should do something about it, but we don't have any real empathy for people who we don't know and are just numbers to us. If it is close to our own lives we may have a stronger reaction as we feel threatened, or concerned that it could happen to our loved ones, but it is not possible to feel real emotions for humanity as a whole.

But I still find that level of callousness appalling. In China an average of 200 people die in road accidents every day. If you don't know who any of them are, how can you possible care about them? Of course one day it could be you or someone that you do care about in the ambulance and this is why, for the common good, in our culture we all give precedence to emergency vehicles. The passive/aggressive nature of Chinese society makes this a less natural thing to do although it does rub against the equally ingrained desire to follow the rules. I am yet to understand why some aspects of authority are obeyed religiously while others, such as all traffic regulations, are blatantly disregarded. But this is why sharing in the lives of other cultures is so fascinating. It is the paradoxes and apparent contradictions that are the attraction. If it was too easy to understand then there would be little to learn from it.

Many foreigners in China complain about the rudeness and thoughtlessness of the local people but I think that most Chinese would be quite shocked if they were told this. It is just a different cultural attitude which in no way implies that individuals are any less caring or lacking in human compassion than people from anywhere else. The size and scale of the country also makes a difference, and while it is easy for New Zealanders to act as if we are one big happy family, the reality in urban China is one of relentless competition- and that is just to get on a bus. When she was British Prime Minister Mrs Thatcher once infamously stated that there is no such thing as society. In China she may well have been right.

What this of course means is that China is the last country in the world that should try to practice communism! It is the 'tragedy of the commons'; everyone would be better off if they all worked together, but imposing a system of working together and sharing, when the underlying text is each for himself, results in the worst possible outcome. China is no longer a communist country in anything other than name and it is Confucius, not Marx or Mao, who has withstood the test of time.

This sense of competition is so ingrained that people respond to it automatically. Without warning the waiting room at Nanjing railway station rearranged itself into a throng of several hundred people pressing toward the gate. All tickets have seat numbers, or if they don't all the seats are accounted for, so I fail to understand the crush to get to the train first. I studied my ticket but was not sure if I was in berth 17 in carriage 2 or vice versa. The attendant in carriage 2 waved me away so I headed for the other end of the train where I was pleased that, as I thought, I had a 'Zhongpu', the middle of the three-tier hard sleeper bunks, which are arranged transversely with an open corridor giving access to a toilet, sink, and hot water tap for tea and instant noodles at the end of the carriage.

Headroom is very limited but the middle berth, unlike the top one, allows a good view out of the window, while the lower bunk is awkward as it can also be used for seating during the day. I am not too clear on the protocol for this as the Chinese seem happy to go to bed at any time of day, but as protecting personal space never seems to be an issue there are probably no fixed rules. The berth under my one was occupied by a woman and child who were both quite short and I perched at the end of their bunk. They seemed intent on sleeping until I produced a laptop which aroused the girl's curiosity, but not for long as it showed her only foreign writing instead of the electronic games I suspect she was hoping for. There was a stiff formality to the start of the journey reflected in the uniformed carriage attendants and freshly laundered linen on the beds.

A bit later in the morning the following day the atmosphere was very different as we pulled into Chengdu station. Our carriage brought to mind a refugee camp with individual dens built in dark corners and luggage and sheets and pillows strewn everywhere. Various pungent cooking smells vied for dominance of the airways. A young law student was still trying to practice his English with me as we disembarked and followed the crowd to the huge modern concourse of Chengdu Dong (East) Station. Where to go now? I knew that the hotel we were booked into was not too far from Chengdu's famous giant panda base which is marked to the north of the city but the only option available was east or west bus station; I chose east and took an escalator to platform 1. There was nothing here in English but there were little maps for each bus number showing its route, none of them appeared to go north and I retraced my steps to try the west station. Eventually I decided on bus 906 from platform 2 which I thought might go in the right general direction. I know that Liz would have told me to take a taxi but, apart from the cost, there is a satisfaction in finding one's own way around and completing the journey unaided.

I was beginning to wonder if bus 906 existed when one finally arrived and with a grinding of gears (it amazes me that in packed cities containing several millions of people they still build buses with manual gearboxes), headed south, the opposite to the way I wanted to go. Not having a very good sense of direction, particularly in China where the sky is uniformly grey most of the time, I find it useful to carry a small compass. But the night before I caught the train I did get hopelessly lost in Nanjing. I tried asking passers-by to show me our position on my street map, but the Chinese seem unaccustomed to maps and wave them away in the same fashion as I do Chinese characters shown me when I don't understand what is being spoken. When I tried asking for where I wanted to go I didn't believe the reply I got, and trudged on in the opposite direction getting more and more tired and frustrated. Eventually I gave in and flagged down a taxi. The next morning, trying to work out where on earth I had got to, I realised that my compass had changed polarity; it must have been affected by a flight I took to Shanghai, and the pointer marked N, I now tell myself stands for 'Nan' as in Nanjing the southern capital (as opposed to Beijing the northern capital).

The compass doggedly insisted that 'N' was the direction the bus was heading and I was considering getting off when it made a U-turn and happily laboured north. I hopped off when I saw a sign 'Panda Base 4 km' and decided that I could do with a walk. I could also have done with something to eat. The staple on Chinese trains is pot noodle sold from trolleys wheeled up and down the carriages and reconstituted from the hot water tap provided at the end of each corridor. I had had that for dinner the previous night but really couldn't face it again for breakfast.

The road I was walking along appeared to be designed as a relief road for heavy traffic but you are never far from food in China. After maybe 3 km I came across a handful of low buildings included a set of rickety wooden tables and chairs outside a doorway emitting smoke and steam. A large bowl of proper noodles in a rich stock with slices of meat and greens and plenty of chilli was the same price as a pot noodle on the train. I continued my journey revitalised but then reached a major crossroads with no indication which way to go. I had come more than 4 km without seeing a single giant panda and I was beginning to regret my decision to walk. All the roads were new six lane highways and boringly straight. When my phone rang and Liz told me that they were arriving at the hotel and that I should take a taxi I was sorely tempted but felt that I had to be close. Half an hour later she rang again to say that they were about to sit down to lunch but it really had to be nearby.

When I finally arrived I realised with a shock of air-conditioned refinement the schizophrenic nature of the lifestyle I am able to lead. I was aware that I looked out of place, hot and dusty in shorts and sandals and with a rucksack on my back, instead of appearing urbane with one of those suitcases with wheels that are now de rigueur but which most owners seem unable to properly control. I had stepped out of the real world into a make believe of glistening polished wood, imitation marble, fantastic fountains and carpets that are actually softer and more springy than the average Chinese bed. While I found the opulence of the hotel other worldly, Liz's colleagues were amused by the whole idea of someone arriving on the ordinary K train. I just enjoyed the contrast of moving from one world to another and happily took my pack off and joined them for lunch in the cavernous dining area. I suppose that both realities are equally valid, but mine is rooted in the lives of ordinary people and gives an experience of something a lot closer to what it is like to be Chinese. My way of travelling may seem somewhat hair-shirted at times, but it isn't just about doing things on the cheap, it is also a genuine attempt to, not just view a foreign country as an outsider, but to be a part of it and share in the lives of people from a different culture.

Sharing in others' cultures is not always a comfortable experience. The road from Kazbegi to Tbilisi is supposed to be spectacular, but I can barely see any of it. I am crammed into the back of a marshrutka where fold down seats enable the little van to seat four abreast in four rows behind the driver and front seat passengers. I realise that they also raise the seats in these vans higher than they should be so that less legroom is required and more passengers can be squeezed in. Consequently it is difficult for anyone of reasonable height to see much out of the windows at the best of times without having to crouch down. I am pleased to get off and consider how to find the city centre. This can often be a problem arriving somewhere new with no idea how far or in what direction you need to go.

I am in no great hurry and enter one of several bakery shop cafes for coffee and Georgian pie, which is pretty much identical to Ossetian pie. I show the waitress a map of Tbilisi centre which is amongst some sheets I printed off before I left home, but she doesn't seem to recognise it. I point out the cathedral and she agrees that it is Sioni, but has no idea how to get there. Two men sit at my table and I show them my map. They ponder it for a long time, try it all ways up, there's a river running through the middle of it for heaven's sake; surely they must recognise their own city, but no. Is it to the north, the south or east or west? They're not trying to be difficult or unhelpful, they really don't know.

I hop onto a marshrutka and show the driver my map. He suggests I get a number 6. I look around but can't see one and get a second opinion from a 169 driver. He says I should catch a 150, which I do, but make the mistake of showing the driver my map. He hangs on to it for a long time before declaring that I must get off and take one of the marshrutkas he points to parked in a yard. But the driver I ask there takes me to an office where there is someone who knows a few words of English. He says I need to go back to the bus station I have just come from. He seems uncertain about the direction but waves at an area to the north of the centre as being where we are. Just then a number 6 comes along and I flag it down and keep my map well hidden from the driver. We seem to be heading north, and as the passenger numbers thin I guess that we are going the wrong way for town. I stay on until the terminus, which is not far, and wonder if I can just remain where I am for the return trip. But the driver wants to know where I am going and out comes the map again. He shouts at the driver of a van just pulling out and I hurriedly pile onto it. It is a few miles to the centre and I get off when I can see the river, from which I can get my bearings. As I wander the streets I see a number 6 and a 150 and even a 7, which was the first one I tried to board. After a lot of walking around I find a friendly cheap hostel run by Indians and Nepalese, and work out exactly where I am on the map.

Chapter Fourteen: The Thrill of the Chase

Georgia claims to be the home of wine, the place where grapes were first grown to be fermented, and I want to go to the Kakheti region which is where this happened and where the wine industry still flourishes. I have decided to visit Sighnaghi in the wine district as it is said to be a very pretty small hilltop town, but I am not entirely happy with my decision to visit Kakheti at all. It means travelling east, not any great distance only about 100 km, but I will have to return through Tbilisi. Taking a long way round I can cope with but actually doing a return trip seems somehow against the spirit of my constant journeying to the west. The problem is that I like Georgia and want to see more of it, but it is a very small country and if I just head straight to Turkey I could easily be there tomorrow. The big distances I did in China and Kazakhstan are well behind me, and now the travelling and the demographics are more intense. It also means that I don't have to see everything that I want to in Tbilisi straight away as I will be back in a day or two.

Needless to say getting to Kakheti will involve taking a marshrutka, and I decide to have a ride on the underground to get to the appropriate bus stop. But it seems that Tbilisi's metro isn't designed for visitors. When I ask for a ticket I am quizzed about my future intentions of using the railway, and when I say that I have none I am told to wait. It transpires that you can't simply buy a ticket but need to purchase a card upon which you put money. I have a similar card in Nanjing, which is good for the buses as well, but in China there is an option to buy single tickets instead, here the system is mandatory. I have put my money in the ticket window and after a few minutes the right kind of customer comes along. As far as I can make out she credits his card with the little extra that I have paid and he uses his card to let us both through the barrier.

Now I am on the longest escalator, as well as the fastest moving, that I have ever experienced. In London, where the tube is very deep two or three flights are used to get to the bottom, but this is uncompromising, straight down into the bowels of the earth. Tbilisi metro was obviously built with proper tunnelling and not the cut and fill techniques which are causing mayhem on the surface of every other city in China as they all want to be next to get an underground system. The station platform, as well as the train when it arrives, is surprisingly short and a little gloomy. The journey is noisy as we rattle and sway between stops, but the system, which was built nearly 50 years ago, is full of character and provides a good feel of what it is like to be a local in this city.

I find the appropriate bus to take me from Tbilisi to the wine producing area of Kakheti without too much difficulty, and it already has the engine running and is about to leave. We do a turn of the block, back past the metro station and stop. It isn't full enough. But now we really are off and going well along the good road surface. The countryside is pleasantly undulating and before too long the road is lined with vineyards. I see a signpost- Sighnaghi 16 km, but we don't take the turning and continue for another half hour. When I see a sign 4 km to the town which we also ignore I try to question our destination. It looked like a quiet country lane and I would not have minded walking that distance, but I am told to wait. We stop at a town at the bottom of the hill and I am directed to another marshrutka which eventually takes me back the way we have just come.

Sighnaghi, with its open pedestrian areas, and large decorated fountain, reminds me of one of those pretty hilltop villages in Italy. I head up a cobbled street past houses with overhanging balconies and terracotta tiles and am woken out of my reverie by an urgent shout. An old woman has spotted my backpack and recognises me as someone needing a guesthouse. She takes me into a yard and shows me the toilet and shower and then goes up some stairs seemingly to the building next door, but at a landing where there is a kitchen, the old wooden steps turn back into the upstairs of the house. The downstairs area is abandoned and desolate. Dodo, as she introduces herself (she is quite old but certainly not dead) shows me rooms crammed with beds to the point that the farthest ones can only be accessed by climbing over those nearer. Outside the large balcony accommodates another five beds and I consider that sleeping in the fresh air may be not too bad. If the place was full it would be horrendous but as I appear to be the only guest, and it is very cheap, I say yes.

It is actually a bit cold at night but I decide that I want to spend a full day exploring the area and tell Dodo at breakfast that I will stay a second night. I might just need another blanket. It seems that in Georgia cheap places to stay (hostels and guesthouses) don't provide linen and I think that most people sleep in their clothes. This strikes me as a bad idea, if for no other reason than that they will require washing more frequently. I have three or four changes of clothing which gets me through a week comfortably. But I have also packed a silk sleeping bag that I bought in Vietnam. I have not often used it but threw it in my pack as it folds into a size not much bigger than a pocket handkerchief and it weighs virtually nothing. I am very pleased that I did, especially when it is hot as it covers me up without the need of clothing in shared accommodation and effectively acts as sheets when none are provided.

The day begins to warm up and I walk a couple of kilometres to a convent where St. Nino, who brought Christianity to Georgia in the 4th century is said to be buried. There is a pleasant little church dedicated to her but next door to it, where she is meant to be buried, a much bigger new church is being built. A carved stone west face is being finished which looks very grand and the whole building appears to be well constructed in a traditional manner and regardless of cost. I just wonder why they need two churches in the same place. The convent building is a large brick structure in well-kept gardens of lawn and roses, but is off limits. There is also a farm and a couple of nuns are working in a vegetable garden, but the main activity is managing tourists.

I follow the signs to the Holy Spring down a few hundred concrete steps. This is where St Nino discovered healing waters and a tiny little chapel has been built to accommodate the spring. The place is full of women and children so I sit and wait for it to become quieter, but instead of them moving on another group arrives. Now there is no chance to see the spring, but I suppose it is more important for them if they really believe that it is miraculous holy water.

Back in town I sit in the square for lunch and order tomato and cheese soup with some bread from the Amsterdam Pizzeria. Well they eat most things in Holland. It occurs to me that my meal has all the same ingredients as a basic pizza but in a different format. Continuing east I come to the very extensive and well preserved town walls. They're actually only a couple of centuries old but curiously encircle an area next to, but not including the town itself. I believe that they were built for the protection of those living in the adjacent lowlands to come up to higher ground in times of danger, as well as for Sighnaghi townspeople, so maybe it was seen as a place for the region to resort to rather than a wall for the town. But suddenly there are claps of thunder and I hurry back to town before the rain gets too heavy. I might sleep indoors tonight.

Dodo's guesthouse is certainly a contrast to where I stayed with Liz in Chengdu last year. When I woke up in the posh hotel 20 floors up I studied the view from the window and gazed out at a tropical pool with a sandy beach, beyond which was green countryside and I could make out some interesting looking paths. After eating as much free breakfast as I could I set out to explore, but found a high wire fence protecting the hotel grounds. I worked my way around it until I spotted a gardener on the other side. I watched for a while and saw him pass through a section of fence which on inspection had been disconnected from its neighbour and was used for taking grass clippings off the premises to be piled up out of sight.

The other side was delightful. Winding country lanes with only a very occasional scooter or van and I soon arrived at a little village. I always like to get to rural areas where I can feel most immersed in a country and here, although I knew that we were surrounded by major highways, I was able to walk for miles and be totally unaware of the city. Of course this couldn't last forever and with a rude shock I suddenly found myself back in the frantic mayhem of noise and traffic that I had suffered the day before. I hopped on a bus but I got confused about the direction with my backward working compass and had to get off and catch a different number back the way I'd come. When I decided that I'd travelled far enough I really had no idea where I was and the only map of Chengdu I could find was so pathetic that it couldn't even be called a diagram. All it showed was three concentric circles to indicate the ring roads and a blob in the middle for the city centre.

I decided on a north easterly bearing and set off on foot again. My route took me along the side of a rather smelly waterway and when that veered to the east I found myself on much smaller roads and had difficulty in keeping on the same bearing as there was a hill in the way. It was hot, humid and dusty. I had been walking for hours and was not even sure that I was heading in the right direction. I hadn't thought to pick up a business card from hotel reception, so even if I had been able to find a taxi I would have struggled to explain where I wanted to go, so I plodded on. The last thing I wanted to do was to go round in circles so I determined to keep north east even if it meant heading away from the hotel. The roads became narrow lanes and after some false trails I found one going up the hill. At the top, to my amazement I could see the bulk of the hotel across a valley filled with trees and tiny contoured and manicured areas of cultivation, too small to be called fields. To celebrate I swallowed the last of my water.

I lost the view of the hotel as I descended and so continued to use the compass but kept ending up in cottage doorways and had to retrace my steps. When a particularly long lane ended at a dwelling I was tempted to take a path through the cultivation. This seemed promising and even had a plank of wood to cross a creek but then ended abruptly and I was forced to turn back. But the track had disappeared and I was stranded in dense bush for a couple of minutes before I could work out the way I had come. A glutton for punishment, I tried another path and this time it came out onto a lane I recognised from earlier in the day as being a pleasant 20-30 minutes from the hotel. Around the corner tables and chairs indicated some form of eatery and the locals inspected me with interest as I sat down and waved away the suggestion of tea. My Chinese managed not just a beer but a cold beer, which hit the spot beautifully. I'd managed to get totally lost and found my way back again. I was pleased with myself. It had been a good day. When I get back I thought I might even try that swimming pool with the tropical sandy beach.

Liz was in Chengdu for an induction conference, organised by the company she works for, before the start of the academic year. I was there to take advantage of the hotel and the travelling to and fro. My qualification as a social worker is of little use in China and so I now consider myself to be semi-retired, with a degree of confusion around the 'semi' bit. Liz had a major presentation to make to the conference and she seemed to be more concerned about what she was going to wear than about what she would say. My priority was to arrange my journey back. While she had been booked onto flights it would be both an extravagance and a waste of an opportunity for me not to travel overland. I knew that I should have bought a return ticket before I left the station when I arrived but I wanted to research other possibilities, as I felt that I should be able to make more out of the journey by stopping off en-route. My plan was to find a destination on the rail line in not too large a place where I could find somewhere to stay and maybe see some of the countryside before carrying on to Nanjing later the following day. After searching all the train timetables I decided on a place called Ankang.

Most Chinese are quite reserved when it comes to starting a conversation, although they are very curious about foreigners and once the ice has been broken will crowd around expectantly, so I was surprised when an attractive young woman on the bus into town asked me where I was going. She gave her name as Tam Sin, or something that sounds similar, and was a teacher in a place that I had never heard of. She said that she would help me to get a train ticket and we headed off together in search of a ticket office, small shops which are dotted about towns and which for a small fee enable one to beat the long queues. Tam Sin wanted to know all about me and where I came from and I realised that we had an unspoken agreement; she was helping me in return for practicing her English. I told her that as a family we moved from England to New Zealand more than 10 years ago and that as our children are now grown up we are taking the opportunity to do other things. She was surprised that the population of my entire country is significantly less than that of Chengdu, but I explained that there are a lot more sheep than people and taught her the expression 'the black sheep of the family'.

Tam Sin constantly accosted passers-by to ask for directions, which bore no fruit but finally she spotted what we were looking for. I asked for a ticket to Ankang, a place Tam Sin hadn't heard of and I struggled to explain why I wanted to go there. The only suitable train had standing room only so I changed tack and enquired about a hard sleeper to Nanjing. This was also 'meiyou' but the ticket seller and Tam Sin engaged in a long conversation at the end of which I was told that I could buy a hard seat ticket on a slower train and should then ask the attendant on the train for a berth. Did I understand? 'Yes', well actually 'no', if there was no bed available on this train why should I not take the faster one and ask the attendant on that train for a sleeper rather than risk 30 hours on a hard seat which, I added, I felt too old to do. I was a little disappointed that Tam Sin agreed quite so readily with this self-assessment. There was no answer to my question but I decided to trust the recommendation of the ticket seller rather than risk being stranded in Chengdu.

I then had time to look around the city, which is meant to be one of the more pleasant in China, but I was not impressed. The centre is a large shade less square of concrete and grass from which broad busy roads go in all directions. There is no other obvious point of reference, no lake or river or visible hills and nor are there any twisting little streets and alleyways. The shops appeared to be the same as in any other Chinese city and a new mall I wandered into could have been almost anywhere in the world.

I needed to decide what I wanted to achieve from chasing my wife around China. I liked the idea of travelling around the country but I had to have a clearer vision of what I hoped to see and gain from the experience. I am not particularly interested in the sights and tourist attractions and I can't be bothered to go round taking photographs. If I did I would want them of people but think it rude and embarrassing to be pointing a camera at the locals. My experience of watching wildlife is to be constantly staring at a spot where someone else claims to have seen something which I just missed. I do have a picture somewhere of a tree in Brunei which I took as a rare monkey in its branches was being pointed out to me, but I never saw it. I like to go walking in the hills but if it was just geographical features I wanted I could have done that far more easily by staying in New Zealand.

So the attraction had to be the people; their culture and way of life. What I really wanted to do was to get to the heart and soul of China and meld it to all the images of the country I have had in my mind from childhood through to 1989 and beyond. A tough task with the very limited language skills I have. Train journeys, especially if they are overnight, are a way of living for a short time with local people and sharing a slice of their life but going from one city to another and only seeing what is in between from the train window was not enough. I was cross with myself that I had been too disorganised to get to a smaller place on my way back to Nanjing as I know from my travels over the years that the truest images of a country and its people are found in the little places, not the cities. This is an added challenge in China as what appear to be villages on a map turn out to be towns of half a million people.

Before I boarded the train I explained to the attendant that I wanted to upgrade to Yingwo and he redirected me to carriage 12 which is roughly in the middle and seemed to be the nerve centre of the team of guards. I was told to wait, which I took as a good sign. I stood with my pack on my back in the area leading to the next coach, which contained the rubbish bins, toilets, and tea making facilities, and tried to keep clear of more boarding passengers, some of whom seemed to be carrying all their worldly goods. Not everyone had a seat and a pair of migrant workers set up a camp behind me as we pulled out of the station. After half an hour I was still stood in the same place and smokers, not allowed to light up in the carriage itself appeared around me. I decided that the aromas of cigarette smoke combined with that emanating from the nearby lavatory were not to my liking, and I sought out one of the guards to say that I was going to the seat shown on my ticket, which was back in the second carriage.

Inevitably when I got there I found that it was taken. The reason was that the young man wanted to sit next to his girlfriend so I should take his seat. This was given as an explanation rather than a request and repeated by all those around who seemed very eager to make sure that I understood the situation. My confusion was not that I didn't understand but that, as all the other seats were occupied as well, I had no idea from whom I should demand that they vacate their place. Eventually one member of the group of youngsters got up and I took my seat. They were a very friendly bunch but also very loud and when one of them proudly produced a tinny music player, I consulted the timetable for the train which I had copied from the internet and decided at what points in the journey I should renew my request for a sleeper.

To my surprise this wasn't necessary as before the next stop I was summoned by one of the guards. Back in coach 12 tickets were being sold from a little office and I finally made my way to the very end of the train where an empty and unlit hard sleeper carriage was appended, seemingly as part of a ghost train that had lost its way. It was used to store many of the items for sale that are wheeled up and down the carriages and my bunk had boxes of fruit under it which the fruit seller periodically pulled out to replenish her supply. A few more people drifted in but the carriage maintained its separate identity and when I left to make tea from the hot water tap further forward, I was bombarded by the bright lights and noise of the other carriages and hurried back to the peace and refuge of the ghost coach.

I was thankful for the knowledge and wisdom of the woman who sold me the ticket and I reflected that even a simple job such as dispensing train tickets can be done with different levels of professional expertise. In many countries these spare berths would be used by the staff to earn extra income but my tickets were clearly issued to the correct value. There is an enormous amount of what we would consider to be corruption in China, which has been part of a way of life for centuries, if not millennia. But the ordinary Chinese people strike me as being extremely honest, although they don't seem to trust each other and always want to lock things up. My experience is that as individuals, people don't even take advantage of foreigners, unlike the government which used to have a blatant separate price structure and even a different currency (Foreign Exchange Certificates) for visitors to the country.

As the train progressed more refugees made their way to my carriage. The separateness of its culture was maintained and new comers respected the unusual peace and quiet. One woman climbed into her bunk and was still there, having barely moved, 24 hours later. But I did have a concern; thinking that it was going to stay almost empty I had 'borrowed' an extra pillow from the top bunk and, sure enough, well into the night I was aware of a couple climbing up there. Words were spoken and a pillow was passed from one bunk to the other leaving the donator without one. I considered making a clean breast of it and offering my extra pillow back to its rightful owner, but I knew that my Chinese couldn't manage an explanation and I was not sure how well received a used pillow would be. I sat tight, or rather laid tight. In the morning I pulled the cover over the pillows but I was aware that the head end of my bunk was raised higher than others and I imagined accusative looks from my fellow travellers. I was pleased when the couple I discomfited got off.

The marshrutka back to Tbilisi only gets packed for the last few kilometres and, now that I know my way around (I've bought my own metro card this time), there is still most of the day left after I have checked back into the friendly Indian run hostel for the night.

Exploring the city I come to the museum which looks enormous and may be very interesting. I do have an interest in things historic and have nothing against museums, but walking slowly and looking at exhibits can be very tiring on the feet and I would much prefer to be looking at the real life of the city, so instead I walk around a supermarket, which gives an insight into Georgian life today as well as being much more colourful than any museum. The delicatessen counter is full of interesting looking smoked sausage and a large variety of cheese, and I am tempted to buy food and wine to eat at the hostel tonight. Hostels differ from guesthouses in that they generally have a kitchen available for guests to use, but I am not going to carry it with me now so I will decide later. I am asked in English if I would like to try some wine. I am not in the habit of refusing a drink but I may feel under some pressure to buy some, and again I don't want to have to cart it all around the city. Instead I ask how she knew that I am English, but she is unable to explain. I take a bottle of water to the checkout and again am spoken to in English. Is it my physical appearance, are some people more Caucasian than others, my clothes- just a plain shirt and cotton type trousers, or something in my manner? She can't tell me, she just knows.

In Liberty Square (previously Lenin), A mounted golden St. George sparkles in the sunlight atop his column. Delving into the backstreets most buildings are full of character and, the centre of town at least, has largely been spared the dull concrete blocks of what Georgians now officially term the Soviet Occupation. But many are in an appalling state of decay. One once fine old brick building overhung with iron balconies has such wide and long cracks in it that I don't feel like staying too long in its vicinity.

I climb up a twisting cobbled street where there is some evidence of remedial work being carried out but the task is daunting. I am looking for a 1500 year old Zoroastrian temple which should be up here. It is roughly shaped as a cube but what I find looks in remarkably good condition and far too tall for the description I have. A little further on I find a map of the area displayed on a board and realise that I have been photographing the bell tower of the nearby church, which is neither Zoroastrian nor 1500 years old. Back down the street I climb steep brick steps and try a big metal door but it is locked. I am on my way down when the door opens and a friendly woman invites me into her home, from which is the only access to the temple. It is just four walls and buttresses, which suggest that there was some form of vaulted roof, but that is long gone and it now has a plastic rain canopy for protection.

Continuing to climb with views across the whole city I get to the massive statue of Mother Georgia gazing across her domain, and on to the commanding site of the fortress which can only be viewed from the outside. I then discover that I can use my metro card to take the very swish looking cable car back down to the river. My map is a little difficult to follow, particularly as it gives very few street names, but I manage to find the Armenian Cathedral and remember to zip the legs back onto my trousers which I had converted to shorts, before entering. It is an atmospheric place emanating faith and fervour, but I am beginning to feel an overload of orthodox churches, although I still find it difficult to pass one by without entering.

There are a lot of beggars in Tbilisi and here they line the streets; mainly old women but some men who just sit with their arm outstretched and palm open. Near to the hostel that I am staying in there is a young girl begging. She is maybe eight years old, looks healthy and not too shabby and lies on a blanket on the pavement, with no sign of any responsible adult. I make my way back to the hostel and she is still in the same position, several hours after I first saw her. There are clearly no proper child protection procedures in Georgia.

Not far from where I am staying in Tbilisi is the Georgian State Pantomime Theatre. I assume that this is some form of performance without words rather than an; "Oh yes it is" "Oh no it isn't" kind of panto and I am tempted to see it. Tonight is a performance entitled St George. From the poster I see that they performed Shakespeare's sonnets a couple of weeks ago. Why? If you take the words away it would be like going to a restaurant and seeing a video of some dishes but getting nothing to eat.

There are twenty odd of us in the audience which is about a quarter full, and nearly as many performers. Everything is minimalist. The slate grey walls are unadorned and the plain black stage is matched by the plain black seating. There is no curtain, no set and the only props are wooden staves. These are used to devastating effect, not just to mime weapons and barriers, but also they provide another dimension as the main characters climb them or are carried upon them whilst they are being held by the other performers. It looks as if you have to be pretty strong to be a pantomime artist. The show is highly stylised music and movement, full of agony and anguish. The minimalism is also taken to the plot which is stripped to a simple struggle between right and wrong. If I'd hoped for a pantomime dragon I would be disappointed; this is serious stuff. There is nothing to distract from the force of the action and the only help that St. George gets is lightning flashes from above as he overpowers an abstract evil in the denouement while the Hallelujah Chorus is belted out: stirring stuff.

In the street parallel to where I am staying there is a string of bars that claim to be from all around the world, but nothing Georgian. There is a British pub ostensibly selling Fullers London Pride. It is not a bad copy of a town pub but of course it can only ever be a copy. I can't get to know the locals by chalking a game of darts and then peering into an old beer tankard to find three reasonably sharp darts with most of their flights intact so that I can take on the winner. The beer is somehow reminiscent of its namesake but is obviously a keg brew; pasteurised and then injected with gas at the point of delivery to give an impression of life.

I am befriended by a woman at the bar who doesn't have a drink but who chain smokes. Her English is not at all bad, but her friendliness seems somehow feigned and I wonder if she is a prostitute. She is not dressed in a particularly tarty manner, unlike most of the young women in China (who aren't prostitutes anyway), but then she is not young. She tells me that she is a grandmother with a 33 year old daughter, which doesn't really sound much of a sales pitch if she is trying to sell sex. If nothing else, I think that she is waiting for me to finish my drink in the hope that I will have another and offer her one, but I am not paying the prices charged here for a very indifferent half litre of beer, and I had to tell the barman to top it up to even get that. I drain my glass and leave. She follows me outside and I see that she goes into the Irish pub next door, presumably to smoke another cigarette.

Chapter Fifteen: The Image Collector

At the start of my trip I was clear about the route I was taking and how I would get there, but I had only planned the first few days in any detail, as much as anything because there is only so much information that I can hold in my head. I need to continue west into Turkey. I had considered the possibility of a side trip to Armenia (the border between Armenia and Turkey is closed because Turkey wants to stay friends with oil-rich Azerbaijan) but I only have about another ten days before I need to be in Bulgaria and I still want to see more of Georgia. After doing what research I can on the computer, I am going to head west, to Borjomi.

There is a rail line and I would much prefer to travel by train but I must either be at the station to catch the 6.40 am, which would mean missing the inclusive breakfast at the hostel or else catch the afternoon train which doesn't arrive until after 9 pm, which is late to start looking for somewhere to stay. So I take the underground to Didube bus station, where I had first arrived in Tbilisi. It would have saved me a lot of trouble if I had known then that it was on the metro. The girl at the ticket window refuses to take back my card and refund my money. I try the other one but get even shorter shrift, which I cannot understand, and she then puts up a closed sign and goes off for her tea break. I give up, there are some battles that you are never going to win, and I now have a new bookmark.

Across the bustling bus station-cum-market a marshrutka is being loaded for Borjomi. Watching the driver reminds me of a job I had when I first left school as a furniture remover. Some of the men would take great pride in loading the contents of a house into a lorry in the most space-efficient manner. He puts my bag in the back and directs me to a single seat behind the sliding side door. This isn't too bad as the folding seat that should be next to me is missing, but he cleverly uses this for more luggage space, including several large cardboard boxes and a microwave oven. Eventually we are all packed in to his satisfaction and head out of the city. The advantage of having every possible space filled is that we don't need to slow down to pick up more passengers, but there is a pang of guilt as we sail past and condemn them to another hour standing in the sun. The large woman behind me periodically gives me a back massage with her knees and, when we do drop off some passengers and the luggage is reorganised, she elects to stand where it had been rather than stay in her cramped corner.

Borjomi feels right as soon as I clamber out of the marshtruka. The air is fresh, the hills are green and a clean white suspension bridge crosses the modest expanse of the Mtkvari River. The main road and a handful of shops are to the north, but I head south over the river and soon come to a sign advertising the Borjomi Hostel. I go through an archway, into a courtyard and up some steps but can get no entry into the building. From the other side of the courtyard, just a few feet away, a woman waves me over and shows me a rather dingy but adequate room. In fact it is a private suite, as the bedroom is accessed through another area with a sofa and chairs, and for the same money as I would pay for a bed in a dorm. She says that her name is Marina and that there are no meals but there is tea and coffee. To prove it she brings me a small cup of sweet sticky coffee that actually goes down quite well.

I resent carrying items which I don't use and one which has yet to see the light of day is my togs. Borjomi exists because of its mineral waters, which are bottled and sold around the world and its traditional market has been the old Soviet Union. After a few false starts I find my way to Mineral Water Park and replenish my water bottle, but after continuing up the river for a couple of miles, past the funfair attractions and through a pretty wooded valley, I come to the swimming pool. Unlike my wife and children I am not a fan of diving into cold water, but this pool is fed by a large bore bright blue painted lead pipe coming down the hill and delivering thermal spring water. It is not really hot like some in New Zealand, but it certainly isn't cold and I stay in it for a good five minutes. I wish that I could find places like this, built on a human scale, in China but it is a struggle when what appears to be a small village on a map turns out to be the size of Manchester.

Of course some Chinese cities are of a more modest size. I travelled with Liz to Zhangjiagang, another town in the Yangtze delta, but one that doesn't even have a railway station and Liz was not at all happy that we had a three hour bus journey to get there. Unlike many cities in the region, it doesn't have thousands of years of history and became established in the 19th century as a small market town. The area developed very rapidly with the economic reforms and in 1993 became one of the few places in the country with permission to engage in international trade. Consequently Zhangjiagang is now a city of over a million people, although figures for Chinese city populations tend to be misleading, as they usually include a large rural area. Strolling around the town I found it to be a pleasant enough place, clean and tidy by Chinese standards and with a network of waterways in the centre which didn't smell as bad as those in many other cities.

The hotel personnel were helpful and I got a pleasant smile from the girl collecting breakfast vouchers, which is more than I expect from the normally robotic Chinese customer service. Liz also commented on the friendliness of the people and I was beginning to question the conclusions that I had drawn about Chinese society, while I was observing passers-by as I sat on a bench in a Shanghai park. I thought that maybe it is a size thing and that away from the biggest cities people are more personable and have time for others in general, rather than just those that they identify with as being part of their group. But Zhangjiagang is still a big place and I have visited much smaller towns without feeling the need to reassess my observations. Then I looked the city up on Wikipedia. What I read seemed just bizarre even by Chinese standards!

Zhangjiagang grew so fast that it was effectively an entirely new city, which I suppose was also largely true of those that had been around for millennia before being rapidly re-developed, but the central government decided that this was to be something special. It was selected to be a unique model city for all of China and pamphlets were given out listing the 10 'don'ts' and 6 'dos' of what the government called 'civilized behaviour'. The new rules actually attempted to address the issues which I had identified, and included areas such as courtesy, showing mutual respect and giving consideration to others. These weren't presented as helpful guidelines but as a code of conduct which had to be followed, and which was enforced to such a degree that visitors remarked on the beauty, cleanliness and friendliness of Zhangjiagang relative to other Chinese cities. According to Wikipedia, clean, friendly cities are such a novelty in China that up to 300,000 tourists visit Zhangjiagang every year to sample the urban utopia. That's an average of nearly 1,000 people a day turning up in the hope that someone will smile at them, or at least not bump into them, as they wander the litter free streets!

The city was also awarded the UN Habitat Scroll of Honour, which apparently recognises contributions to housing development. Amongst many others it shares this honour with The Shack Dwellers Federation of Namibia, King Carl XVI Gustaf of Sweden and Grozny, a place which less than a fortnight ago I was doing my very best to avoid as it is reported as being so dangerous. But the real issue in all this is: if the Chinese Government believes that the rules it proscribed are necessary to ensure civilised behaviour, what is its view of the 99.9% of its people who don't live in Zhangjiagang? The answer must be that it agrees with me that there is a fundamental flaw in the way that society in China has developed. The passive/aggressive model of each group of people pursuing their own ends regardless of the impact on others is becoming increasingly unworkable as the country modernises. The absence of a sense of social responsibility has resulted in polluted waterways, air that is dangerous to breathe, and roads that easily become gridlocked into a pathetic blaring of horns as no one will give way.

One apparent exception is behaviour on city buses, where a seat will always be found for an elderly person or anyone else in special need. On one occasion an elderly man who was offered a seat viewed my grey hair and insisted, despite my protestations that I take it, resulting in another young woman having to give up her seat to the original beneficiary. But this is nothing to do with having any empathy for those in greater need; it is simply a result of people acting in the way that they have been told to. I even remember the public information commercial shown on Chinese television in 1989. It was so lacking in subtlety that I found it hilarious: a very heavily pregnant woman boarded a bus on what seemed to be a particularly hot and humid day, and became increasingly uncomfortable having to stand. Various men were shown in close-up studiously trying to pretend that she didn't exist until eventually one of them called her over to take his seat. But he only had one leg! He swung on his crutches to a place where he could lean against something and was shown wearing the beatific smile of someone bathing in his own goodness.

We actually came very close to Zhangjiagang when we were in China then, although the city would not even have existed at that time. We had caught a ferry from Dalian in the north east of the country to Shanghai and then made our way to Wuxi, which is another ancient Yangtze delta city and where the Shanghai to Nanjing rail line crosses the Grand Canal. We were delighted to find passenger ferries operating from there on the inland waterways, and we were even more pleased to manage to get a ticket to go somewhere that I pointed to on the timetable. In those days there was often a presumption that foreigners could only go to places identified as being suitable for them, rather than being free to roam as they pleased, and even now many simple hotels aren't allowed to accept international guests.

After several very enjoyable hours watching the commercial traffic on the busy canals we arrived at a pretty waterside village just as all the local schoolchildren were breaking for lunch, and trooped past us giggling at the sight of aliens from a strange world. We found a little café by a pond which we entered to the complete shock of the owner who was the only person there, but five minutes later the place was packed as it seemed that word had spread of strange beings and everyone wanted to get a look at us. Waiting for the boat to return and take us back to Wuxi we were approached by a young woman who told us in broken English that she was the school teacher and that we were the first foreigners to visit their village, which we learnt was called Beiguo.

At that time there was a whole network of ferries operating and it was the only way to get to places like Beiguo. When I returned to Wuxi I walked the length of the canal through the city but found no evidence of any boat services still operating. I love travelling on boats but it seems that the Chinese are on a mission to get rid of all the world's ferries. Their mania for road building has destroyed their inland waterways passenger services, done away with the Yellow Sea ferry we caught and forced us to ride on buses in South East Asia all the way along the Mekong. I needed to get to Myanmar as a matter of urgency as China is now there, busily laying mile after mile of slick tarmac and will eventually make river transport obsolete.

With a free day in Zhangjiagang I decided to try to find Beiguo again. I was surprised how easily I got a bus ticket to such a small isolated settlement even though I had forgotten to bring the Chinese characters for the village which I had printed off. In fact everyone I spoke to in the city seemed to be able to understand my poor Chinese and I wondered if comprehending foreigners was one of the 'dos' that the citizens were obliged to follow. This may not be as silly as it sounds as it could be that the prevailing attitude in China results in people making no real effort to try to understand what is being said to them.

But when I got off the bus I was not sure if it was even the same place. I was in a medium sized town and, apart from the waterway, I recognised nothing. It didn't look new, but I suppose that a quarter of a century is a long time and buildings in China do seem to age quickly, either from poor construction or neglect. There were a handful of small terraced cottage type dwellings near the canal which were obviously original, but these were dwarfed by the more recent development. Most houses and factories did look as if they had been built at the same time, and were clad in small white ceramic tiles. Despite the whole town looking well worn, it occurred to me that, as our original visit had been a quarter of a century earlier, before most of present day Beiguo had been built, I had probably been there before most of those who now consider themselves to be locals. I was stared at with expressions of mild shock, rather than the complete amazement on the faces of the villagers in 1989. It may well be that we are still the only foreigners to have visited Beiguo, but with easy road connections and a big city nearby, I did not appear quite as remarkable as we did on our previous visit.

I was a bit disappointed that nothing looked as I remembered it and I had to admit that the image that I had in my mind of that original experience had been distorted by time and was inaccurate. That image I feel was part of the collection which forms like layers of sediment over the years and becomes part of my sense of who I am and where I have been, so it is disturbing when it is shown to be an invention with little basis in reality. But then what is real? Maybe my recollections have value in that they represent significant ideas or attitudes. In the same way that dreams can be concrete manifestations of abstract ideas or thoughts, my memories can be a synthesis of what those experiences meant to me. The images I carry in my head aren't a true picture of the event as it happened but a piece of abstract art containing the essence of the reality.

I'm getting a headache thinking about this, but I still wanted to acquire more of these experiences and find other little places in China for my mind to distort. Liz was supporting a new centre opening in Tianjin and then going on to meetings in Beijing. These are both huge cities and I needed to plan where I wanted to go. I bought a road atlas of China but I could not find one in Pinyin (that is using the alphabet), so it is just an incomprehensible muddle of Chinese characters. I also bought a train timetable and I developed a system to enable me to plan journeys. First I use the internet to identify a train I may want to catch and get a print out in Pinyin of all its stops. I then use the train number to find it in the timetable, which gives me the stations written with Chinese characters. By comparing this with the print out, I can match the Pinyin to the Chinese by checking the arrival and departure times. The tricky part is to then match the characters in the timetable with those in the road atlas following the route of the railway line. Well, it makes a change from doing a crossword.

Using this method I decided on a place called Shangqiu as a suitable stop. It is roughly half way to Tianjin which meant that I could reach it comfortably in a day and then carry on to Tianjin the following day without the need for a sleeper. I couldn't discover much about the place on the internet, which I took to be a positive sign as I just wanted to stay in a typical ordinary town. On ctrip, which is a major Chinese website for travel needs, I found a cheap hotel and printed off a map showing how to reach it from the railway station, but before I booked I thought I should go up the road to the ticket booking office and confirm the train.

'Meiyou'. I had alternatives but got the same response. I asked why these trains were so full and was told that students were travelling back to resume their studies. I was then concerned that I wouldn't even get to Tianjin and hurried to the apartment to make new plans. Back at the ticket window I had a print out of all trains from Nanjing to Tianjin. I asked for a Yingwo (hard sleeper) on T186 without success and finally settled for a 'D' train. These are superfast but with a maximum speed of 250KPH they are not as superfast, and therefore not as expensive, as the 'G' trains which Liz uses. The ticket cost more than the overnight sleeper train or slower day train with a night in a hotel half way. It also seemed much less adventurous and I had again failed to break the journey between major cities. This, it seemed to me, was essential to my aim of getting to what I can feel to be the quintessential China.

It was evening when we arrived at Tianjin Nan Station. Another problem with the bullet trains is that they arrive at new stations which are miles out of town. I had printed off a Google map with public transport directions to the hotel that Liz was booked into and accordingly I ignored the buses outside the station and walked North West in search of a 110 bus. It soon became apparent that I was not going to find any bus on the new highway I was trudging along and I reluctantly flagged down a taxi. It already had a passenger but I pointed to the next part of my instructions, a station on a light railway and they told me to get in. It should only have been an 18 minute bus ride so I was relieved when after 20 minutes the other passenger got out, paid the fare, and the meter was reset. I hate taxis at the best of times. Some people like to sit back and be ferried around in style but it just makes me feel uncomfortable. Most of all I hate the meter, which seems to accelerate as time passes draining away my money, and which I have difficulty in not constantly watching. It shouldn't have been far but on and on we went. It got dark and still we didn't stop. It was hot and stuffy and I felt more and more agitated. I sat forward and communicated my unease but the driver just waved us on further.

When we finally stopped I waved my piece of paper at him. 18 minutes by bus, three quarters of an hour in a taxi. Explain. Of course he couldn't but I don't think that he metaphorically as well as literally took me for a ride, but then I was stuck. The next instruction was a one hour train ride but I couldn't still be that far away. I wondered if I had shown him the station where I should have got off instead of where I should have started, in which case the hotel would only be about a kilometre away. He hadn't yet zeroed the metre so I asked to be taken to the hotel. It was several kilometres later, but nothing like an hour's train ride when we finally arrived. The only explanation is that the directions I had were entirely fanciful and I had been trying to follow a route which simply did not exist. This is a problem in China where so much development is happening so quickly that even internet maps are out of date before they are downloaded (or maybe uploaded, I get confused with the terminology). Of course Liz thought that my having had to take a taxi, and via some out of the way point, was hilarious.

As all hotel rooms these days have double beds there is no problem with my staying at hotels Liz is booked into but unfortunately they will often only provide breakfast for one person. I argue that as she will probably get lunch provided it makes sense that I use the breakfast coupon, but she tends to get a bit possessive about these things, leaving me to roam the streets to find sustenance. I had been wandering around Tianjin admiring the classical style of much of the new architecture and looking in confusion at buildings from the early 20th century, which have been spared the spread of high-rise development because of their historic interest as relics from a European enclave, but which are now gently rotting and crumbling. I felt a sudden pang of hunger and realised that I'd forgotten about breakfast. It then occurred to me that, unlike everywhere else I have been in China, there hadn't been the constant bombardment of the sight and smell of food in every other doorway. While Tianjin has consciously been creating a stylish international city it has carelessly stamped out its Chinese identity. All over the world cities strive to preserve their Chinatowns and present the colourful vibrant streets and alleys as a tourist attractions, but as I searched for a simple bowl of noodles in Tianjin, I realised that the quintessential Chinese character has been discarded in favour of European style and bakery shops selling overpriced coffee.

I walked past a classical stone building which struck a passing resemblance to Buckingham Palace. It was clearly no more than a few years old and I wondered what civic function it performed. When I reached the front I was shocked that it was no more than a bank, namely the Everbright Bank, but on reflection London is full of grand buildings erected by firms such as Lloyds or Barclays in the nineteenth century. Were they placed on new wide thoroughfares squeezing out what had then typified London, maybe cobbled alleyways, chimney sweeps and jellied-eel stalls? I suspect that they were.

The comparison of modern China with industrial revolution England is intriguing. Dickens description in Dombey and Son of the devastation caused by the construction of the railway in London is repeated everyday throughout China as the cities expand. In England the landscape was changed forever as people moved from a traditional rural existence to the new factories where, for the first time they earned a wage, albeit a pittance. In China the same thing is happening but on a far grander scale. When we first came to the Country in 1989 about 80% of the population were rural peasants. Today, as China like Britain before it becomes the workshop of the world, the urban/rural split is about 50/50. That means that roughly a third of the total population of the Country has moved from the countryside to urban areas. The numbers are mind-boggling; the migration to the ever expanding cities in two or three decades, has involved a significantly larger number of people than every man woman and child in the United States.

The majestic buildings in Tianjin, clearly built regardless of expense, looked as if they belonged in the 19th century and seemed out of place in a modern city, but then they are based on the same classical architecture that exists in London and would have been viewed as ancient when it was built 200 years ago. What they signify (together with the massive statues that adorn the centre) is the same civic pride which built the grand cities of Europe but which is difficult to conceive for us brought up in times of national decline and cost-cutting. In a few short years Chinese peasants have transformed themselves into sophisticated urbanites and the streets are crammed with fashion shops and hairdressing salons but, as in industrial revolution Britain, the riches are created by a large number of poorly paid workers and poverty as well as wealth is growing. It may have been an impossibly inefficient system, but in 1989 there were no beggars on the streets.

Still searching for breakfast I consulted the city map and headed north, where it looked as if the streets ran closer together and followed an older grid pattern. Finally I found what I was looking for. Down a little street I came across a group of workers sitting on stools shelling hardboiled eggs around a large bowl on the concrete floor, and got an affirmative to my request for noodles from the woman who appeared to be in charge. It took a long time coming but when it did it was piled high with some kind of meat in gravy, egg omelette, and shredded cucumber, which I am not particularly fond of.

I started to eat under scrutiny, avoiding the cucumber as much as I could, but clearly failed to meet expectations as the woman then brought an even larger bowl into which she tipped my meal. This buried the meat, egg and cucumber under a mound of thick, tagliatelle-style noodles and I was encouraged with energetic signs to mix it all up with my chopsticks. I followed orders but not to her satisfaction and she took the bowl away from me to do it herself, but deposited half the egg on the table in the process. She then disappeared into the kitchen, presumably to have more egg added. By this time I was not feeling nearly as hungry as I was when I came in but knew that I had to do justice to the meal, and any chance of being fussy about eating cucumber had long gone. When I put down my chopsticks some minutes later my bowl was inspected and I was given a nod of approval. I paid exactly one tenth of what the hotel breakfast would have cost. Including any service charge!

Revitalised I found the river which the city celebrates and which acts as a point of reference for everything else. It looked surprisingly clean and free of unpleasant smells and there were not only anglers trying their luck but also bathers. Whatever the appearance you wouldn't find me swimming in it. Walkways and landscaping line both banks of its serpentine course and its companionable width allows for plenty of crossings. More than that it is an exhibition of bridge design and construction; I started at a substantial stone structure embellished with gold paint and guarded in each corner by contrasting large bronze equestrian sculptures. Heading north there was a stylish pair of suspension bridges pulling their cables from opposite banks before, in complete contrast, I came upon a life size meccano iron lift bridge finished in pastel blue and unashamedly showing all its workings in the form of gears, levers, chains and pulleys. This was complemented by an adjacent giant Heath Robinson looking clock, displaying its mechanism and showing a zodiac face topped by a personified golden sun linked by a crane-like structure to a silvery moon. But I was looking further on to a double arch supported by slender threads and which intriguingly changed its graceful geometry as I got closer until I realised that, contrary to my assumption, it was asymmetric. The shape of the next one was reminiscent of Waterloo Bridge but the profusion of statues along its length made me think of St Charles Bridge in Prague. I wanted to turn off at the next bridge which at first looked dull in comparison, but as I drew near the simple white painted metal framework giving picture window views was striking in its simplicity, and more endearing than the miniature Forth Road Bridge which I could see in the distance.

Having spent a day walking around the city, the following day I planned to go a bit further afield by catching buses. I hopped onto the first one that stopped but the route seemed designed to disorient the passengers, as it constantly changed direction and I failed to follow where we were with my street map and compass. After 30-40 minutes I spotted what looked like proper China and hurriedly got off to explore. The narrow street seemed cleaner and more orderly than it should, but had the right intensity of colour and smell. Fruit and veg. stalls overflowed into the alleyways flanked by suspended strips of bony bits of butchery and the fruits of the sea, dominated by light grey crabs, some of which were intent on escape and were controlled by judicious use of wooden sticks.

I escaped the crush of shoppers into a park where grown men were gyrating to tinny discordant music while rotating what appeared to be lavatory ball cocks on pieces of string. On closer inspection I saw that they were actually tops balanced on string which is attached to and controlled by a stick in each hand. The other masculine activity on view was whip cracking with a length of chain, which was uncomfortably loud and life threatening to anyone in the immediate vicinity. The further I delved into the maze of narrow streets and alleys the scruffier and smellier it became and the more I liked it. I recanted what I had said about Tianjin; the central area may no longer be Chinatown but overall it is a city of character and style, which is more than can be said for most in modern China.

All I really knew about my position was that I had ventured east of the river. I wanted to get to the west railway station, which was over the other bank, as I was leaving from there the next day. My plan was to see if I could find a bus at the station which matched a list of bus numbers that I had noted from the stop near the hotel and which I could then catch the following morning. After walking west for over an hour I finally found the river at a point where it bifurcates. The left arm was the direction I wanted but to the right was the apogee of Tianjin river bridges. Giant legs at an angle of 120 degrees spanned the flat bridge surface whilst, to complete the symmetry, a third rose vertically from their summit, at the top of which was the hub of a massive bicycle wheel; Tianjin's answer to the London eye.

I am not keen on heights but it was such a glorious blue sky sunny day that I bought a ticket. It was not until I hopped into the moving capsule that I realised that not only was I the only person getting on, but that the other 47 cars all look as if they were empty as well. I suddenly felt very alone as the mechanism dragged me inch by inch away from solid ground. At first it seemed that it would take forever to complete the circle but in fact I was back in just over 30 minutes, so I suppose it moved at nearly twice the speed of the minute hand on my watch. The view of Tianjin cannot really compete with that of the Thames even on such a beautifully clear day, which may be why there were no other takers. The lovely weather I was told was not entirely down to good fortune. Tianjin was hosting the World Economic Forum and, following the success of the method for the Beijing Olympics, key polluting factories had been temporally shut down to improve the air quality. I take it as a positive sign that the government is at least embarrassed by the extent of pollution, an issue that didn't concern the British Government when it was forging ahead with its industrialisation.

Borjomi has nothing like the London Eye but it does have a tourist office. Given the importance of tourism to the economy and its potential for growth, I am surprised that there are not more of these. Artur is very helpful and supplies me with maps and leaflets. I decide to go on a trip tomorrow to Vardzia, a place which I had hoped to get to but which is difficult to access by public transport. Artur also tells me that if I were to stay another day he would recommend that I visit Bakuriani, a ski resort which can be reached by a narrow gauge hill railway.

I am up bright and early but cannot really see anywhere for breakfast. A restaurant is open but only shows a dinner menu, which isn't really what I want, but from the next door comes an irresistible smell of freshly baking bread. Inside all is activity as a team of women shape lumps of dough which are delivered to the oven and later retrieved to be added to the pile of flattish loaves cooling on wooden shelves. I select one that has just come out of the oven and head over the suspension bridge to the grocers where I buy garlic sausage, cheese, and a couple of pieces of fruit to make it all healthy. I sit on a bench by the swiftly flowing river and get through less than a quarter of what I've bought.

There is just me and a young German couple on the trip. If my mental arithmetic is correct, more than half of the money that Talumi, the driver collects from us will go on fuel for the van. After a quick look around a local monastery, the next stop is a huge fortress at Athaltsikhe, but it has been restored to such an extent that any sense of past glories or tragedies has been erased. There is even a hotel inside built of fort-like stone. The fun part is working out how to get from one end to the other as new bits have been built inside blocking what seem obvious routes. At one point I see Talumi who has moved the van to a different car park. I go to speak with him and an official who watched me doesn't want me to come back in, despite showing him my ticket. I am not having this and use my best Anglo-Saxon, which he may or may not understand, to tell him so. He doesn't pursue the matter (or me), and I climb to the top of yet another tower with wood and iron staircases and concrete landings.

When we are all back at the van I assume the privilege of age and take the front passenger seat, from which I can admire the view without getting a crick in my neck. We continue up the valley which now has bare hillsides and drive around the Jersey and Guernsey looking cattle, which evidently prefer tarmac to grass. There are about half a dozen of them expectantly crammed into a bus shelter and wearing that vacant expression that people assume when waiting at a bus stop with no control over when their transport might arrive. Khertvisi Fortress is our next port of call. This is a proper crumbling castle that hasn't been interfered with. According to the information board a fort was first built here by Alexander of Macedonia, which I assume refers to Alexander the Great. The current building is obviously much more recent but was started about a thousand years ago, so has no doubt seen some life through the ages.

Generally speaking the older and more steeped in the past things are the more appeal they seem to have (with the exception of suspected Tbilisi sex workers), but Vardzia is such a strange place that associating it with recent history and the present, actually increases its curiosity value. Talumi stops and points to it across the river. At first I don't see but then I realise that the rocky hillside is completely pockmarked with caves. It was begun in the 12th century and developed into a huge complex on no less than 13 floors and it still has a functioning monastery today, as well as being a popular tourist site.

Stairways with safety rails have been built to cater for the needs of tourists but this doesn't lessen the impact of the place. When I come to an area cordoned off for the present day monks I descend into the cliff face down dimly lit passageways with handholds dug out of the rock on either side. When I eventually emerge I am by the church which, unlike the other caves, has been excavated to a significant height and with a smooth finish. I could be in any ancient orthodox church, not one that has been carved out of a solid lump of rock.

I cannot help but wonder how the Horseshoe Monastery in China would have compared if I had actually got to see it properly, instead of laboriously travelling there and staying for two nights only to not get round to entering what I had come to see. I also wonder where to go next. There are two border crossings into Turkey; one is just 20 km down the road from here but reports on the internet suggest that there is no public transport either side of it. Artur in the tourist office advised that I go to Batumi on the Black Sea coast from where it is easy to catch a bus through the more major busier border. It seems to be a choice between the sensible option and the more adventurous. I have discovered a third possibility on the internet, which is to not go through Turkey at all. There is a ferry that goes from Poti in Georgia right across the Black Sea to Bulgaria. I have e-mailed the company to ask what days it goes and what it costs but I think that this is very much a long shot.

More immediately, I keep thinking about the narrow gauge railway I was told about at the tourist office. I can't be this close to it and leave without having a ride and I resolve to go tomorrow, Artur talked of it as a day trip but I will stay overnight in Bakuriani. I no longer have time available to contemplate a side trip to Armenia and it now very much feels that I have broken the back of the journey and, having crossed the Caucasus, am literally as well as metaphorically on the downhill leg. I suspect that I've been deliberately dawdling through Georgia as a reflection of my ambivalence at reaching the end of the trip. It is a bit like reading a thrilling novel, where you want to get to the end but also don't want it to finish, as giving up the fictional characters can be like suffering a minor bereavement.

Chapter Sixteen: Seeing the Wood for the Trees

I replace the remains of yesterday's bread with a fresh loaf from the bakery to go with my cheese and garlic sausage, which looks as if it will last the whole week at the current rate of use. Half an hour's walk brings me to the station and the little train arrives. It is an overhead electric line and the pull-me-push-you engine is slowly pushing the two coaches up to the platform. The driver reverses his side mirrors for the trip back up the hill and the waiting passengers climb aboard. I seldom miss an opportunity to travel on a narrow gauge railway and they are all somehow idiosyncratic. This line was originally built in the 19th century when the Russian royalty took a shine to the area but the locomotive and rolling stock are modern. The width of the carriages seems to be quite ambitious and they roll from side to side on the narrow bogies as people move about.

We set off and quickly gain height above the road which stays by the river, as the track is benched into the hillside. The train is purposeful but unhurried and maintains what would probably be a good pace for a long distance runner. Soon we start to carve a way through mixed forest and then enter lush greenery before the landscape opens to reveal a little station. The line twists and turns to maintain a steady gradient, it is nothing like as dramatic as the Darjeeling Toy Train, but nevertheless a delightful journey and conducted at the right pace to fully appreciate it.

Striding out of the station I find that I am ahead of my fellow passengers but have no idea which way to go and pause to see what the majority view is. I am pleased that after a few minutes I see a building labelled as the Bus Station, as it is from here that I need to take my bearings. I am going to try one of the recommendations in the Lonely Planet guide. In the past I have deliberately avoided these, as they tended to attract young people only intent on meeting other foreign travellers, and who consequently completely avoided having any meaningful contact with the people of the country that they were ostensibly visiting. In recent years I think that the readership has become much broader although the books are still geared to the needs of the budget traveller, a category that describes me well.

Some are much better written than others and I do get irritated when I come across judgements that have probably been influenced by how the writer happened to be feeling that day, what the weather was like or perhaps where he or she enjoyed a romantic interlude. The best guidebook I have come across is the South American Handbook, the biblically thin pages of which are just crammed with useful information. Unfortunately it is of very limited value if you happen to not be in South America.

My final beef about the Lonely Planet books is the weight of them; they're like bricks, why on earth do they choose such heavy paper for something you need to carry around with you? But this is no longer a problem for a hi-tech person such as me. I may have brought the wrong SIM card for my phone so that now I can only use it as a camera, but the little computer I have with me works a treat. If I was even more technically savvy I could probably get it to display the words 'Don't Panic' in large friendly letters as, instead of getting a book, I have bought the Georgia chapter of the Lonely Planet guide that covers the region, as a download. Since I arrived in this country, and have had more choice over where to go rather than just covering huge distances to the west, it has been very useful and, after consulting it on the train, I need to go 800 metres to the west of the bus station to find the Edelweiss Guesthouse.

This is heaven; not only my own room but my own bathroom, and a little south facing balcony with a view of the hills, that still have patches of snow in sheltered north facing clefts. The place is clean and tidy, all the wallpaper is properly stuck to the walls, and there are solid wooden stairs and doors as befits a ski resort. The out-of-season price for full board is very reasonable and I ask them to put my slightly smelly bag of cheese and sausage in the fridge. Lunch is at two o'clock, which gives me half an hour, just time for a shower.

The water has got hot and I am about to step in when there is a knock at the door. The last time that I ignored a tap on my door because I was in the shower was at the hotel where I stayed in Turpan, and resulted in me losing my passport, as they then forgot to hand it to me and I forgot to ask for it. I will go into the bedroom and just pull on a pair of trousers, but as I emerge from the bathroom the girl is already in the room, but only fleetingly and I call out 'sorry' at her rapidly disappearing figure. But why am I apologising? I didn't invite her into my room. It is a kind of Male Original Sin that anything that could be remotely to do with impropriety is automatically by birth-right the fault of the man.

Back in the shower I realise that there is no soap and I resolve that straight after lunch I'll find a shop and buy a bar. The conveniently small piece that I had, got left in my wash bag on the train in Astrakhan and I have been relying on bits left in bathrooms since then. I dry myself on the little travel towel that I packed, really only for very occasional use and think that I should have found space for something more substantial. As I leave the room I see a pile of things on the landing obviously left for me by the maid. There are large towels, two little bars of soap, a toilet roll and sheets and I leave it all on my bed. After a rich vegetable soup, some spicy mince made into sausage shapes, mashed potato, salad, cheese and fruit I return to find only the towels where I had left them. Clearly once they were sure that I was safely out of the way in the dining room the girl had returned, made my bed and put the toiletries in the bathroom. I really do love this place.

I find a tourist information office in town and they sell me a map with detailed walks marked upon it. This means that I will have to stay another night and get into the hills tomorrow. I am running out of clean clothes again but there is no chance of finding a laundry here and, noticing that the balcony has a piece of cord strung across it, clearly for drying clothes I decide to make full use of my bathroom and do it myself. If Liz were here she would send me out to buy washing powder, but I think that one form of soap is pretty much the same as another and I don't want to acquire any more packing. Unfortunately there is no plug for the sink so I use my travel towel to block it as best I can and the little bar of soap lathers easily in what I imagine is soft mountain water. With the washing strung out, now it really feels like home.

The great thing about having meals provided is the chance to taste local dishes that I wouldn't know how to order in a restaurant. When I have finished my cheese dumplings I say that I will be staying a second night as I want to go for a walk tomorrow. The girl, who can speak some English offers to provide me with a packed lunch, but I don't want to be fobbed off with a few sandwiches and say that I can get back by two o'clock, but she then says that breakfast is at ten! That's ridiculous. She negotiates with the kitchen on my behalf and we agree breakfast at eight.

The map that I was sold is splendid, but the different coloured routes are so heavily marked that they obliterate any other detail. I manage to work out where I am and set off confidently on the yellow route as soon as I've finished breakfast.

After about an hour of climbing in bright sunshine I catch up with a couple of other walkers and hear the woman asking her partner in English for their water bottle. I make a comment about mad dogs and Englishmen and stop to talk with them. They are revisiting Georgia after having lived here some years ago. He tells me that he worked in the British Embassy and his wife for the British Council and that they had been in Georgia from 2001 to 2005, which was before and after the Rose Revolution. They say that they would never have encountered a foreign tourist in those days and are clearly very impressed with the progress that the country has made. I ask how they believe it has been achieved and am surprised at their reply: *"By levying taxes"*. They describe the country after independence but before 2003 as being lawless and run by gangs. The police and presumably other government employees as well, weren't paid but relied on their positions of power to extort money from whomever they could in order to feed their families. They told me that the roads were difficult to navigate and full of potholes and that it was a rare occurrence if the electricity, gas and water supplies were all working properly at the same time.

I was aware that after 2003, when Shevardnadze's government was forced to resign in what was dubbed the Rose Revolution, the country was run by Mikheil Saakashvili, who served his allotted maximum of ten years (two terms as in the USA) as president. He made huge progress, although remaining a controversial figure, and I had been puzzled at just how this had been achieved. If there had not been a proper system in place to collect taxes, then the implementation of one would explain how the new government was able to fund projects and move from a crime ridden society to a relatively peaceful one. Presumably not everyone is happy as those with money are now footing the bill.

My new companions tell me that the British Embassy, and I assume those of other governments, were concerned at some of the methods used by Saakashvili to curb the power of the criminal gangs. They say that proper legal procedures and respect for human rights were not always followed in the push to establish a society, which paradoxically was able to be more transparent and give greater weight to these very issues. I suggest that perhaps this is a case where the ends justify the means and, in the language of Sir Humphrey, the old diplomat indicates that on a personal level, seeing how the country has been transformed, he would not necessarily disagree with me.

In contrast with this meeting my next encounter, as I continue uphill and under a ski lift, is with two shepherds moving their flock further up. They come over and shake hands with me but I am unable to understand anything they say. They have a pair of large white dogs, but the sheep seem compliant and not bothered about me as I come through them from the opposite direction. A little further on I walk through what I take to be their home, although it has more the feel of a camp than a permanent residence, and I am eyed a little suspiciously by the women there.

I've now climbed over 500 metres and I can see a small village which is the lowest point on my route, nearly 700 metres down in a steep valley. What I can't see is how to get there. My track has petered out leaving an assortment of brown lines along the grass which I hopefully try to follow, but they are clearly animal tracks and lead nowhere. I try to lose height, regardless of direction, but the going is getting more and more difficult. I pass through a wooded area where I cling to the trees for support and pick up a stick to aid my balance, but I am beginning to think that I should have turned back.

The undergrowth becomes thicker as I bush whack my way through and my legs get stung and scratched, but the only option that I now have is to get to the bottom of the valley where I hope to find a path. There is a creek heading down and I remember a New Zealand hunter's adage to follow water to find a way out, but it is too steep. I am a little concerned that if I were to fall badly and break a leg it could be some time before anyone came near to here and my phone is only good for taking photographs. Eventually I reach the bottom and am relieved that there is no inaccessible gorge to negotiate, but neither is there any kind of path. But after a short while one emerges on the opposite bank, and I am saved. The sun is shining, the stream sparkles and life is good again.

When I reach the village it is like stepping into a bygone age. The wooden houses are spread out amongst roads of packed down earth and each has an assortment of animals; a few cattle, a couple of pigs and a collection of hens. I suspect that they are largely self-sufficient and rely on horses for transport. In fact walking the few kilometres back up to Bakuriani exactly half the traffic I see is equine, although it could be argued that two horses (one ridden and one being led), one car and a van, does not amount to a statistically significant figure. I have been aware of the time and I get back to the guesthouse at two minutes to two, more than ready for lunch.

The bucolic charm of Georgia is a delicious antidote to the intensity of living in China. When we left Tianjin Liz and I actually travelled together for once. I waited at the railway station for her having found that the 868 bus would get me there, although catching one was surprisingly difficult. The first I saw didn't even come into the inside lane as I waited at the stop. Another came soon after but the driver ignored my waves and I double checked that I was in the right place. When I spotted the third 868 I stepped out in front of it and flagged it down. The few others who had managed to get the bus to stop alighted soon after and the driver asked me where I was going. When I told him he lit a cigarette, put his foot down and didn't as much as glance at another bus stop until we reached the terminus.

Newly built Tianjin West Railway Station is magnificent. In the upstairs waiting room the vaulted roof stretches the length of several train carriages and is illuminated at both ends by huge multi paned arched windows reminiscent of Saint Pancras. It is curious that China is using railway stations to express its national prestige in the same way that Industrial Revolution Britain did, and even adding retro touches of Victorian England. This is a modern cathedral of concrete and glass, celebrating progress, whilst at the same time displaying a solidity and permanence not usually associated with modern structures, particularly those built in China.

Liz arrived by taxi and we boarded the express to Beijing. 'Express' means the slow train and she only reluctantly agreed to the hour and a half journey after I had pointed out that the 30 minute bullet train arrived at Beijing many miles from the city centre. As always seems to be the case, there were others in our seats but the group of aging labourers rearranged themselves and proceeded to ask where we come from and how old I am, as they eyed my grey hair. Liz now sees normal life in China as being abnormal and insisted that I take a picture of her sitting with the other hard seat passengers, while she worked on her laptop. She thought that her colleagues would find it amusing that she was on an ordinary train amongst ordinary people. I coped with the embarrassment of this with thoughts of how young Chinese use their cell phones on trains and buses to sneak a snapshot of the oddity of a foreigner.

Beijing was busy and the hotel we were in was the size of the town where we live in New Zealand. I wasn't too sure if all the shops and restaurants were really a part of it, or if the hotel actually only occupied a relatively small part of the building it was in. One of my tasks when travelling with Liz is to identify places to eat while I wander the streets. On our first visit to China we would eat in the scruffy little basic places and usually enjoyed the Northern Chinese cuisine. We were advised not to choose eateries too close to the hospital next to where we worked, as these could be frequented by patients with all manner of diseases, and wherever we went we carried our own chopsticks as a hygienic precaution. But Liz now demands more up-market establishments which are harder to find. We could have eaten in one of the hotel restaurants but I thought I would see what else was available as I wanted to have a look around the area. As everywhere in China the streets were full of food being cooked and I identified one establishment which I felt had the right ambience for what I knew Liz would want. I then put my glasses on to see what kind of food they served and realised that it was just another hairdressing salon. We ate in the hotel.

I made a note of a dozen bus numbers from the stop over the road in the hope that it could help me to find my way back from wherever I got to. I wasn't really sure what I wanted to do in Beijing, but I certainly needed to find my way to Tiananmen Square. We were there the last week-end of May in 1989 a week after martial law had been declared in Beijing, in an attempt to contain the student led demonstrations. We had travelled from Shenyang where we were teaching English in a medical university, to see what all the fuss was about. The huge square was by no means crammed with students but was dotted with small encampments waving banners and flying flags. I remember being disappointed that the good natured demonstration was fizzling out, as crocodiles of students were led to the railway station for free rides home. Despite martial law having been declared the atmosphere was calm with no suggestion of violence and, although some people spoke passionately, the atmosphere was more that of a holiday.

The first bus I caught from the hotel started off in the right direction but then turned north and I needed to head south. I then found a bus that brought me close to the centre, but what looked like just a couple of blocks on the map turned out to be a half hour walk as the scale of the city is just so big. I saw a 104 bus going in the opposite direction before I got off, which was one of the numbers I noted on the stop by the hotel. When I reached Tiananmen Square I found barriers all around so that I couldn't cross the road and get into the Square proper. There had to be a way to get there but I couldn't work it out and I ended up back where I had been 20 minutes earlier. There was an entry to the underground and I could see another over the road but ticket barriers were in between. I could have caught a train, come back to the same station and taken a different exit but, apart from that being silly, I wasn't sure if being over the road would give me access to the Square anyway.

I could see across to where in 1989 we sat with a group of young people and talked about the changes they wanted to happen. They spoke about corruption but acknowledged that that had been an ingrained part of the system for millennia in China. They wanted political change but were unclear what this would be. Although international media dubbed the protests a pro-democracy movement, the protesters were aware that among the rural Chinese, who represented 80% of the population, the government was very popular and that 'one person one vote' was not likely to advance their cause.

Paradoxically it was the opening up of China that was causing feelings of resentment. Students in particular saw that people who were not necessarily well educated were beginning to make money. In the freer economy there was a perception that market traders were getting rich just by selling jeans, and they worried that they were going to miss out. It is a sad reflection of human nature that material concerns seem to motivate people more than issues of principle and ideology. Of course any large demonstration incorporates people representing a variety of views and beliefs, and some of the demonstrators were passionate about wanting more openness and freedom to do what they were actually doing at the time; expressing their own views. I have no doubt that many of those young students were driven by a conviction that they were demonstrating for a worthy cause. Regardless of what they wanted, they certainly didn't deserve what they got.

I finally arrived. There were not many people in the Square, probably because of the maze one has to negotiate to get here. The last piece of the puzzle involved an underground pedestrian crossing which came up to a police manned security check with the obligatory x-ray machine. What are they trying to protect in an open space? Are they frightened people may smuggle in their sleeping bags and set up camp again? I think that must be it; Tiananmen Square is such a focal point that the authorities want to guard against it ever being used again as a meeting place for dissenters. The centre of China's capital city is now linked throughout the world with the awful events it witnessed on 4th June 1989 and this, sealing it off as a security area full of police and army, only goes to perpetuate that association. To be fair none of it was at all aggressive. The soldiers all looked to be in their teens and carried cell phones on their belts instead of guns and the little electric police vehicles, with big wheels and no doors, looked so much as if they belonged in toy town that it was difficult to view their occupants as any kind of threat.

It was exactly a week after our visit in 1989 that news started to dribble through that the fun and excitement had turned horribly wrong. The information came by word of mouth and short wave radio; BBC World Service and Voice of America, and the Chinese we knew were totally stunned. The army was loved; toddlers were dressed in miniature uniforms, the news that the People's Army had turned its guns on the people was impossible. At first even the most sophisticated of those we knew just couldn't believe it and only accepted what had happened when undeniable eye witness reports began to be circulated. People were in shock and turmoil.

All our students had been sent home and no one knew what might happen next. There was a real fear that the country could revert to something like the Cultural Revolution, which was still very clear in the memories of anyone over 30, and people we were friendly with apologised that they were worried about being seen with us, as foreign influence was being blamed for the demonstrations. Crowds took to the streets with no idea of what they wanted to do or see but not wanting to miss anything. On one occasion we joined the masses in the city centre of Shenyang, but when we were spotted a space opened up all around us and moved with us like a spotlight as, with nothing else to see, we became the focus of attention. We still get stared at in China but in those days we were regarded the same as if we were little green men who had just arrived from Mars. The crowd was looking for some action and, feeling extremely uncomfortable and unsure what might happen next, we made our way as quickly as we could back to our bikes and escaped.

So there I was; back in the one spot where I saw world history in the making. I felt, quite illogically, that this gave me some kind of ownership of the place, but the Square is now dull and sterile and I had no wish to linger. On that previous occasion the Forbidden City was forbidden, closed to the public to discourage tourists like us from visiting Tiananmen. I had walked too far and my legs were too tired to do it justice but I could wander through part of its vastness on my way to find the 104 bus.

Beijing is not an easy city to navigate ones way around and I was feeling pretty pleased with myself as I boarded the bus, for working out that it would take me back to the hotel. That is until everyone got off miles short and the driver turned the engine off. Another 104 arrived, so clearly the first one only completed part of the route for some reason and this one would take me to where I wanted to go. We started off well enough but just as I began to relax we seemed to be turning further away and, checking the compass, I found we were travelling in the opposite direction. Then I spotted another 104 travelling on a completely different road. We then seemed to be heading back to the centre and some things looked strangely familiar. I got off and found myself exactly back to where I got on. I didn't want another 104 and walked north until I found a different bus route on my list. Eventually I arrived back at the hotel stop aboard an 837, with a 104 just ahead.

Really there is no choice where to go next in Georgia. Unsurprisingly I have not heard back from the shipping company and I never thought that it would be a realistic option anyway. And I am not going to ignore an interesting border crossing on my doorstep in favour of relatively dull marshtruka rides. I am actually quite looking forward to hitchhiking; it will remind me of my youth. The first step is to get back to Borjomi. If I catch the train I won't be there until the afternoon with a long way still to go, so I am at the bus station to get the nine o'clock, which either left early or doesn't exist. When I do get a marshtruka it completes the journey in half an hour, five times quicker than the train, and the slow pace that I enjoyed coming up I would have found frustrating with an unpredictable day's journey ahead of me.

I only have a short wait by the side of the road before a bus to Akhaltsikhe arrives and it terminates at the bus station with large signs advertising Ozlem Ardahan bus company routes to Turkey. I enquire inside and it becomes apparent that, as indicated on the internet, if these buses ever existed they certainly no longer do. I walk along the road towards the border until I am clear of buildings and choose a spot to hitchhike. The very first car stops.

Osman tells me that he is an architect specialising in restoring churches and is on his way to a local monastery. Like many Georgians he is deeply religious and tells me that I am his guest and that he will treat me like Christ. I hope that we can gloss over the crucifixion bit. He wants to take me to my destination but relents when I get through that it is in the next country. Osman's English is not very good but he is an intelligent man and wants to communicate. I am surprised that he is both passionate about his country and ambivalent about independence, although I suppose that the early years were far from good. But he has no ambivalence about Saakashvili who he describes as a sadist and a maniac. I rather mischievously ask him his opinion of Stalin. He hedges and says that it is difficult to judge the man 60 years after his death. As he has just compared Mikheil Saakashvili to the Roman Emperor Caligula, I find this a poor excuse, and he eventually makes a clear statement that Stalin, unlike

Georgia's recent president, was not a sadist. I think that the whole beautiful country is in denial about its most famous son; Uncle Joe certainly has no place amongst the Georgians that I have had the pleasure to meet on my travels.

Part 5:

Chapter Seventeen: Arcadia

I get through the border from Georgia to Turkey with ease and find myself, well, nowhere. I am just on a country lane beyond a closed barrier which opens with surprising infrequency to release the odd vehicle. I did see a line of trucks on the Georgian side so I will just have to wait until they filter through and hope that one will pick me up. There is a group of men in a field next to me who seem to have set up some kind of camp and one of them asks me in good English if I would like to join them for a cup of tea. I'm a fairly trusting person but I am always a bit wary of people hanging around international borders as it is a time when travellers are most susceptible, before they get a feel for the country they are entering, but nothing is happening where I am and I sit on a plastic stool and accept tea in a small curved glass of a type found throughout Turkey.

I tell them that I am heading for Ardahan, which I believe is the first town where I can get back onto public transport, and they say that they will help me get a lift. They start handing around large chunks of bread with some filling and I suspect that I will be offered one soon. This could lead to me being asked for an exorbitant sum of money or else to my feeling indebted to them, and I am not keen on either of these outcomes. Fortunately the Edelweiss Guesthouse returned my sausage and cheese which I quickly produce to pre-empt the situation. The Borjomi bread is well past its best but I am pleased with myself for averting an awkward moment. I am about to return to the roadside to thumb a lift when I get called at to come. One of the men has stopped a smart Mercedes minibus with a group of Georgians going to Cappadocia. I check what this is going to cost but it seems that they are willing to take me to Ardahan and I gratefully clamber aboard.

There is no dramatic change in crossing the border, which is hardly a surprise as this part of Turkey has had periods when it formed part of the

Kingdom of Georgia, and at other times, back on the other side in Georgia, the region was under Ottoman rule for much of its history. It is probably more unusual that the area is now divided between the two countries, although the terrain is rugged enough to form a natural frontier. We continue to climb and reach patches of icy snow where there are spectacular views across the hills and when I reach Ardahan it does feel like a new country. To go west from Europe to Asia should be wrong but the layout of this little market town, packed with individual grocers' and tin ware shops and with men dressed in old fashioned jackets and hats, does feel more oriental. Most of all there is the change in religion, which I am acutely aware of as I find a basic hotel room next to the Mosque, with its electronic blasts calling the faithful to prayer through day and night- or at least when I expected to be asleep.

Ardahan is certainly a whole world away from the enormous teeming cities of lowland China, but on my return from Beijing I did finally manage to arrange to visit a smaller place. With a bit of a sense of adventure I got off the train at Qufu West, which is a new station on a high speed line. These tracks for superfast trains are built in mainly elevated sections with long straights and smooth curves, easing a route through the country regardless of where the towns are situated. Consequently they take passengers very quickly to nowhere. New stations have been built several miles away from the towns that they are meant to serve, and I was relieved to see a bus which I assumed would make the journey into Qufu town.

When I saw what I took to be the Ming Dynasty walls I was tempted to get off, but the bus was still full and if it terminated in the centre of town that would be more convenient. But then we seemed to be heading away from the centre and I could see a long, straight and not very interesting road ahead. When I looked around I found that most people had actually got off and I cut my losses at the next stop. I sometimes enjoy the uncertainty of arriving in a new place with nothing booked and seeing what turns up, but I have learnt that in China hotels booked in advance on the internet are much cheaper than any rate that can be negotiated by coming in off the street, and also many hotels are not allowed to take foreigners. I was booked into the one star Huangchang Hotel at a very good price. As long as it is reasonably clean I'm not too fussy where I lay my head and I was sure that it would be an interesting contrast to the up-market, but large and impersonal hotels I stay at with Liz.

Unfortunately no one in town had ever heard of it. I got a taxi to take me to the address and the woman driver pointed to a derelict site. She asked around but with no success but then I remembered that the website, ctrip, had sent me a confirming text message with a telephone number for the hotel. I felt that this was not the best time to play at trying to speak Mandarin so I dialled the number and handed the phone to the driver, who then drove one handed while following spoken directions. We arrived in a side street just inside the city walls and not very far from where we had started. Taxi drivers don't expect a tip but she had gone beyond the normal call of duty and the meter hadn't even reached the miserable 5 Yuan flag fall, so I gave her a larger note which I think she appreciated. The small hotel was undergoing renovations but was adequate for my needs and I dumped my bag and set off to explore.

I chose to come to Qufu because it appeared to be a smaller place about half way between Beijing and Nanjing. After I had bought the train tickets I looked it up and found to my dismay that it is a major tourist destination as it is the home town of Confucius. The Confucius Temple as it is known (although the man himself was secular and had no special interest in religion) covers 12,000 square metres and occupies the whole of the middle of the town. It is surrounded by a wall which it takes a good half hour to circumnavigate, so the actual city centre is a hollow square squeezed between the Kong family temple and the town walls, which are remarkably intact. The Confucian mansion is still lived in by the descendants of the great man but was not built until the middle of the Ming Dynasty, 2,000 years after Confucius died.

I liked Qufu. The size of it seemed to me to be on a more human scale than the vast Chinese cities. Although it is an important tourist destination

I appeared to be the only foreigner in town and consequently I was a point of interest to small children and old men riding around on tricycles. They proceeded at a steady walking pace and twisted their heads like sunflowers tracking the sun on a bright summer's day to get the full measure of me. Tricycles in various forms are the preferred transport in Qufu, both pedal powered for the old men and electric for business use. They usually come with a pick-up style body attached and carry all the goods to and from the shops. The modern family has a scooter type of tricycle, with smaller wheels and streamlined fairings, but still with the same luggage carrying capacity, which is used by young mothers to convey their children to school. Looking at the bustling activity along the lines of little shops hunched under overhanging roofs selling only the basic necessities of life, it was easy to imagine that, apart from the tricycles, the scene could have been very similar in the time of Confucius.

Having explored the entire town centre at least twice it was time to venture a little further afield so I hopped onto a bus to see where it would take me. At first I took little notice of a man of about 40 who was cleaning a wooden bracelet with an old toothbrush, but he engaged me in conversation and actually had very good English. When the bus terminated I found that Ricky, as he introduced himself was a kindred spirit. It was the first time that I had met anyone doing the same as myself; catching a bus simply to see where it would go. We had arrived on a newly built but deserted four-lane highway, which is the way in which Chinese towns and cities expand. They first put in the entire infrastructure, including avenues of fully grown trees which have to be supported with wooden structures until they take root in their new environment, and then wait for developers to move in. No doubt this will become an urban area before very long with tower blocks of apartments and shops or else an industrial park of factories and warehouses.

There were some fields and I wondered if I might find a country road to explore, but Ricky was unimpressed with the area and he resolved to catch the next bus back. I quickly weighed up my options and decided that the opportunity to spend some time with an intelligent Chinaman with such a good command of English was too good to miss and so we headed back towards town to see what was at the other end of the bus line.

There were some very big fields of maize growing which looked to me like highly organised large scale farming but Ricky thought it was a collaboration of individuals rather than big business. A bit like a commune I suggested, tongue in cheek. China has worked for centuries on the principle that it has such huge reserves of cheap labour that, what would be cost efficient ways of doing things in other parts of the world, are at best unnecessary and could actually lead to social unrest by creating too many idle hands.

This attitude extends to the cities where everywhere people are given jobs that involve doing nothing. The most obvious are security guards. They don't just protect banks and civic buildings but loiter around ordinary blocks of flats in their officious dark blue uniforms. There are very few jobs in China that don't entail wearing some kind of uniform, as appearance is always more important than substance. Any shop, other than an individual enterprise, whether it is a bakery, a chemist's or a hairdressing salon will have its own livery. Sensibly street cleaners wear bright orange overalls and their numbers swell in the autumn to cope with the great leaf harvest. Many cities, including Nanjing, have an abundance of trees which give some relief from the summer heat, and when the leaves fall it provides a bonanza of employment opportunities. Not one is allowed to remain on any road or pavement as they are gathered up and sent I know not where. Maybe they are strewn over a wooded area but it is as likely that they are put in landfill or even incinerated.

The reliance on manual labour makes rural China a trip back in time as modern labour-saving farming methods are eschewed, but the migration to the cities must have left the countryside denuded of able bodies and Ricky told me that the government is now trying to encourage people to stay in rural areas. Freedom of movement through the country is not a right in any case and permits to live in certain cities are highly valued but, in what strikes me as being quite patronising, Ricky told me that country folk are given trade-ins on their old televisions, whether working or not, for fancy flat screen models as long as they remain on the land. I'm not convinced that he was right about this as it is the kind of myth that spreads easily amongst city dwellers, but if it is true then at least it seems that the government is trying to use a carrot instead of a stick, and exerting control through some form of consensus rather than force.

In the past movements of the population have been controlled by what is known as the Hukou System. The identity of each individual is described by where they belong geographically and specifically whether they are urban or rural. This distinction has literally meant the difference between life and death as millions of land workers died of famine in the Great Leap Forwards while city dwellers, effectively an elite class, were given enough food to at least keep them alive. This system still exists in theory but its enforcement has been relaxed in order to supply the factories with the labour they need.

As ever in China the scale of things is mind boggling with an estimated 260 million people working away from where they should be and having the status of illegal immigrants. This means that they don't enjoy the same rights as bone-fide citizens, such as health care and education. As their children do not have access to local schools where their parents live, they are often sent back to the family village to attend school and stay with their grandparents. This I suppose is why I seem to be two or three times the age of most Chinese as I wander around the major cities; the old and the young are in the villages, but it must also put more pressure on those left to work the land, and I suspect that there will soon be an agrarian revolution in China with the introduction of modern farming methods and machinery.

Confucius is the most popular historical figure in China Ricky told me. We were sitting outside the entrance to his temple; both too mean to buy a ticket to go in. Most visitors are in groups, probably on works outings, as the Work Group in China, though not as all-encompassing as it was when we belonged to one in 1989, is still a very paternalistic organisation and provides for the social as well as the physical needs of its members. Many tourist attractions in China are quite expensive and certainly beyond the means of a typical citizen, but they exist almost exclusively for a domestic market and are frequented by coachloads of workers being given a day out.

Not only is the complex of buildings called a temple but Confucius himself is translated into English as a saint. I thought he was an atheist! Ricky suggested that people need to have something to believe in and while organised religion was discouraged in communist China, Confucianism was an acceptable alternative. So an aura of religious fervour has been created around a purely secular historical figure to help people cope with their need for some kind of creed without the bother of a God figure. I think that this is an interesting lesson in understanding a Chinese way of addressing a problem. As long as you get the packaging right the substance doesn't really matter. Appearance is everything.

The family, which long after Confucius died became hugely rich and important on the strength of its association with the great man, is referred to as Dukes of Yansheng. How well would that of gone down in the Cultural Revolution? Ricky was unsure but felt that the monuments may not have fared too badly as, despite all the trappings, it is not actually a religious site. That the family is still alive and well is an achievement in itself after 2,500 years. And it is not just the descendants of Confucius who are still alive. Talking to Ricky I began to realise how important he still is to the whole Chinese way of life and thinking. My understanding of him as someone who promoted social order and obeying the rules is only half the picture. The other part is that he saw this as an individual responsibility which doesn't need to be imposed from above. His teaching on living in harmony and knowing ones place would be music to the ears of any government, and if the Chinese Communist Party decided to go easy on Confucius that may have been a very wise decision.

Perhaps it is the recognition of peoples' need to have some person or object that can be revered that has allowed Mao to remain such a respected figurehead with his distinctive features still appearing everywhere, including on every Chinese bank note. In contrast, the leadership in recent years has merged into a grey background of business suits, and the Communist Party seems determined to never again be ruled by an out of control cult figure. Mao now performs a similar function to that of the British Royal Family in the UK as a convenient symbol of the country; but being well and truly dead he has even less power than they do.

Ricky told me that the leadership is elected every five years and (the same as the President of the United States) can only serve two terms, which effectively means that there is a complete change every ten years. This should ensure that any dictatorship is conducted by the Party and not an individual, although it appears that Xi Jinping is being allowed to act in a more presidential and less purely businesslike manner, as for example when he is photographed coming down the steps of a plane with his wife. It may just be that he is a more personable character than his predecessors, or perhaps Mao Zedong is now sufficiently confined to history that the Party feels it can relax a little in its vigilance to ensure that no individual hi-jacks the whole show. Even 40 years after his death Mao needs to be handled with the care afforded to a dangerous object, as he is used as a convenient figurehead, but no one wants his history to repeat itself.

The communist government allows the major religions to function in the country, but doesn't grant freedom to those wanting to participate in what it views as cults. The most well known of these is Falun Gong, who I have met peaceably campaigning in Wellington city centre, but there are more extreme sects whom it seems have preyed on the susceptibility of simple country folk wanting something to believe in. Throughout the world religion causes conflict, or at least is used as an excuse for it, and the Communist Party will not have forgotten China's own history. The Taiping Rebellion, which was centred on Nanjing, was led by a charismatic (and presumably schizophrenic) religious fanatic who claimed to be the brother of Jesus Christ. He established a Heavenly Kingdom in the middle of the 19th century which lasted for 14 years before finally being put down with the help of foreign powers, most notably Britain and France, and with a greater loss of life, mostly civilian, than was sustained in the whole of the First World War.

The Taiping Rebellion is officially presented as having been a justifiable uprising against a cruel and corrupt dynastic regime and it is viewed as the precursor to the eventual fall of the Qing and the creation of the Republic. There are streets named after it and a museum in Nanjing dedicated to it, which is the only one I have visited that has been in continuous operation since before the Cultural Revolution. But the Communist Party in China is now the establishment, not the revolutionaries, and it is understandably wary of out of control religious cults.

On 28th May 2014 an innocent woman was bludgeoned to death in a McDonald's restaurant in Shandong Province. The perpetrators were reported as not looking like a gang of thugs; one was a father with three of his children. They belonged to an illegal group the name of which is translated as the Church of Almighty God and is also known as Eastern Lightning. The doomsday nonsense they spout is unimportant but they claim to have several million followers, and it seems that this group of cult members randomly decided that their victim was a 'demon'.

In most branches of McDonald's around the world the killers would have been swiftly overpowered by the much larger group of customers before they caused too much harm. But this was China. The lack of responsibility that the average citizen feels for their unknown neighbour, and the fear of confrontation in Chinese society, conspired to allow the tragedy to happen. Instead of intervening, the crowd watched. Chillingly one of the spectators recorded the whole episode on his phone and posted it on the internet. Without that technology the incident would probably have been quickly forgotten by most people, but hearing the woman's screams before she ended up lying dead in a pool of blood, as others quietly stood and watched, finally sparked an angry response from 'netizens'. They in turn were dubbed as 'keyboard heroes', with the inference that it is easy to be brave when your safely behind a computer screen.

Strangely to my mind the discussion in the media was about whether an individual in that situation should put themselves at risk by taking some form of action. In the world that I come from I would expect the onlookers to use their greater numbers to act together, but in China no one seemed to consider this as a possibility. That the issue was raised at all suggests that other ways of thinking and behaving are permeating Chinese culture, which is inevitable as it forges stronger links with the rest of the world, and will no doubt bring positive and negative changes. This was very much an isolated incident in what, considering the huge urban areas, is a remarkably safe country with very little violent crime. The avoidance of confrontation which is deeply ingrained into the culture is, at least in part due to the overriding need to safe 'face'. If there is a falling out between people inevitably one will come off the loser, which is no fun in any culture, but catastrophic to the Chinese, and with the stakes so high individuals are brought up to bear all manner of small injustices philosophically.

It sometimes seems that all Chinese people think and say the same thing, maybe as a result of being fed propaganda, and perhaps the Confucian principal of respecting authority makes the populace very open to suggestion. It was therefore refreshing to talk to Ricky who had the ability to take a broader and more objective view of his country and its customs. Sitting on a park bench in the shade of an ancient tree we watched the crowds paying obeisance to a man who lived several hundreds of years before Christ. I marvelled that they were clearly so fervent in their devotion and not just idle tourists, albeit to a man who didn't even believe in a god, let alone claim divinity or Sainthood for himself.

Ricky suggested that Socialism had been presented as a belief system to replace religion, but that one result of the economic reforms has been a change in philosophy to one based largely upon the pursuit of wealth. Consequently this has left many with a kind of existentialist void, which has fed into a revival in religious belief including Confucianism. I left Qufu feeling that I had perhaps inched a little closer to understanding China.

I somehow feel resentment towards Turkey. Before I even left home I had thought that the most interesting part of the whole journey would be travelling through the Caucasus, and I have particularly liked my time in Georgia. Turkey now seems an anti-climax as the final stretch through to Bulgaria, and this is perhaps why I have left little time to traverse the country. I have formed a plan to take the morning bus to Erzurum, which is on the rail line and from where I can catch an overnight train to Ankara. The line should go through to Istanbul, but due to extensive upgrades taking place on the rail system this section is currently non-operational, so I will have to use the bus again from there. Liz flies to Bulgaria next Saturday and I have told her that I will be there no later than Monday.

Turkey has always had a bit of a bad press in our culture and maybe this has also had a subconscious influence on me. I am surprised to read that the Seljuk Turks actually originated in the Kazakh steppe, to the north of the Caspian and Aral seas, the region that I travelled through a fortnight or so ago. In the 10th century a group moved into Persia where they took control, and then spread west to modern day Turkey. Here they set up the Sultanate of Rum, that being the Arabic for Rome, as this land had been the centre of the Byzantine Empire. The Seljuk Turks had converted to be Sunni Moslems and became the focus of the Christian Crusades, which is probably where the negative connotations started. Constantinople, the capital of Byzantium and the last remnant of the Roman Empire, held out until 1453 when it finally succumbed to the Ottoman Turks and became Istanbul, 1,000 years after Rome itself had declined and fallen.

The Ottoman Empire was a very real threat to European countries and that no doubt reinforced the prejudice against the Turks. The collapse of the Ottoman Empire was both a cause and an effect of the First World War, which put Turkey on the opposing side. In New Zealand (and Australia) the most significant and sensitive battle of the Great War was not in Flanders but Gallipoli. The flawed plan of Winston Churchill, who was First Lord of the Admiralty, to seize control of the Dardanelles resulted in the wholesale slaughter of ANZAC troops by Turkish forces and is now remembered as the antipodean Poppy Day. It would be hard to overestimate the historical importance of that campaign: for the majority of New Zealanders it contributed to the formation of a national identity beyond being an extension of Britain. On the other side, the Turkish military commander, Mustafa Kermal, became a war hero and later, as Ataturk, the founder of the modern state of Turkey.

The bus I board in Ardahan is a rustic model which would be better if it was a bit longer, to accommodate the number of seats it has, and my knees are hard against the seat in front. But the countryside is lovely; hills of rolling grassland give way to forests of pine stretching as far as the eye can see, and now we are in a valley alongside a white water stream. Wherever there is a flat piece of land it is being farmed in a traditional manner with hand tools. Grass is being cut by scythe and turned by rake before being piled into hay ricks. The road surface improves and we are bowling along amidst a mountain landscape of jagged peaks in sombre shades of brown and purple. I take back all that I said about Turkey; this scenery is as good as anywhere I've been.

Attractive countryside is much more to me than a pretty picture. Travelling in China I was constantly striving to get to and feel a part of the rural landscape, and this appears to be a major driving force in my travels. It is like a quest, but to find what? Perhaps some remnant of a childhood image of perfection, maybe a storybook picture of a rural idyll, or glimpses of sunny harvest days from the rear window of an Austin 7 or Jowett Javelin. Whatever its provenance it is a deep-seated desire to travel back to an imaginary Arcadia, and maybe a simpler, if not gentler age.

Chapter Eighteen: Heart and Soul

My pace of travel requires greater urgency than I have given it the last couple of weeks, and this is exciting in a way; that I have to keep moving towards my destination with no time to loiter gives more of a sense of purpose to the journey. I am not good at languages and usually manage to learn 'hello', 'please' and 'thank you' when I get to a new country. But now I am so intent on the journey that the words I have had to acquire are Otagar (bus station), istasyon (train station) and otel. At Erzurum I find a minibus said to be going to the centre but it is full to the point of people standing, or rather crouching, in the back. I let it go. I stand by a bus stop for a couple of minutes, but I am pretty sure that I am to the west of the centre so I start to walk east. According to the guide I consulted, Erzurum is an ancient town and has quite a lot of interest, and I spy what looks like a cheap hotel, but first I have to find the istasyon.

It is a good walk from the otagar but the weather is fine. As Erzurum is at an altitude higher than the top of the Tararuas, our local mountains in New Zealand, and they easily outstrip Ben Nevis, it can be horrendously cold in winter. The railway station is fairly centrally located and is a fine building of brick and stone. Having become accustomed to Chinese railways it is strange to find this station bereft of people and the man in the ticket window watches as I approach. I explain my needs which he double checks and we discuss what class of sleeper I require. I am reaching for my money by the time he gets around to looking at his computer and tells me that tomorrows train is full. So where else can I catch a train to? Nowhere; this whole edifice exists to service the needs of one miserable train a day in each direction. The only ticket I can buy is for the following day. Reluctantly I trudge back to the Otogar. I had been looking forward to getting back on the rails and a sleeper train would have taken me most of the way across the breadth of Turkey. Now it will all have to be on buses. I buy a ticket to Erzincan to get me a bit further on my way.

Erzincan is meant to be a town of well over a quarter of a million people, but from the otogar there is no sign of any of it. Before I look for the town I first need to get my next ticket to take me further west. The ridiculous system in Turkey has upward of a dozen different companies operating out of the bus station, each with their own buses running at different times and with no central ticket office. I enquire at the first one for Istanbul and they are keen to sell me a ticket for a bus just about to leave, but I have not forgotten my lesson from Mineralnye Vody and I realise that it is the bus that I have just got off. It is another 20 hours to Istanbul, which I could happily cope with on a train, but not a bus. I try to establish what time tomorrow I could go to Ankara- they all seem to either leave or arrive in the middle of the night and I abandon the idea of getting a ticket for the next part of the journey tonight. I really need to find internet access and devise a new plan.

In China my plan was to build on the partial success I had had in Qufu, of getting closer to what I felt to be the essence of the country. Liz was due to go to the earthly paradise of Hangzhou, which sent me to studying the train timetables. Hangzhou was the capital of China for about 150 years in the 12th and 13th centuries and greatly impressed Marco Polo when he visited. It is said to have had a population of a million and been the biggest city in the world at that time. I made the same claim for Angkor for a similar period when travelling through Cambodia, which was supported by research, so I need to check my facts: according to Wikipedia Hangzhou was the world's largest city for just a few decades, while Rome had a population of a million citizens more than a thousand years earlier, so it was perhaps not so remarkable.

The Nanjing City Museum claims that "The strategic status of Nanjing was just the same as Rome of western civilization". Hangzhou can't compete with Nanjing for past importance as our home city has been the capital of China during the reigns of six different dynasties. It acquired its present name, which means south capital (as opposed to Beijing in the north), when the Ming Dynasty established their capital in the 14th century and built the longest city wall in the world, most of which is still intact. With the fall of the Qing Dynasty in 1911 Nanjing was again the capital city and, apart from a few years when the government moved to Sichuan Province because of Japanese occupation, it remained so until the communist takeover in 1949.

There was a new high speed line being built to connect Nanjing and Hangzhou, both huge cities in the vast Yangtze delta, but until it was finished the bullet trains did a zigzag course via Shanghai. Studying the timetables I realised that there was an alternative; a different route of old line which kept west of the enormous Taihu, which is a very large lake believed to have been formed by a meteor impact more than 70 million years ago, which accounts for its distinctive round shape. As always in China the scale is breathtaking. Taihu has an area of 2,250 square kilometres as opposed to Windermere, the largest lake in England, which covers a pathetic 14.7 Km Sq. This rail line is a similar distance but takes twice as long as the superfast alternative and I thought that I could leave the day before Liz and find a smaller place to stay overnight.

About half way is Xuancheng, a town that even our Chinese friends hadn't heard of, which I found encouraging. Annoyingly nothing quite fitted; the trains either left too early or arrived too late, and the hotels I could find online were a bit more expensive than I really wanted to pay. I considered just stopping off and having a look around and then carrying on to Hangzhou for the night, but again the train times were such that I would only have had a little over an hour to explore. By the time I got anywhere I would have to go back to the station. The Google map showed several hotels marked in Xuancheng which I couldn't find mention of on the internet, and which I assumed to be smaller and cheaper establishments. I couldn't get there until nearly 6 pm and would have preferred to have arrived earlier with no hotel booked but, while I like the satisfaction of planning a trip and then seeing it appear in reality, there is also a little bit of a thrill to not knowing where one will end up. I bought a ticket for K101 which would have left Beijing the night before and have travelled over 1350 km when I alighted at Xuancheng.

That K101 had travelled all night looked all too obvious. I pushed past the usual bevy of smokers in the entrance to my carriage and negotiated the assortment of luggage, which appeared more like piles of refuse. Evicting a middle aged woman from my seat I was disappointed that it was in the middle of three, but my Chinese did not extend to asking for a window seat. The youth next to me constantly jiggled his knee, presumably from some nervous affliction rather than a desire to be irritating, while the plastic coated girls opposite ate anaemic chips from Kentucky Fried Chicken bags. Both window seats in our group were occupied by middle-aged women who, I imagined, were the type who find their way to the front of any queue. The train itself seemed tired and sluggish as we pulled out of Nanjing; this felt like it could be a long journey.

But I gradually adjusted to the leisurely pace of K101 and its occupants, as dull city buildings gave way to a watery landscape dotted with whitewashed villages and decorated with splashes of bright yellow oil-seed rape. A Chinese railway carriage is a community which develops its own individual character as the journey progresses. This one was relatively quiet as many of the passengers slept but there was a constant movement of people to the hot tap at the end of the carriage where cardboard tubs of instant dried noodles were revitalised. Uniformed staff pushing metal carts of food which had started off hot, fruit and snacks such as sunflower seeds and vacuum packed chickens' feet, a local delicacy, made regular trips through the chaos. Trains do have a dining car but this seems primarily for the use of the crew and, as a typical train has 16-18 carriages with over 100 seats in the majority of them, plus an allotted number of so many hundred standing passengers, navigating laden trolleys through the throng is the only practicable option of ensuring that there is always food available, which there seems to be absolutely everywhere in China. We were also treated to one of the crew selling toothbrushes with a long sales pitch that was surprisingly effective. A pair of beggars, one blind led by another with one leg, had less success.

Xuancheng was unremarkable, which isn't a criticism. I had read that it has a long history but, as everywhere in China, the main street layout is clearly of recent design to accommodate several lanes of traffic. I found an adequate hotel easily and in fact the town seemed to be full of them. I was unsure why this was, as there is little to attract tourists and no more obvious business than anywhere else. Wandering around I found an area which seemed to belong to an older pattern of narrow alleys, crowded with the usual food stalls and hairdressers. I enjoyed strolling through what I felt to be the proper China and stopped for a bowl of noodles and a beer at a typical little eatery, with plastic stools set on a bare concrete floor and the cooking conducted in the doorway where the steam was easily dispelled.

I was actually finding that all Chinese towns were beginning to look the same. The process of urbanisation is one of revolution rather than evolution, with the old bulldozed away and a new grid pattern of multi-lane streets, lined with high rise blocks, superimposed. What appears to be old and original China is in fact the traditional shops and businesses taking root in the new environment, like grass growing up through concrete. In a sense this is encouraging as it demonstrates that it is the vibrant colourful alleyways, and not the plate glass high street shops, that are still the natural demonstration of Chinese enterprise. Opposite where we live in Nanjing is an area that was clearly designed to be an attraction to visitors, with single story traditional style whitewashed buildings, but instead of tacky souvenir shops it is a jumble of clothing repairers and simple eateries belching steam across the narrow street, itself crowded with delivery tricycles. Despite the best attempts of urban planners the real Chinatown doesn't have to be sought out, it is irrepressible.

My train to Hangzhou was delayed for three hours and by the time it arrived I felt that I had fully exhausted all the possibilities of wandering the streets of Xuancheng. I wasn't really sure why I had stopped there in the first place and what I had gained from the visit. Wikipedia told me that the town has over 2,000 years of history, but it would be more accurate to just say that people have lived on the same spot for that time. There is nothing to see, or even to feel of any connection to the past. It is a smaller city but still has a population of more than a quarter of a million, and as such failed to fulfil in any way my desire to be immersed in rural China.

Like Nanjing and Xuancheng, Hangzhou is an ancient town with millennia of history but you really wouldn't know it by just looking around. As it seems everywhere in China, the city is dominated by skyscrapers and six-lane highways, although again a kind of impromptu Chinatown has quickly developed at the bottom of some tower blocks with bubbling cauldrons of street food, overflowing fruit and veg. shops and hairdressers. From the number of plastic electrically powered spinning barbers' poles in every Chinese town, getting ones hair cut should be an almost daily event. I actually think that it may be for some young people. Girls and boys alike have their hair dyed different colours, styled and puffed up. When the hot humid summer is replaced with the bitter humid winter and the girls put away their miniskirts and hot-pants, it is not always obvious who is what. Many of the boys have soft features and little or no facial hair, and Chinese girls are not known for being big-bosomed. I once spoke to a teacher who told me that she had taught a student in her class for a whole term and was still not absolutely sure of his or her gender.

Statistically not all of the boys who would be assumed to be gay in a western culture can be homosexual, and it is perhaps refreshing that they don't feel the need to dress and act in a macho manner, although they are clearly conforming to some kind of fashion statement, and the older generations appear far more traditional and conservative. A legacy of communism is that gender roles are not firmly fixed and women can be seen labouring alongside their male counterparts on building sites throughout the country, and playing cards together on street corners. I would not be surprised however if, as one feminist observed, it is still always the woman who has to clean the toilet.

The main attraction of Hangzhou is the West Lake, and it is pretty, but to my mind it would be nothing without the backdrop of hills behind it. And this is where Hangzhou does seem special; many cities in the world are surrounded by mountains, but here it is the city that surrounds the hills. The West Lake draws Chinese tourists by the coachload. They trail behind a leader holding a brightly coloured flag and invariably they are issued with identical hats to seal their identity. Sometimes they are loaded into electric vehicles, like stretched golf carts, which take a dozen people at a time. These completely quiet carriages don't run on the roads or even use the bicycle lanes; they navigate their route along the pavement and are potentially lethal. The lake is said to be the inspiration for classic water garden design throughout China and beyond to Japan and Korea, but it only forms a small part of the area to which it gives its name, as more than 90% of the West Lake Scenic Area consists of bush covered hill ridges, steep valleys and even a few small villages set in tea plantations. The whole area, which the city surrounds in a horseshoe shape, covers a staggering 60 sq. km. and the peaks rise to 1,350 feet, which would certainly qualify as mountains in Britain.

I caught a bus to the pretty whitewashed village of Longjing (dragon well) which is famed throughout the country for its tea. Mountain climbing in this part of China doesn't require ropes or ice axes as there are always stone steps leading to the top. The most sacred of all the sacred mountains in China is Tai Shan, which has been worshipped for over 3,000 years, and for the last two millennia has required any appointed Emperor to make the ascent to receive a Heavenly Mandate. This concept is different from that of the Divine Right of Kings in that it is based on merit and not heredity. To gain the Mandate of Heaven an aspiring Emperor has to demonstrate that he is able and powerful, and it can be withdrawn if he fails by, for instance, not being able to prevent a flood or famine. There are between six and seven thousand granite steps to the top of Tai Shan (accounts vary so I assume that those who have tried to ascertain the exact number have lost count before reaching the summit). After I had been up there, while breaking a journey on my way to Beijing, I had pretty well had enough of climbing up stone steps.

Consequently I tried to seek out quieter paths in Hangzhou, and found an isolated track behind one of the many temples that dot the hills and valleys. Soon I found myself in a tea plantation and wondering what conditions the plants need, as they were growing in terraces at all elevations and facing all directions, in sunshine and in shade. Then my path petered out. I retraced my steps a little way and tried an alternative route which took me to an area where the tea shared the hillside with a cemetery, another dead-end! I had come up a long way from the valley floor and I was reluctant to go all the way back down. According to my map there was a good path at the top if I could just reach it, but the higher I went the steeper and more overgrown the terrain became. I don't know why I always get myself into these situations. I hauled myself up with the aid of some thick bamboo and finally burst through the undergrowth onto a paved path, to the utter amazement of an old man who was standing with one leg raised above the horizontal, resting his limb in that of a tree.

This is not an unusual sight. I have a theory that different exercise regimes were promoted by the Communist Party but changed as quickly as fashions in teenage clothing. The recipients of the latest wisdom stuck to what they had been taught, so that now individuals perform strange rituals depending on the time that they were indoctrinated into their particular form of exercise. Some, such as the morning assemblage of elderly residents in every park performing tai chi, may have a sound basis to them but others are just bizarre. People can be seen going in circles punching parts of their bodies as hard as they can, swinging their arms in an exaggerated manner or concentrating on keeping a steady pace while walking backwards. Any possible health benefits must be far outweighed by the potential risks. Exercise is taken very seriously in China, and what look like children's' playgrounds with brightly painted equipment that are dotted around the cities, are actually outdoor gymnasiums, used by the elderly to raise their legs when they can't find a suitable tree, or to twist their bodies in some other ritualised routine.

Trying to appear unruffled from my bush-whacking, I bade the man with his leg in the tree and his mouth agape 'good day' and followed the main path up and down stone steps to little pavilions with views over the city and a helpful sign in Chinese and English explaining how to hike. Its message boiled down to putting one foot in front of the other. Further on an even more helpful sign explained that if your waist measurement is greater than 100 cm. then you are suffering from a condition known as 'beer belly'. Fortunately there is a cure which is to go hiking for at least 40 minutes a day 5 days a week.

I have come across many of these information boards on my travels around China, my favourite being one I saw near the port city of Dalian. Entitled Upside-Down Standing for Fitness. It explained that we spend too long in a vertical position and gave a long list of disorders that we suffer as a result. The sign proclaimed the importance of relieving pressure on joints and organs by becoming inverted by whatever means possible, but warned against getting too carried away too soon, and advised that a beginner should start from simple upside-down standing under a teacher's guidance and protection.

I walked for a couple more hours without coming to any roads, but had to increase my pace to get out of earshot of a man behind me carrying a particularly tinny sounding radio, which was playing traditional Chinese music. As nature abhors a vacuum the Chinese seem to abhor silence, and from the other direction I came across a group of youngsters who, clearly having forgotten to bring a radio, were yelling at the tops of their voices to ensure that peace and quiet could not gain any kind of hold.

It may be not so much a hate of silence as a love of noise. Being one in 1.3 billion, just about all of whom think and act the same as oneself because that is the Confucian way, can be suffocating. Individuals need to spend all their money on the most distinctive clothing and haircuts, let off the loudest cacophony of firecrackers when they wed, and yell at the tops of their voices from mountain peaks just to tell themselves, let alone anyone else, that they are here. Despite the noise I really enjoyed my outing. There is something about getting up into hills that I find strangely relaxing, even when it is mainly climbing up stone steps, and I felt much better for my walk. I descended through more tea gardens and past another mustard yellow temple to catch a bus back to the centre of town.

I couldn't leave Hangzhou without having a trip on the Grand Canal of China which is arguably a much more significant achievement than the Great Wall. Like The Wall, it was built in several sections over the centuries, but it was the Sui Dynasty Emperor Yang Huang who in the 7th century had the vision of a continuous waterway linking the grain rich south of the country with the Yellow River, and on to what is now Beijing. The Chinese invention of the pound lock, just over a thousand years ago, enabled the route to be shortened by crossing the hills in Shandong Province but at over thousand miles in length it is still the longest as well as the oldest working canal in the world- by a long chalk.

The modern water taxi I caught was built in a traditional style, but without all the fancy carving that is seen on trip boats on the West Lake, and which I think looks ridiculous. I sat by the window on the wooden slat bench and, as always, felt content to be on the water. The canal starts (or finishes) at the Qiantang River, which must be at least half a mile wide in Hangzhou and empties into the same estuary as the Yangtze. The Qiantang is best known for having the world's biggest tidal bore, which at its height in autumn attracts surfers from around the world, and often kills them. I got the boat from a jetty behind a skyscraper near the centre of town and we headed north along a prettified route with elaborate sculptures decorating the numerous bridges. It was surprisingly wide for a canal, perhaps a similar width to that of the Thames in London, and consequently felt much more like a river, although there was no shortage of commercial traffic.

Barges loaded to the point that water lapped over their gunwales carried mainly aggregate, presumably to feed the ubiquitous road, rail and building construction. The cabins at the back displayed the colourful bunting of the daily wash, an indication everywhere in China of habitation. Compared to the hardships of many in the country, I think that running a canal boat here could be a pleasant enough life and would certainly provide a much more comfortable place to live than the back cabin of an English narrowboat. Towering above us loomed a huge bare hulk and it took me a few moments to realise that this was the same as the other barges I had been looking at but without a load, and it gave an indication of the huge weight that these vessels carry.

The trip finished just beyond a steeply arched and very graceful stone bridge which, unlike the rest of the area, was genuinely old. Crossing the bridge brought me to a narrow cobbled street running between plaster and wood buildings which could possibly date back to the late 20th century. Whether this was a Chinese restoration, which very often involves erecting vaguely similar structures next door to those that previously existed, or just a folly didn't matter to me. There was no proper link to the past and no real feeling of history to this little touristy area.

It was also in Hangzhou that I had seen the ultimate in this fraud; not far from a cable car up into the hills is a café with a board outlining its ancient history and importance. That the building doesn't even pretend to look old is unsurprising, but the real audacity is that the famous old restaurant had no connection with the area- it was situated miles away- they've just appropriated the name! One of the draws of travel is to get that feel of history and connection to the past which gives us a sense of identity and belonging, but that requires a stimulus to the imagination that is not achieved with any sterile modern building, regardless of what old-fashioned shape it is made into.

Nor am I going to get much of that cosy connection to the past where I am now. Catching a city bus from the otogar I finally find Erzincan and discover a dull town. It's not its fault; it has an ancient history but has been destroyed by earthquakes. But it's still dull. The most devastating earthquake was a massive 8.2 on the Richter scale which flattened the city in 1939. The damage was so extensive that the site was abandoned and the present town built to the north of it. Consequently it is a victim of mid 20th century town planning, when it seems architects from around the world conspired to give us the most uninspiring buildings that their imaginations could muster.

On the off chance, I find my way to the dusty istasyon on the edge of town, just in case the train that is full from Erzerum has a berth available from here. It is well into the evening and I think at first that the ticket office is closed, but then a man appears, and then another and another. The three of them apply themselves to selling me a ticket, goodness knows what else they have to do, and there must be huge excitement when the daily train arrives. I request a couchette, which seems to be the equivalent of a hard sleeper but they think that I would be more comfortable in the more expensive option, but they then say that this is not available. I tell them that a couchette will be fine. We are just on the point of sale when they realise that the only available berth is in a woman-only section. I give up.

Wi-fi is not readily available in this town but I find a hotel more upmarket than the one I have booked into that has it, which seems to be a good reason to stop for a beer. After studying online maps, timetables and descriptions of places, my new plan is to go to the interesting sounding town of Amasya, and from there continue to Istanbul without going through Ankara.

Chapter Nineteen: As You Like It

I have learnt to make a mental note of bus numbers when I need to return to where I have come from and I get back to the isolated Erzincan otogar without incident. The bus I am offered to Amasya does not leave until the afternoon. I may do better with another company, but I ask about going to Sivas, a bigger town which I had noted was on my route. There is a bus waiting to leave and I am on my way again.

I have in mind that I should accelerate my progress the further west I get, not just because I am getting short of time but also as I imagine that it will become more populous, less scenic and not as exotic as the eastern end of the country. To be fair it is holding up very well. The farming looks more organised here but no less pleasantly pastoral as we roll along through acres of wheat, maize and sunflowers, punctuated with the terracotta roofs of isolated dwellings. Patches of snow are no longer visible on the hills and I expect that we have dropped quite a bit in altitude, but the horizon remains invitingly rugged.

I have no problem in getting an onward ticket for Amasya and only see the otogar at Sivas, where I finally finish off my garlic sausage while waiting for the connection. I still have a bit of bread and cheese left and it seems a long time ago that I bought it for breakfast in Borjomi. It is evening when we reach Amasya, but my good impression of Turkey has not diminished. We have climbed over mountain ranges, through lush valleys and past small towns and villages with houses painted in pastel shades of pink, green, yellow and orange. The countryside is clean and diverse, the roads, where they're not being repaired, are good and the modern buses run like clockwork.

I find it sad that the rail network in Turkey isn't used more for passenger traffic and, while in China they try to operate the bullet trains like jet-liners, here they have similar aspirations for the buses. Each company has its own livery and logo and all the personnel wear uniform shirts and ties (they don't seem to employ women). Each bus has at least one conductor, whose job is more like that of a flight attendant. On this bus the conductor is a small, agile middle-aged man whose uniform includes a bow tie, which makes the poor fellow look like a clown. There is actually more leg room than there is on an economy flight and TV screens are built into the seat backs, the operation of which is sadly beyond my technical expertise. The aisle between the seats may be narrow but, as the countryside flashes past, I watch the conductor load a little trolley which he wheels between the seat rows to dispense coffee and cake and soft drinks. It is all very comfortable, but I can't help thinking back to the rollercoaster ride I had on the sleeper bus from the Chinese/Kazakh border to Almaty, and feel that the journey would have been far less memorable if it had all been in the style of a Turkish bus.

Is it important that journeys are memorable? I like to think that I live for the present rather than storing images for later reflection, but I don't much care for the idea that I won't be able to recall where I have been or what I have done. I suppose that a lot of it will inevitably fade and distort with time and that what remains as being memorable has some greater significance, either for its impact upon the senses or because of its importance to a grander scheme. Before I left Nanjing I was preparing for this trip and I was also on a quest to get to what I considered to be the heart, or perhaps the soul, of China which I sensed resided in the simple way of life of country folk.

With time running out I needed to go to Shanghai and I woke up looking forward to the day; I often have no kind of schedule and have to decide what I am doing as I go along and it made a pleasant change to have my time fully mapped out and clear tasks to complete. After an early breakfast I went down to the metro and smiled to myself as I watched a neatly uniformed guard stand to attention and salute the driver as the train arrived. Clearly engine drivers are held in higher esteem than they are in many other countries, although all they do is sit there as the whole thing can operate automatically. But there is more to it than that; it is the

Chinese love of uniforms, hierarchies and kowtowing to ones superiors that again shows what an unsuitable country it is to have a communist system of government; all the animals want and expect some to be more equal than others.

At the railway station I found that my train to Shanghai was delayed. You can set your watch by the bullet trains but the old expresses, which often travel a route of thousands of kilometres over several days, can be subject to delays and I think only manage to keep to any kind of timetable by having liberal stops at stations along the way where time lost can be made up. Forty minutes behind schedule but I was on my way. I turfed a young man out of my seat after he and his mates had studied my ticket to see which of them should move. The other two had only a short reprieve before identically dressed young women, in flower patterned jackets, claimed their places and stowed their identical white and gold wheeled suitcases under our feet.

The delay had put some pressure on me and I walked as quickly as I could to find the travel agency issuing a ticket for Liz to fly to Europe for the school summer holidays. Having been in China for a little while I knew better than to look for a high street shop, and correctly interpreted what looked like a street number on the address I had, as being the 22nd floor of a tower block. Travel agents always seem to need a long time to sell a ticket which, for anything else, is sold from a kiosk at the end of a queue. The only difference is that greater sums of money are usually involved and in China cash is still king. The ATM's, as in most countries, limit the amount you can withdraw but in China there seems to be no limit to the number of times you can keep feeding your card back into the machine. Consequently I was travelling with a huge wad of notes stuffed into my back pocket which I was relieved to finally exchange for a piece of printed paper.

With no time for lunch, my next stop was the Russian Consulate across town and housed in a beautiful old building overlooking the river and next to the Bund. But, after having to put my bag in a locker outside, presumably to prevent me from taking a bomb into the Embassy, I was directed to a dingy windowless room where a week ago I had queued to apply for a Russian visa. To my relief I regained my passport without any more bureaucratic posturing and felt that I was back on schedule.

I took a longer metro ride to the modern Hongqiao Station, to the west of the city, which only seems to handle the superfast trains. I had got my ticket in advance as, despite the station having at least 11 booking offices each with a double figure number of windows selling tickets, it can still be a long queue to get served and time was of the essence. By default a system has been created which has effectively created first and second class railway stations. My outward journey was from the tired looking Nanjing Station with its permanent population of homeless beggars and passengers surrounded by all their worldly goods, to the equally down-at-heel Shanghai Station. My return on the fast train started at the plush modern terminal where most of the travellers are smartly dressed business people, most of whom wouldn't so much as spit in the litter bins.

Spitting is a Chinese habit that I think all foreigners find repulsive, especially when you can hear someone behind you hawking up phlegm which could end up anywhere. The only place where the pavements are free of globules of phlegm is Zangjiagang, where it is one of the 'don'ts' of 'civilised behaviour'. I arrived at Hongqiao with just enough time to get through the x-ray machine and find the right platform gate from where I knew that my 'G' train would leave dead on time, and cover the 300 km journey to Nanjing in just one hour and seven minutes; a third of the time, but at three times the cost of my outward journey. My arrival station was Nanjing Nan (south), in a similarly refined and modern setting, and which Liz views as being her railway station as opposed to the one that I usually use.

Liz had not been home long, having just flown down from the cold of Changchun, but I had previously prepared a meal which we enjoyed before donning backpacks and heading back to Nanjing Station. The following week was the Mayday holiday which, as it fell on a Wednesday, had been combined with Monday and Tuesday, and the week-end made working days. Liz had arranged to take these as time off in lieu which meant that we had a 5 day holiday. I had put a lot of time into planning this but still had some concerns as Liz does not always take a philosophical attitude to the trials and tribulations of travelling into the unknown and, despite my best efforts on the internet, the finer details of our journey were yet to be discovered.

We were booked on an overnight train to Jingdezhen, which is the nearest railway line to Wuyuan, which in turn is the main town in the county to which it gives its name and which is reputed to have exceptionally pretty villages, an emerging domestic tourist industry based on home-stays and a network of old postal roads providing walking links between the settlements. I couldn't resist it.

The train would be on time as it starts in Nanjing and we were invited to board half an hour before the scheduled departure. When I had been at the station 12 hours previously and my train to Shanghai had been delayed, I had been eager to get going and irritated at the enforced wait, but once darkness had fallen it was a different place. We settled into our soft sleeper and I gazed at a scene of romance and mystery. Ghostly shadows elevated the mundane of daylight to an arcane richness in which the long and turbulent history of the place could be felt. I made out a train of old coaches finished in dark green with a broad yellow stripe, a type that was found right across Asia and Eastern Europe and which had carried many of my dreams. I loved it.

The morning daylight revealed verdant hills and sparkling white villages. It seemed less crowded than most trains I have been on but of course, travelling with Liz, we were in the soft sleeper carriage which on my own I would view as an extravagance. The dining car was next door and was serving passengers, so when I eventually persuaded her out of the compartment we got bowls of noodles in a rich brown broth with a rubbery fried egg floating on top. Fried eggs less well cooked can be too much of a challenge even for the Chinese to manipulate with chopsticks.

Jingdezhen is heralded as the porcelain capital of China but first impressions were of just another big sprawling town. The roads were not quite so wide or the traffic quite as heavy as bigger places like Nanjing, but this was compensated for by continual use of horns, creating a cacophony that we could barely make ourselves heard over. We then had the first gap in my planning; I had learned that the bus to Wuyuan does not leave from the main bus station and that where it does depart from is not far from the railway, but I hadn't been able to establish in which direction. We waded through the usual clamour of taxi touts and asked a waiting bus driver who gave us a general direction to walk in. To me wandering around, getting lost and wasting time looking for a bus is all part of the joys of travelling, but Liz is not at all tolerant of this attitude and if we were going to enjoy the few days holiday then finding transport, accommodation and food needed to be a clean slick process, which was why I had gleaned all the information that I could find on the computer.

And there it was; a little bus station with little buses, but at least bigger than those awful minibuses, these seated about 20. My information was that the villages close to Wuyuan become packed with Chinese tourists, while equally interesting places further north are relatively untouched but still provide simple rooms to stay in. This was what we were aiming for as what I really wanted was to get closer to rural China, I was less interested in seeing identified scenic spots than in just being able to stroll around and relax in the countryside. Once there, the prospect of being able to walk from one village to another was hugely appealing. Ideally I wanted to get to Guankeng from where there is a straightforward route to Lingjiao, from which Dalikeng can be reached with the help of a guide. I then realised that if we could get a bus to Qinghuan instead of Wuyuan we could make it a circuit but going the opposite way around.

I asked for Qinghuan in the expectation that we would discover that there is one bus a day which had already left, but I got a positive response. Liz, who has a better grasp of Chinese than me, said that we had to wait about an hour until 10 o'clock, but then we were bundled aboard and we were off; brilliant. Bowling down the main street Jingdezhen revealed its glory as the china capital of China, with blue and white porcelain everywhere. We stopped at traffic lights which were encased, not just the lights themselves but the whole thing from pavement up, in patterned chinaware, and the street lamps as well displayed classic scenes of mist shrouded mountains on their ceramic poles.

I was really feeling pretty pleased with myself and, although Qinghuan was a singularly uninspiring place where we failed to find a famous 800 year old bridge, I felt that my planning had paid off when we reached Dalikeng. The bus driver said that he had a home-stay and we followed him along a river which was little more than a babbling brook. We crossed a bamboo bridge to his establishment which, a bit to my disappointment, was more of a small hotel than a home-stay, but Liz was happy with it, and keeping Liz happy was a major objective.

No roads meant no cars and no car horns, but it was not even 6 o'clock in the morning when I was woken by a hell of a racket coming from outside by the river. I didn't want to disturb Liz by opening the curtains so I dressed quietly and went outside. It was a beautiful morning and I sat on an old stone bridge and watched village life gather pace. At frequent intervals along the river worn steps led down to lines of flagstones which may well have been there for hundreds of years. Squatting in that way, with feet flat on the ground, which Chinese people seem to find comfortable but is a painful balancing act for me, the women of the village were wreaking their fury against the daily wash. They wielded lengths of wood, somewhat larger than a rolling pin, and brought them down with all their might on the innocent laundry, and it was these thwacks of wood on river sodden clothing that had awoken me.

Outside the village shop three old men in blue Mao suits sat on a tree trunk supported with stones at either end which, like the men themselves, had sagged and become bowed over years of use. A fragile looking woman tottered towards me balancing two large red plastic buckets on the ends of a bamboo pole. It was only after she had passed that the stench of the night soil hit me and lingered for what seemed an unreasonable length of time.

The next part of my plan was a walk to Hongguan which was reported to be 15 km over the hills, and where I thought we could get a home-stay, but my research stressed the likelihood of getting lost without a guide. The bus driver-cum-hotel proprietor said he would arrange this but I suggested to Liz that if we just found a path and kept going east we should get there. She sensibly pointed out that wandering aimlessly in the hills would make her anxious which in turn would cause me to become irritable and it wouldn't be much of a holiday.

Finally our promised guide arrived. Laoso was a cheerful little man wearing thin canvas shoes and a brown jacket and carrying a plastic bucket with a megaphone in it, the significance of which we never established. He first led us to his house in a back alley, which was an opportunity for us to have a proper look inside the home of a local. The village is predominantly made of stone, but inside Laoso's house the walls were lined with well made wood panelling. Daylight came from, not so much a window as a large hole, high up in the wall and covered with a roller blind. A gallery formed the upstairs sleeping accommodation allowing the light to penetrate downstairs, where the walls were adorned with A4 size yellow and red certificates which I couldn't decipher. There did not appear to be any heating and it must be freezing in winter.

For the majority of Chinese people living conditions are still very basic, although the new city apartment blocks contain heating, air conditioning and inside toilets. There is an area of Nanjing that is being developed near where we live; adjoining the piles of rubble, brick dust and general refuse there is evidence that some buildings continue to be occupied. It may be that it is a long process to re-house everyone, or perhaps some people are reluctant to give up their neighbourhoods, where there may still exist some sense of community, and move with their one-child nuclear family to an isolated flat in an impersonal tower block. The loss of community identity caused by replacing East London slums with high rise living has become clichéd and blamed for all manner of social ills, but most Chinese welcome progress and their country's advancement in the world.

The sense of community in China is hard to pin down. There does seem to be some neighbourliness in the little streets and alleyways where most doors are left open in summer and even the toilet at the end of the street is communal. Modern city living can be heartless and I get the impression that there are few mechanisms for strangers to get to know each other. The communist system structured society around the work unit allocated to each person, which literally provided an identity card and also catered for the need to feel a sense of belonging. The entrepreneurial drive of many Chinese which has been allowed to develop with the opening up of the Country has changed the face of business, and has dealt another blow to the way that communities are organised. Having effectively abandoned communism, China has to accept the negatives with the advantages of a capitalist society, which makes it susceptible to the Marxist concept of social and economic alienation.

There is no evidence at the moment in China of any of the social ills which are found in the inner cities of many other countries; no one plasters the walls with graffiti, adolescents are generally respectful to their parents and, despite the prevalence of opiates before the People's Republic was founded, if non-prescribed drugs are available it's certainly not obvious. The strength of filial ties which promote an orderly and respectful society are hugely important in China, but these are also stretched as one child families are separated from their traditional village communities and migrant workers flock to the cities. The Chinese pride themselves on their ability to put up with hardship, which they describe as a preparedness to eat bitterness, and I have no doubt that when winter comes to Dalikeng the villagers just grin and bear it, but the threat to harmony is how to cope with the emotional and societal changes more than the physical challenges.

Laoso didn't speak any English but he was good at communicating. He got across that he lives alone but has children and grandchildren in the village and wanted to know what family we have. He offered to carry one of our backpacks but as he was only half the size of Liz, let alone me, we turned him down. He did seem disappointed that I also turned down his offer of a cigarette despite his strenuous efforts to get me to accept. I think that smoking is some form of male bonding ritual in China, but I have given up once and have no intention of having to do so again.

Dalikeng is becoming a tourist destination but, unlike some of the water towns in the Yangtze delta which I have visited, it is still a proper living community, the real China that I have been searching for. In fact it is more authentic than most English villages, many of which have become pretty dormitories for large towns, with no real life or sense of community of their own. Travelling in other countries can often seem more a journey through time than space and I wonder if that is part of the attraction; to return to an idealised image of how life in rural England used to be. Here I felt that I had found some of that elusive bucolic idyll from childhood. That it was only experienced through stories and tantalising glimpses from a car window, and probably never existed in reality, hadn't lessened the need for me to lie under the greenwood tree in my own Forest of Arden, and find "tongues in trees, books in the running brooks, sermons in stones, and good in everything".

I am also pretty happy with Turkey, and would like to spend more time exploring the countryside but I need to press on. As soon as I arrive at the bus station at Amasya I buy my next ticket. There is a suitable bus to Istanbul leaving late tomorrow morning and I am pleased to find that the journey time is now down to less than ten hours. Amasya, squeezed between bare rock faces in a deep gorge, is a delight. I try a hotel by the river but they have no vacancies and I wander around for a while before I come across another, which is too expensive. It's well into the evening and I need to find somewhere to stay and then get something to eat, but budget accommodation does not seem to be plentiful. I then spot, down a side alley, not an 'otel' but a 'pansiyon'. The young woman standing outside looks as if she was expecting me, and I suppose she saw the approach of a potential customer with a backpack. She leads me into a courtyard neatly laid out with rustic wooden dining tables and chairs. The three storey building is wood framed with white plasterwork and smells of old mothballs when we enter. We walk past various pieces of old furniture which appear to have been collected to match the character of the building rather than for any function they might perform. I am shown a room upstairs which overhangs the courtyard and am told that there is a bathroom across the landing for my exclusive use. I love it, it is exactly what I want, and I am not at all bothered that they have lost the key to the room.

Back in the courtyard I ask if they have a menu and she tells me that they serve just one traditional dish, which I agree to have despite not understanding the description. She shouts at, I assume her partner, to do the cooking while she manages paperwork at the next table. After some time he brings a knife and fork which he carefully places in front of me, but is not satisfied with the spacing and makes an adjustment. The food when it arrives is a bowl of small twists of stuffed pasta covered in soured cream. This is presented on a large flat rectangular plate which also contains square shaped dolmades, which I had always thought to be a Greek dish, but is probably equally Turkish. It is all beautifully, if perhaps a little obsessively arranged and, washed down with a glass of local wine I thoroughly enjoy my meal and appreciate the surroundings.

The place is a curious mixture of top quality chic and pragmatic make-do, and I wonder if this reflects the respective influences of him and her. It is said that opposites attract but the impression here is that they are trying to pull in different directions. I would guess that he may well have features of an obsessive/compulsive disorder and that the fine pieces of furniture, which are of no use other than as decoration, are his influence as he tries to create a perfect upmarket establishment. He is the dreamer, the artist, the chef who fell in love with the beautiful old building, but she has her feet firmly on the ground. I watch her deal with a mound of paperwork with cool efficiency. She is an attractive well-dressed woman but with no frills, pure pragmatism, and is running a no frills budget pansiyon where the books have to balance.

It will be late when I get to Istanbul and I would have preferred a ticket for an earlier bus, but it is pleasant to have an unhurried walk around the town of Amasya which has a distinct personality, wedged as it is between rock formations which force the buildings to tumble on top of each other. Breakfast is the same as every other breakfast I have had in Turkey; hard-boiled egg, feta cheese, olives, tomato and cucumber with plenty of crusty white bread and black tea. The difference here is the presentation, as each item is displayed in its own asymmetric bowl and the whole arranged on another large rectangular plate. I may have over-rated the efficiency of the hostess, as I struggle to find anyone to pay my bill to before I leave and am on the point of leaving money in my room when another woman finally arrives in the kitchen, and I can settle up before making my way to the otager.

Chapter Twenty: Vivisection

It is dark when we finally reach Istanbul. It is a city that I have visited before and love; so rich in history the past seeps out of the buildings and becomes part of the present. The bridge over the Bosphorus, the divide between Asia and Europe, is lit with red and blue and I can make out one of the traditional ferries plying its route beneath us. This is not just where the continents start but the crossroads of the world, with the Black Sea and Russia to the north and in the opposite direction the Mediterranean and Africa.

The otogar is a nightmare. We are already later than I was told we would be and we are now stuck in a gridlock of coaches. Clearly the bus station, vast as it is, cannot cope with the number of vehicles using it and I am becoming increasingly frustrated. I am pleased that I had the sense, knowing that it would be late when we got here, to book a hotel on line so all I should have to do is catch the metro a few stops and walk for half a mile. At last we reach the right bay, we have been more than half an hour inching around the otogar and now, before I do anything else, I need to get my last bus ticket. The first company I ask only goes to Bourgas in the evening but I try another and get a seat on the nine o'clock tomorrow morning. It is already past ten at night so Istanbul, and really the whole width of Turkey from east to west, will have been a brief visit. It deserves longer.

I could also have happily stayed a bit longer in the delightful Chinese village of Dalikeng but I was looking forward to the walk over the hills, even though showers were forecast and it was raining hard when our little procession got underway. At first laoso led us along the moulded edges of paddy fields, but then we reached a path heading up into the hillside and we started to climb out of the valley on time-worn stone steps. I couldn't but feel that filing along with umbrellas raised detracted from the intrepid intent of the venture, but soon the skies cleared and we had perfect walking weather. Liz commented that she did not realise it was uphill. I don't know what she expected as, other than the road up the valley that the bus had come in on, we were totally surrounded by high peaks. But I was also aware that this was her break from work and tramping in the hills is really a pastime of mine rather than hers.

The river system flows from north to south and travelling east we crossed two valleys to reach Hongguan. Liz said that I had made her walk over two mountains, but I think that she felt a sense of achievement as well as having seen some beautiful countryside. Everyone in China has a mobile phone and even Laoso was no exception. At our request he arranged accommodation for us while we were walking and in the village led us down a narrow alleyway, with the high damp stone walls of the buildings blocking out the sunlight, to what was perhaps closest to a bed and breakfast. There were several rooms but no other guests and the extended family also ran a shop next door where they sold us beer. Most Chinese beer is unremarkable but very cheap, and it comes in satisfyingly large bottles. The one exception I have found is the Tsingtao stout, which at 6.8% is probably a copy of the strong foreign extra Guinness and is equally as good.

The village was a tightly packed jumble of three story dwellings with much of the stonework blackened and crumbling and lending a mediaeval feel to the place. I doubted that most of the villagers had seen a foreigner before and they were very curious. In much of China people just stare at us but here they really wanted to try to talk, even if they couldn't think what it was they wanted to say. In the centre of the village we found a barn like building, just inside the open door of which was a great mound of freshly picked tea. I decided that we should take advantage of the lack of any idea of privacy in China by wandering inside. There we found an array of whitewashed brick furnaces roasting the tea leaves to varying degrees and, ignoring the look of shock on the faces of the workers, I casually did a circuit of inspection while Liz took some photos.

I suspected that Liz didn't really want another long hike and we'd already done as much as I realistically expected we would, so after breakfast the next morning I suggested that we just walk further up the valley to Lingjiao, where there should be another home-stay. Over the river from Hongguan a new road had been built and, while many of the village buildings were decaying, smart new houses were going up in this area. There was no traffic on the road but we stayed on the true right bank of the river and followed paths skirting fields of paddy and oil seed rape. We passed through a hamlet of whitewashed houses and said hello to a group of old men sat on a wooden bench. They just stared back, apparently unfriendly but maybe dumbstruck at the strange apparition of fabled creatures from other lands.

On reaching Lingjiao we found a shop and asked about a home-stay by showing the Chinese characters for it, which I had printed off as part of my preparation for this trip. We were told that we were in the right place and were taken upstairs onto the flat concrete roof, off which a basic room afforded views over fields and hills. I left Liz there and explored a route up the valley head which I thought was the start of the path to Guankeng, which ideally I would have liked to have followed if we had had another day. Most of the afternoon was spent sat on the roof reading and soaking up the picturesque scene of tea pickers on the hillside, a water buffalo being used to plough a paddy field and a woman burning the straw from the rapeseed. Then a storm came and we retired to our room and counted the seconds between giant stomach rumbles and blinding Polaroid flashes.

Heavy rain continued throughout the night and we woke up to a fresh landscape of waterfalls and cataracts as the rainwater coursed through the village irrigation system. The bus to Wuyuan was on time and sailed down the new road, past Hongguan and then stopped. The road further on had not yet been built and there was a sea of rich red mud with a truck stuck in it up to its axles. Gradually other vehicles appeared around us and there were more on the far side of the divide. A truck driver marched back to his vehicle after an inspection of the scene and set off purposefully, as if to battle. To the huge amusement of our driver he got completely bogged down next to the first casualty. Most of the passengers remained seated and the conductress had been shouting down her phone, so I assumed that there was a plan, and I realised what it was when we saw another bus approach from the opposite direction. We picked our way through the mire and boarded the newly arrived vehicle which had already turned around, and we were on our way again.

We had a few hours to spend in Jingdezhen before boarding our overnight train to Nanjing. Liz does not share my interest in aimlessly wandering the streets and so we set off to find a coffee lounge. All around the world cups of coffee are sold for outrageous prices, in New Zealand a flat white costs more than the meat pie it accompanies, but in China, where there is no history of coffee drinking, this has been taken to a new extreme. Every town now seems to have coffee lounges which provide comfortable seating and internet access, and in which people may sit for hours in return for paying truly exorbitant prices for their coffee.

Signs written in English often contain mistakes which can be humorous and I have come across whole books of collections of them in foreign language bookstores in China. The mistake is usually as a result of letters being copied incorrectly, although the really funny stuff comes from computer translations. I also think that Chinese lacks the richness and diversity of English, so that one word or character has to perform many different functions. This can often result in giving a translation where an inappropriate word is provided, although the meaning may still be guessed. An example I liked was when Liz queried how she should properly use the swimming pool in the hotel where she was staying which had a sign forbidding Horizontal Swimming.

Here they had obviously bothered to make sure that they had a correctly spelt English word by putting a handful of letters through a spell check and we entered the M T Coffee Language. It served its purpose, although our coffee and sandwiches cost about the same as the previous day's dinner bed and breakfast. It is as if there are parallel worlds which occupy the same space in China but operate to different rules. I notice this particularly when meeting with Liz's colleagues who frequent expat bars where the prices bear no relation to the real life of the majority of Chinese people. But there is also a very wealthy middle class in cities like Nanjing and Hangzhou and a different level of service has been created to help them to spread some of their riches. Most starkly there is the urban rural divide, formalised in the hukou system. Travelling from one to the other can seem like a leap through several centuries.

It had been a good few days and I felt that I had finally found the experience that I was searching for; to be in and amongst the ordinary unchanged life of China. The still undeveloped villages of Wuyuan County had enabled me to get to that elusive rural heart of the country, which I had observed through train windows but had not previously been able to touch and smell. That we were in China was almost irrelevant, as the fascination for me was the simple rusticity, which was as much evocative of the richly pungent England of a Thomas Hardy novel as of anything more oriental. The attraction is to a traditional rural life that is conducted at the natural pace of the seasons but, ironically for a travel fiend, is inhabited by people whose horizons are limited to what they can physically see.

I know its romantic twaddle, but it is imagination more than the reality that fuels the drive to explore far off places. The exotic is not made of concrete and clay; it is constructed from layers of experiences each sparking some vivid arcane image. This became most obvious to me when I got the opportunity to spend a few months working on Pitcairn Island. People from all over the world are intrigued by this tiny isolated community, but not because of any reality of the islanders daily lives. Pitcairn's claim to fame is that it became the home of the survivors from the mutiny which occurred on HMS Bounty, and the current population are all descendants of those mutineers. But it is not as straightforward as that. The real historical events pale into insignificance beside the Hollywood re-enactments, and it is the tinsel and glamour of the cinema that has made Pitcairn such an exotic destination. A mutiny on a British naval vessel in the 18th century is a dry fact of very limited interest to most people, but images of human passion and conflict acted out and projected onto a large screen made The Mutiny On The Bounty a household phrase. The power of fantasy trumps earthy reality every time.

If I had found my own Arcadia I then had a problem; what to do next? If the hunt was over then there was no point in continuing the chase. I needed to find some other focus because I didn't want to stop travelling. Maybe I would have to become a conventional visitor and seek out the tourist sites. The problem was academic as my time and energy was taken up in planning the big journey that I am now enjoying. After our trip to Wuyuan I had just 2 weeks before leaving Nanjing to travel overland, I suppose mainly along what is referred to as the Silk Road, which has a nice exotic sound to it.

And now I'm nearing the end of that journey and I need to draw some conclusions from my attempt at dissecting myself as a travel addict:

Starting at the top of the head, the challenge and thrill of the unexpected can be hair-raising. But I avoid rather than seek out danger, as I did when choosing a route through Malaysia, and again in the Caucasus where I skirted around Chechnya. I'm certainly not an adrenalin junkie and really prefer more cerebral activities, which brings us to the brain. Before even leaving New Zealand I'd identified being on the inside and living a puzzle as an attraction of travel, the need to solve the logistics and the satisfaction of seeing plans coming to fruition. Looking inside the travel addict's skull, the left hemisphere is happily slotting together the jigsaw pieces from guide books, visa requirements and train timetables, while the right colours in the imagined scenes and seeks out a reality to fit its desired fantasy.

Moving to the eyes, they see everything flickering before them and drink it all in. This is what I termed the lazy paradox; that far from demonstrating an adventurous outgoing nature, the traveller simply boards a bus or train or plane and watches the world go by; it is a television set with smell, touch and excellent 3D imagery. But the smells are telling. The nose is the most nostalgic of organs and is searching for some link back to childhood, or even to a previous age, which has become synthesised into an olfactory utopia. It is sniffing out links to a personal past but also connections to our common history, searching for the scent of where we have come from and who we are. It is a quest for an Arcadia which has most likely only ever existed in the imagination, and so must always be a forlorn attempt to find the end of the rainbow, but nevertheless one that has to be pursued.

But now we've sliced into the heart which is full of all these romantic notions and eager to gain authentic experiences of the exotic. And it doesn't have to be all roses and bosoms; travels through the old USSR did the job equally as well, with its clinical cold war glamour redolent of dirty deeds, brassy blondes and steel-edged espionage. Moving lower, the travellers loins reveal the lust and desire for new experiences and the fulfilment of fantasies. Unlike the eyes which are passive receivers, here is the driving force, the engine of travel which delves into dark corners and secret places.

Structure is needed and the traveller's skeleton provides that framework. This shows the satisfaction of studying maps and guidebooks, trawling through the internet for information and then turning it all into something which can be seen, smelt and touched. But all these bones have to make sense of what is sensed and this is the done by the spine. The backbone is the connection for ideas and opinions, and the touchstone which judges all that is seen and heard.

The spine can be stiffened or relaxed by contact with other cultures and the opportunity to briefly share in the lives of people whose lives have been very different from that of the visitor. It can become rigid and opinionated and it is always in danger of forming or conforming to stereotypical images, but there is also self learning to be had from reflecting on the essence of one's own character, and what remains constant away from the natural environment in which it was developed. The traveller is forced to re-evaluate personal views and prejudices and the sense of self is strengthened, keeping the individual standing tall and erect.

Cutting open the digestive tract we see that, rather than the hackneyed notion of life being a journey, we can view a journey as being a life, which develops its own personality as it progresses and becomes a mechanism for change. In this case it is a long and convoluted one as it winds its way through the intestines. At first this seems an unsuitable metaphor, as what starts out at the top is hopefully considerably more attractive than the end result, and it is expected that travel will be an enriching process. But not everything is expelled, nutrition is gained and some of the memories and experiences are used to revitalise the whole body. Over time much is forgotten and excreted as waste, but what remains is the material which forms the building blocks of the individual. This is the collection of assorted images which are built up in layers, as if by a three dimensional printer, and shaped to fit the character and reaffirm the identity of the traveller.

While travel can induce change, there is also the notion that living in a constantly moving kaleidoscope of change is a way to stand still. The idea that change is a life force running through the veins and arteries which can be fed a constant variety of scenery and cultural experiences to distract it, so that it leaves the host body alone and the traveller can remain untouched. By changing the environment with constant movement, the natural processes of aging and moving on to other stages in life can be halted, and travel can be a convenient mechanism to avoid taking on the responsibilities that come with maturity.

Opening up the guts reveals the more worthy aim of meeting a challenge, demonstrating an ability to act independently and getting a buzz from simple survival. Okay, it might not be trekking through the Amazon rain forest or crossing the Kalahari by camel, but there is still satisfaction to be gained by navigating through an alien world, and coping with whatever obstacles are presented, as a lone traveller relying only on personal resources. There is also a feeling of well-being to be had from being lifted above the mundane of daily life to see the wood for the trees and feel a part of something much bigger, a citizen of the wide-wide world with a panoramic view of life in all its diversity.

Which brings us finally to the feet; bruised and blistered but triumphant. The legs may do the legwork of turning all the plans and dreams into actuality, but it is the traveller's feet that set out to conquer the world, pacing out the distances in order to get the full measure of where we live and belong. Trying to get to grips with the size of the world, and consequently ones place and position within it, is a major incentive to travel. But there is also the notion that if one was ever to succeed at this, the world would become unbearably and frighteningly small, which lends an exciting element of danger to the whole enterprise.

There do seem to be some common themes emerging. One is that the drive to travel is a quest for what is always going to be unattainable. Whether that is an attempt to gain a full understanding of the world we live in without losing the vital sense of wonder at being in it, finding some utopian rural idyll from an imagined childhood or maintaining constant movement to, Canute-like, turn back the tide of change and achieve immortality- it ain't going to happen. And because it won't happen the thrill of the chase can go on; striving for an impossible goal ensures that there is always an unfilled need. That these things are unattainable doesn't detract from the drive to try, and to revel in the exotica of imagining where the next trip will take the traveller. The journey is more important than the destination, or as the inveterate travel addict Robert Louis Stevenson put it, *"To travel hopefully is better than to arrive"*.

The other common theme that has emerged in the vivisection of a travel addict is the establishing or reaffirming of the individual's identity. The sense of achievement in completing a challenging task may be a part of it, but it is more the way in which the experiences gained and memories collected become the sedimentary rock at the core of who the traveller is. Visiting unusual places and being amongst people from different cultures demands that the thinking traveller forms views and opinions and, odious as they may be, makes comparisons. This in turn requires an understanding of self and a constant need to reflect upon one's own origins and value base. In this way the traveller is forced to become a free thinker, develop their own ideas and draw their own conclusions. Away from one's own environment it is not possible to merge with the background as part of an amorphous mass, and inevitably the individual has to reassess who they are and where they fit in the world.

It is not only soul searching and developing independent ideas and values that is important to gaining a sense of belonging and personal identity. While fantasy and the world of the imagination are crucial to the traveller's experience, the solid reality of geography and gaining that feeling of being inside and a part of the whole physical world is equally important. Travel provides a release from the boundaries that usually tie us and provides an unblinkered view that can intensify the feeling of being alive. Paradoxically it is this literal sense of being a part of, and belonging to the natural world, that is more abstract than the cultural and emotional need for identity. As Lord Byron wrote: *"To mingle with the universe, and feel what I can ne'er express, yet cannot all conceal"*

I am still getting a thrill from my journey to the west, although European Turkey is pretty dull compared to most of the country. There is a distinct change when we cross the border into Bulgaria, from open farmland traversed by wide rolling roads, to a landscape of forest and hills with rocky outcrops which we navigate along dusty twisting lanes. This is Strandzha Nature Park, which is at the top of the list of protected areas in Europe. It is a rugged part of the world but, with rounded hills covered in ancient oaks, it's not hugely dramatic and only reaches an elevation of 700 metres.

The importance of Strandzha is its flora and fauna; nearly half of all the species of mammals in Europe live in its luxurious woods, including Jackals, wolves and wildcats. The reason for the huge diversity of life in the forests is political as much as geographic. Having bizarrely travelled west out of Europe into Asia when I entered Turkey, I am now back in Europe and still travelling west but entering what was part of the Eastern bloc. This was the iron curtain between East and West, but oddly a piece of it where the hemispheres were the wrong way round. Maybe I could use my backward working compass here. The point is that, as it formed such a sensitive border, the area was left to be wild and remote and escaped the ravages of most of the 20th century. Soon after the collapse of the communist regime the Bulgarian Government designated the area a nature park ensuring its continued protection, and I hope to see more of it while I am here.

Annoyingly the bus stops for half an hour when we are actually in sight of Bourgas but I am able to check the e-mails and find no reply from Liz about the time of my arrival. When I last spoke to her she was changing planes at Moscow and moaning about the Aeroflot flight to Sofia, where they had not given her a drink and only offered smelly fish for breakfast. She should now have collected a hire car and driven to Sozopol, an ancient little town on the Black Sea coast about 30 km from the much larger city of Bourgas.

There is no sign of her when we arrive at the bus station and there is a little bus bound for Sozopol. I wait until the last moment to board in case she is about to appear, by which time it is so crowded that I am wedged in by the front door, It is like being back in China. In a way I am pleased that I am completing the last part of the journey by bus and foot instead of being met, as it reinforces the satisfying feeling of having fully managed a very complex journey relying only on my own resources.

I remove my sandals to take a short cut across the beach. It is good to be at the seaside, although I am aware that I must look out of place as I splash through the lapping waves with a pack on my back. I need to be by the sea as away from the shoreline, where the sand has not got wet, it is hot enough to burn my feet and so soft that it is hard work to trudge through. I might strike as being an odd figure, a dusty traveller amongst all the holidaymakers, but the sunbathers are taking little notice of me, it is not like being back in China where a foreigner is a constant curiosity. The mighty Yangtze in Nanjing flows into the Pacific and I am now paddling in sea water that connects with the Atlantic, so I have travelled right across the world's biggest landmass. I have come (most of) half way around the world in 40 days.

Liz is pleased but surprised to see me. Apparently I said that I would be arriving on Monday, and today is Sunday. Oh well; as I recall Phileas Fogg did exactly the same thing.